# NEW RACE POLITICS IN AMERICA

Foreign migration to the United States is dramatically altering the demographic profile of the American electorate. Nearly a third of all Americans are of nonwhite and non-European descent. Latinos and Hispanics have recently eclipsed African Americans as the largest minority group in the United States. Between 1990 and 2000, Asians doubled the size of their population to more than 4 percent of Americans. Although immigration has altered the racial and ethnic composition of every state in the nation, surprisingly little is known about the consequences of this new heterogeneity for American politics. This book explores the impact and political consequences of immigration. After considering the organizations that mobilize new citizens to politics, the authors examine the political psychology of group consciousness for political mobilization. Finally, they consider the emerging patterns and choices of new voters.

Jane Junn is Associate Professor in the Political Science Department and the Eagleton Institute of Politics at Rutgers University. She is the author of *Civic Education: What Makes Students Learn* (with Richard Niemi; 1998) and *Education and Democratic Citizenship in America* (with Norman Nie and Ken Stehlik-Barry; 1996), which won the Woodrow Wilson Foundation Award, American Political Science Association. Her research interests include political participation and elections, education and democracy, immigration, and racial and ethnic politics.

Kerry L. Haynie is Associate Department Chair and Associate Professor of Political Science at Duke University. He also codirects Duke's Center for the Study of Race, Ethnicity, and Gender in the Social Sciences. He is the author of *African American Legislators in the American States* (2001) and coeditor of *The Encyclopedia of Minorities in American Politics, Vols. I and II* (2000), and he has written several articles for political science journals.

# New Race Politics in America

## UNDERSTANDING MINORITY AND IMMIGRANT POLITICS

Edited by

**Jane Junn**

Rutgers University

**Kerry L. Haynie**

Duke University

**CAMBRIDGE**
UNIVERSITY PRESS

CAMBRIDGE UNIVERSITY PRESS
Cambridge, New York, Melbourne, Madrid, Cape Town, Singapore, São Paulo, Delhi

Cambridge University Press
32 Avenue of the Americas, New York, NY 10013-2473, USA

www.cambridge.org
Information on this title: www.cambridge.org/9780521670142

First published 2008

Printed in the United States of America

*A catalog record for this publication is available from the British Library.*

*Library of Congress Cataloging in Publication Data*

New race politics in America : understanding minority and immigrant politics / [edited by]
Jane Junn, Kerry L. Haynie.
   p.   cm.
Includes bibliographical references and index.
ISBN 978-0-521-85427-6 (hardback) – ISBN 978-0-521-67014-2 (pbk.)
1. Elections – United States.   2. Immigrants – United States – Political activity.
3. Minorities – United States – Political activity.   4. Race – Political aspects – United
States.   5. Ethnicity – Political aspects – United States.   6. United States – Emigration and
immigration – Political aspects.   7. United States – Race relations.   8. United States –
Ethnic relations.   9. Pluralism (Social sciences) – United States.   I. Junn, Jane.   II. Haynie,
Kerry Lee.   III. Title.
JK1965.N48   2008
324.089′00973–dc22        2007036208

ISBN   978-0-521-85427-6 hardback
ISBN   978-0-521-67014-2 paperback

For our daughters
Eve Junn and Juliet Champagne
and Olivia Haynie

# Contents

# Contributors

**Marisa A. Abrajano,** Assistant Professor, Department of Political Science, University of California, San Diego

**Kristi Andersen,** Professor, Maxwell School, Syracuse University

**Niambi M. Carter,** Visiting Assistant Professor, Department of Political Sciences, Duke University

**Dennis Chong,** Professor, Department of Political Science, Northwestern University

**M. Margaret Conway,** Professor, Department of Political Science, University of Florida

**Jeronimo Cortina,** Assistant Professor, Department of Political Science, University of Houston

**Kendra Davenport Cotton,** Ph.D. Candidate, Department of Political Science, University of North Carolina at Chapel Hill

**Victoria M. DeFrancesco Soto,** Assistant Professor, Department of Political Science, Northwestern University

**Rodolfo O. de la Garza,** Professor, Department of Political Science, Columbia University

**Jeffrey D. Grynaviski,** Assistant Professor, Department of Political Science, University of Chicago

**Fredrick C. Harris,** Professor, Department of Political Science, Columbia University

x

**Kerry L. Haynie,** Associate Professor, Department of Political Science, Duke University

**Jane Junn,** Associate Professor, Department of Political Science, Rutgers University

**J. Alan Kendrick,** Graduate School, University of North Carolina at Chapel Hill

**Dukhong Kim,** Ph.D. Candidate, Department of Political Science, Northwestern University

**Gerald F. Lackey,** Ph.D. Candidate, Department of Sociology, University of North Carolina at Chapel Hill

**Pei-te Lien,** Associate Professor, Political Science and Ethnic Studies at the University of Utah

**Monique L. Lyle,** Ph.D. Candidate, Department of Political Science, Duke University

**Elizabeth Matto,** Research Associate, Eagleton Institute of Politics, Rutgers University

**Paula D. McClain,** Professor, Department of Political Science, Duke University

**Brian D. McKenzie,** Assistant Professor, Department of Political Science, Texas A&M University

**Jennifer L. Merolla,** Assistant Professor, Department of Political Science, Claremont Graduate University

**Shayla C. Nunnally,** Assistant Professor, Department of Political Science, University of Connecticut

**Thomas J. Scotto,** Assistant Professor, Department of Government, University of Essex

**Valeria Sinclair-Chapman,** Assistant Professor, Department of Political Science, University of Rochester

**Janelle S. Wong,** Associate Professor, Department of Political Science, University of Southern California

# Acknowledgments

This volume has been longer in the making than we planned, due in no part to the people who supported this project. The book began with a gathering of scholars at a conference on minority voting and U.S. politics held at the Eagleton Institute of Politics at Rutgers University in early 2004. The meeting was held at the Eagleton Institute with generous contributions from the Walt Whitman Center, the Department of Political Science, and the Eagleton Institute. We thank our colleagues Rick Lau and Richard Wilson in the Political Science Department for supporting this project both financially and intellectually. Ruth Mandel, the director of the Eagleton Institute, provided human resources and a warm environment in which to hold the meeting. Michelle Horgan helped coordinate the event, and we thank her for her efficiency and good cheer. We also thank Dana Brown, Nadia Brown, Hannah Holden, and Anna Murphy for their fine work as research assistants.

The authors of the chapters in the book benefited from the wise counsel of conference discussants. We thank Cristina Beltrán, Michael Hagen, and Rogers Smith for their thoughtful reflections and for sparking discussion and critical revisions in each of the chapters. Two of our colleagues who were involved in the initial conference, Vince Hutchings and Nicholas Valentino, were unable to include their work in the book, but the creativity of their analysis produced much interesting dialogue. We are grateful to Paula McClain and her colleagues for contributing their chapter and joining the book after the conference was completed. We also thank two anonymous reviewers for Cambridge University Press for their insightful critiques and helpful comments.

It has been a tremendous pleasure working with Ed Parsons at Cambridge University Press. He convinced us early on that the topic of "new race politics" was one that desperately needed more scholarly footing. He has been a wise and tireless advocate, and we are grateful for his guidance. Faith Black and Bonnie Lee of Cambridge University Press helped us navigate the many phases of book production, and we thank them for their expertise and willingness to help at every turn. We also thank Laura Lawrie for her great skill at editing the manuscript.

Our partners David Champagne and Mina Silberberg have aided us in innumerable ways, but perhaps most significantly in sharing with us the conviction that understanding new race politics in a diverse and multiracial society is among the most important imperatives for political science. Our children, to whom we dedicate this volume, are testimony to this resolve. We wish for them a new race politics in the United States that more faithfully lives up to democratic ideals of fairness, tolerance, and equality. The future of America's diverse democracy lies in the hands of the next generation, and we hope they develop a new race politics with an innovative spirit and an enduring commitment to political equality.

# 1 New Race Politics

## The Changing Face of the American Electoral Landscape

Democracy in the United States always has been characterized by dynamism – states entered and attempted to leave the union, political parties were born and faded away, and the composition of the electorate underwent continuous alteration as women, minorities, and young people were included as eligible voting citizens. The United States is experiencing another set of changes that portend a potentially important reconfiguration of American democracy, and among the most significant is the introduction of a substantial number of immigrants to the polity. Overwhelmingly from Latin America and Asia, immigrants and their children currently make up more than 20 percent of the U.S. population. As a consequence, more than one-third of Americans consider themselves to be a race other than white. What difference will an estimated twenty-two million potential new voters – the combined total of the eleven million foreign-born Americans who became naturalized citizens since the 1990s and the eleven million who are eligible for naturalization now or within the next few years (Fix, Passel, and Sucher 2003) – make for campaigns, election outcomes, political identities, and democratic representation? To what extent will blacks, Latinos, and Asian Americans engage in a racial pluralism forged in identity politics? Should we expect racial groups to cohere politically? To what extent can racial identity be used to mobilize Latino and Asian American populations? Alternatively, will the majority population engage in a countermobilization response to increasing numbers of minority Americans? The dynamic racial and ethnic environment of the nation alters the racial context of politics, taking us beyond the black-white divide in American politics, and changing how we think about race and ethnicity.

The nation's current demographic makeup stands in sharp contrast to its ethnic and racial composition of twenty-five years ago.[1] Once the nation's largest minority group, the percentage of African Americans remained virtually unchanged between 1980 and 2000, increasing only slightly from 11.7 percent to 12.3 percent. In contrast, Latino and Asian American populations have experienced explosive growth, with Latinos replacing African Americans as the largest minority group in the United States. In 1980, Latinos made up 6.4 percent of the American population, but by 2000, the percentage grew to 12.5 percent. The U.S. Census Bureau projects Latinos will constitute a quarter of the total U.S. population by 2050. Although Asian Americans still account for a relatively small proportion of the population, they are nevertheless among the fastest-growing minority groups in the country, more than doubling in size from 1.5 percent to 3.6 percent of all Americans in 2000. The size of the Asian American population is projected to double again to 8 percent by 2050.

Unique geographic patterns of foreign migration to the United States are also noteworthy, for immigrant populations are highly concentrated in some states, and growth rates vary substantially among locations. Immigrants are concentrated in states with disproportionately large electoral significance, drawn to the immigrant gateway cities of New York, Los Angeles, San Francisco, San Antonio, Miami, and Chicago. The large number of electoral college votes held by California (fifty-five), New York (thirty-one), Texas (thirty-four), Florida (twenty-seven), and Illinois (twenty-one) always has garnered these states a great deal of attention by political observers, and now the changing demographics of these states have focused even more attention on them. For example, the percentage of Latinos residing in California, Florida, Illinois, New York, and Texas exceeds their proportion at the national level (12.5 percent). In some instances, the difference is dramatic – over 30 percent of the population in both California and Texas is Latino. The percentage of Asian Americans residing in these electorally important states also is worth noting, with the percentage of Asian Americans living in California (10.9 percent) nearly triple the percentage of Asian Americans at the national level.

All new immigrants, however, do not reside in traditional "gateway" metropolitan areas, and although there are a number of metropolitan areas

---

[1] Percentages are from U.S. Bureau of the Census, 1990 Census of Population and Housing, and U.S. Census Bureau 2000. The racial classification system used by the U.S. government in the census includes "Hispanic" as ethnicity rather than race. Although there are important distinctions between the terms "Hispanic" and "Latino," the authors in this volume use the term "Latino" to refer to people in the United States with Latin American heritage.

that continue to be popular destinations for new Americans, these cities have experienced relatively moderate growth in immigrant populations compared with a set of "emerging gateway" locations (Singer 2004). In contrast, "reemerging," and "preemerging gateways" have seen a significant increase in the number of immigrants settling in their cities. These new immigrant destinations include locations as diverse as Atlanta, Dallas, Raleigh-Durham, and Las Vegas. New patterns of immigrant settlement foreshadow a dynamic political environment in traditionally white-black and mostly-white locations, signaling the potential for multiracial coalitions of voters. The changing face of the American population is thus the starting point for the study of a new race politics in the United States.

## A NEW IDENTITY POLITICS IN A DYNAMIC RACIAL ENVIRONMENT?

What are the political consequences of these changes in the racial landscape of the United States? Political theorists have taken up anew the question of how "identity politics" will influence the conduct of contemporary government. Political theorists such as Amy Gutmann (2003), Seyla Benhabib (2002), and Iris Marion Young (2002) signal optimism in the democratic possibility of political coalitions based in race and ethnicity. Alternatively, another perspective best exemplified by Huntington (2005), argues the growing diversity will have the negative consequence of creating ethnic balkanization. The expectation that demographic shifts will produce political consequences is based on prior examples of ethnic-based collective action and the gains in political equality that often have accompanied such action. The notion that people with shared ethnic and racial backgrounds naturally will join together is intuitively appealing. Public celebrations of ethnic identity and the successful collective action strategies of African Americans during the Civil Rights movement are but two examples of the palpable appeal of racial identity in inviting group mobilization. Equally compelling is the normative premise linking citizen participation with political equality; more voice, particularly among those traditionally disadvantaged, will lead to more favorable political outcomes that enhance equality. The presence of a critical mass of racial minorities signals the possibility that disadvantaged groups can better mobilize individuals and increase their input in democratic politics. Grounded in this way, it seems reasonable to hope and expect that political mobilization around race can produce higher levels of political participation among minority Americans.

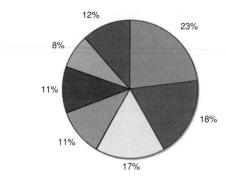

12%

23%

8%

11%

18%

11%

17%

☐ Chinese,except Taiwanese     ■ Filipino
☐ Asian Indian                  ☐ Vietnamese
■ Korean                        ☐ Japanese
■ Other

**Figure** 1.1. Composition of Asian Population: 2000. *Source:* U.S. Census Bureau.

In analyzing the significance of race for voting, scholars have most often utilized the mutually exclusive racial categories of black, white, Latino, and, to a lesser degree, Asian American. The U.S. government classifies "Hispanic" as an ethnicity rather than a race, and people who identify as one of the categories of "Hispanic" can be of any race. There is some confusion about the definitions of the terms race and ethnicity, and how they are related. Although authors sometimes use these terms interchangeably, the term "ethnicity" commonly refers to one's cultural background or country of origin, whereas "race" is most often used to describe the larger grouping into one of the four categories of white, black, Latino, and Asian American.

Because the influx of a large number of Latinos and Asian Americans is a recent phenomenon, we know surprisingly little about their patterns of voting participation, partisan affiliation, and group mobilization. In an attempt to go beyond the black-white binary, analysts most frequently have combined what are often highly distinctive groups – Mexicans and Cubans, or Japanese and Vietnamese – into the panethnic racial categories of Latino and Asian American. Yet there is tremendous diversity within the larger racial categories, and Figures 1.1 and 1.2 present breakdowns of the national origins of Latinos and Asian Americans in the United States in 2000. Although the vast majority (66 percent) of Latinos are Mexican, a third are from other locations. The ethnic diversity among Asian Americans is even more pronounced, and no single group constitutes a majority of the population. Not only does country of origin differ to a substantial

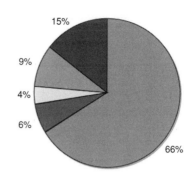

**Figure 1.2.** Composition of Hispanic Population: 2000. *Source:* U.S. Census Bureau, Current Population Survey, March 2000.

degree among Asian Americans, but so, too, do language and religion. Although most immigrant Latinos in the United States share Spanish (some from South American nations speak Portuguese), there are differences in dialect, as well as variation in adherence to the Catholic Church. Similarly, there are important within-group differences in terms of immigrant status and socioeconomic status. Similarly, there is important variation within the category of "black" or African American, and more than 15 percent of the foreign-born residents of the United States come from a sending country in the Caribbean or Africa. Although positive stereotypes of West Indian values and high levels of economic assimilation among the well-educated African immigrant population are widespread and familiar, foreign-born blacks nevertheless face a continual struggle against racism shared with native-born African Americans (Kasinitz 1992; Waters 1999; Foner 2001; Rogers 2006).

To be certain, the ubiquitous use of the "big four" racial categories of white, black, Latino, and Asian American has produced political consequences. In the wake of the recent shift in demographics, a continued reliance on such a categorization of America's newest voters also has theoretical implications in that such a classification system limits our ability to understand the new race politics. The use of the "big four" racial categories speaks not only to the state's need to measure race and enforce race-sensitive policies but also to the stark reality of continued ignorance and racism regarding ethnic diversity. Despite significant progress in racial equality over the last half century, the persistence of racial stereotyping

has produced political and economic inequality among individuals categorized by race. Such categorization signals the continued importance of
race in American society for things material as well as psychological. For
example, in a recent study by the Kaiser Family Foundation, more than
twice as many blacks, Latinos, and Asian Americans than whites report
experiencing racial discrimination in everyday social interactions, including being threatened or attacked, insulted or called names, and treated
with less respect. Although ethnicity may be a primary identification for
immigrants and their children, the imposition of racial identities by the
state has the political effect of instituting a racial hierarchy. The ubiquity
of the four racial categories has theoretical consequences as well. In order
to assess the contours of the new race politics in contemporary America, it
is important to explore more deeply the connection between politics and
the multiplicity of identities within American society.

## ECHOES OF OUR PAST AS A NATION OF IMMIGRANTS

A large influx of new voters and the presence of ethnic voting blocs, however, are far from unprecedented in the history of the United States. Robert
Dahl's landmark 1961 work on New Haven, Connecticut, is a study of the
politics of ethnicity, political identity, and assimilation (Dahl 1961). Despite
what Dahl characterized as the "astonishing tenacity" of ethnic factors in
political behavior, the importance of ethnicity was soon eclipsed by the
prominence of race in American politics. Between 1881 and 1930, the
United States experienced a massive influx of foreign immigrants, when
27.6 million people arrived in America. For the most part, these newest
entrants came from countries in eastern, central, and southern Europe,
in particular Italy, Austria-Hungary, Russia, Poland, and Germany. The
fractious events of the Civil Rights era and the struggles of African Americans against racism speeded a reconfiguration of the political landscape
from multiple ethnicities to a binary analytical lens of black and white,
the change reflecting the realities of stratification and inequality between
people categorized by race. By mid-century and into the 1960s, second-
and third-generation Italians, Irish, and Jews – groups marked as distinctive from and less desirable than the white Protestant establishment –
continued to assimilate through educational certification, diversified labor
market participation, dispersed residential settlement, and intermarriage,
moving from the categorization of ethnic to white ethnic to simply white
(Ignatiev 1987; Waters 1990; Alba 1992; Jacobson 1998). The assimilation
of these groups contributed to the decline in interest in ethnic voting. In

addition, the demise of most of the powerful political machines reinforced the shift from a focus on ethnicity to a focus on race.

Although they came in fewer numbers, immigrants from China, Mexico, and the Caribbean also found their way to the United States during the early twentieth century, although federal immigration policies of the 1920s made it more difficult for Asians and Africans to enter the country (King 2000; Tichenor 2002; Ngai 2004). For the most part, it was America's big industrial cities such as Boston, New York, Chicago, Pittsburgh, Milwaukee, St. Louis, and San Francisco where immigrants settled. By 1930, one-half to three-quarters of the populations of these cities were composed of immigrants and their children. These newest residents found work in the industrial sector in automobile plants, garment factories, and construction, quickly forming a new working class with ethnicity and immigrant status at its core.

Like many of America's newest immigrants, those who entered the United States in the early twentieth century found themselves at a disadvantage. The difficulties they faced made integrating into the political system challenging. A large number of these immigrants did not speak English and were poorly paid. These factors hampered their ability to involve themselves in the democratic system. In addition, the political system as it stood in the 1920s was, in many ways, not very welcoming to new participants. As a response to mass immigration, many states instituted restrictive electoral laws such as literacy tests and property requirements in order to limit immigrant participation (Sterne 2001). States play a pivotal role in determining the process and ease with which immigrants will integrate into the system. In many cases, states have been and continue to be stringent in conferring the full rights of citizenship upon immigrants (Aleinikoff 2001). The passage of California's Proposition 187 in 1994 limiting social services to illegal immigrants is an example of the active stance states often take regarding immigrants.

In the wake of the recent surge in foreign migration, one pivotal question facing the nation is how will new immigrants integrate themselves into the political system? The immigrant experience of the early twentieth century suggests a path new immigrants might follow in order to integrate themselves fully in the democratic system. Much attention has been paid to the role of the political machine and its party bosses of the early twentieth century as well as unions in bringing the ethnic-based working class of this time period into the political system. Networks of civic associations also played an important role in bringing new residents into politics and acted as "alternative yet mutually reinforcing modes of incorporation" (Sterne

2001, 34). The political party machines of the early 1900s did a great deal to mobilize America's newest residents and integrate them into the political system, providing immigrants with much needed services, including jobs, financial assistance, and mediation. The assistance immigrants received and the one-on-one contact immigrants enjoyed with the parties provided a connection between the government and America's newest citizens and a link to the political system. Similarly, unions such as the Knights of Labor and the American Federation of Labor (AFL) played an important role in teaching immigrants of the early twentieth century how to participate in the democratic process. Labor leaders of this time period held that participation in the electoral process went hand-in-hand with employment in industry (Sterne 2001). Immigrant union members were indoctrinated with the notion that industry and politics were indelibly linked. The role of the civic association in immigrant political incorporation in the early twentieth century often is overlooked, for not all immigrants came into contact with party machines or labor unions. For many immigrants, it was associations such as settlement houses, ethnic groups, neighborhood organizations, and churches that provided immigrants with a civic education and brought them into the democratic system. These organizations were more accessible to immigrants, offered solidarity among fellow newcomers, and more specifically addressed their needs (Sterne 2001). In all these ways, immigrants were brought into the political system in the early 1900s, and their incorporation had a dramatic and lasting effect on the political landscape.

The entrance of these immigrants into the United States, most of whom were working class and living on a modest income, coincided with another pivotal phenomenon – the Great Depression. The combination of an economic depression and heavy foreign migration resulted in a significant readjustment in the party loyalties of the citizenry and the contours of the political party system. With the beginning of the Great Depression in 1929, an already financially insecure immigrant population found themselves depending more on the assistance of the state. There were only so many services parties, unions, and civic associations could provide. In Franklin Delano Roosevelt (FDR), immigrants found a sympathetic leader, and the "New Deal" promised much-needed assistance in the form of a social security program and public works projects, for example. Thanks to the parties, unions, and associations, America's newest citizens became educated in and motivated to participate in politics, and in many ways, the affinity immigrants felt for the Democratic Party was actualized through active political participation (Sterne 2001). This influx of a large number of new citizens supportive of the Democratic Party resulted in a significant shift in the contours of the political party system.

The election of FDR in 1932 had momentous consequences, and the formation of the New Deal coalition ushered in the fifth party system and the realignment of the nation away from the Republican Party toward the Democratic Party. As Burnham (1970) noted, realignments tend to occur when the existing party system is unable to cope with social, economic, or cultural problems facing the country. As a result, realignment occurs when the electorate's party loyalty undergoes a lasting change thereby transforming the minority party into the majority party. As Kristi Andersen argues in her study of the creation of the Democratic majority (1979), the realignment that took place at the start of the FDR presidency was not the result of a conversion of large numbers of Republicans to the Democratic Party. Instead, the shift in the party system was the result of significant demographic changes in the United States. In particular, the mobilization of large numbers of new immigrants (many of whom were urban, Catholic, and "blue collar" workers) infused the Democratic Party with new supporters. The combination of an economic depression and the emergence of an active immigrant pool, therefore, changed America's party system to what is still present today. The political effects of America's recent experience with immigration are now in the making, and it is to the electoral consequences of the new race politics to which we now turn.

## THE ELECTORAL CONSEQUENCES OF IMMIGRATION

When considering the effects of a large influx of immigrants into the United States, the natural question to ask is how integrated into the political system will these immigrants become? Will they become citizens and how will they engage in politics? Trends in naturalization suggest the pool of potential participants in the political system is expanding, and many of America's newly naturalized citizens possess qualities that make active political participation likely. At the same time, there is a large pool of immigrants not yet naturalized, and it remains to be seen which of these future citizens will become politically incorporated.

Naturalization is the process by which immigrants are invested with the rights and privileges of American citizenship. Following a period of time in which rates of naturalization were trending downward, there has been an increase in the rates of immigrants becoming citizens. In 1970, 64 percent of the nation's legal immigrants became American citizens, but this dropped to 39 percent by 1996. But by the end of the 1990s, the percentage of immigrants who have naturalized has risen to 49 percent, and by 2002, the number of naturalized citizens stood at eleven million (Fix, Passel, and Sucher 2003a, 2003b).

Who are these newly naturalized citizens? In general, immigrants from Europe, Canada, and Asia have been the most likely immigrants to become citizens once they entered the United States. By 2001, approximately 65 percent of the immigrants from Canada and European nations had naturalized, and the percentage of Asians who chose to naturalize increased between 1995 and 2001. By 2001, 67 percent of Asian immigrants become U.S. citizens. The story is different for immigrants from Mexico and other Latin American countries. Although the percentage of Latino immigrants who naturalized was lower than immigrants from Europe and Canada, there has been an increase in the number of Mexicans and Latin Americans who have become citizens. By 2001, 34 percent of Mexican immigrants became citizens – an increase of 15 percent. The proportion of Latin Americans who became citizens also rose from 40 percent to 58 percent between 1995 and 2001.

In general, America's newest citizens possess moderate levels of English proficiency, education, and income. Of those who have recently naturalized, 48 percent report that they speak English very well. In terms of education, 91 percent report having at least a ninth grade education, whereas more than a third (35 percent) have a college degree or higher. In terms of economic standing, poverty rates among newly naturalized citizens are fairly low with only 11 percent living below the federal poverty level (Fix, Passel, and Sucher 2003a, 2003b). Rates of naturalization show no signs of slowing in the near future. An estimated 7.9 million immigrants are eligible to naturalize and become citizens immediately. The remaining immigrants (approximately 2.7 million) are soon-to-be-eligible to become citizens, and most of them are of the age to become citizens. Once the five-year residency requirements are satisfied, they will be eligible to naturalize. This means that the American population will be absorbing approximately eleven million newly naturalized citizens in the next five years.

This large number of potential citizens possesses markedly different characteristics from recently naturalized immigrants. Among these future citizens, 60 percent possess limited English proficiency compared to 52 percent of the recently naturalized immigrants. Regarding levels of education, 25 percent of soon-to-be-naturalized immigrants have less than a ninth grade education compared to 9 percent of those immigrants who have recently become citizens. Poverty rates among these sets of immigrants also differ. Many more immigrants currently eligible to become citizens have incomes below the federal poverty level compared to the percentage of the recently naturalized (Fix, Passel, and Sucher 2003a, 2003b). Once again, patterns of settlement among future citizens deserve attention. As indicated earlier, recent immigrants to the United States have tended to settle in states of electoral importance. The same can be said about America's future citizens. Of the nearly millions of citizens that are eligible to naturalize, three-fourths live in states with the largest number of Electoral College votes: California, New York, Texas, Florida, New Jersey, and Illinois.

What is the significance of these trends in naturalization for those interested in the political implications of immigration? First, naturalization rates provide an estimate of how many of America's newest residents are legally eligible to participate in the political system. With a large pool of newly naturalized as well as a substantial number on the verge of becoming citizens, we see a large number of potential participants in the political system, many of whom reside in states of great electoral importance. Second, the background of America's future citizens also says much about the likelihood of these newest citizens participating in the political system. Scholars consistently find that socioeconomic factors such as level of income and education affect one's likelihood to participate in the political system, although among naturalized citizens, the relationship between socioeconomic resources and voting is less clear. The extent to which models of voting developed from the experiences of native-born and white Americans helps to explain the political behavior of blacks, Latinos, and Asian Americans – among them, America's newest voters – and what factors help to mobilize minority voters, are the subject of the chapters of this book.

## MOBILIZING IMMIGRANT AND MINORITY VOTING

A number of themes animate the book and are woven throughout the individual chapters, and all are grounded in the reality of growing racial and ethnic diversity of the U.S. population. Although many of the effects of this new race politics have yet to manifest themselves, the research discussed in this volume analyzes the potential significance of an increasingly racially diverse American polity. One significant theme is the character and development of strategies to mobilize citizens into politics either through traditional mobilizing institutions such as political parties, but also through the influence of political elites, mobilization of voting through media advertisements by candidates for office, and coethnic outreach efforts. In the early twentieth century, party machines, unions, and various civic associations played an important role in educating new citizens and bringing them into the political system. It remains to be seen what role these traditional groups will play in incorporating America's newest citizens. We begin such an exploration in this volume.

A second theme of the book concerns the political psychology of group membership and racial consciousness among members of racial and ethnic minority groups. The study of racial consciousness in contemporary politics has focused almost exclusively on the African American political experience, and emphasized the high degree of political cohesion among blacks in the United States. The extent to which Latinos and Asian Americans – the two newest and fastest-growing minority groups in the country – will follow a similar path of racial consciousness remains unclear. Furthermore, there is little systematically known about the implications of this group consciousness for political mobilization and voting. Early-twentieth-century immigrants to the United States developed voting blocs with the aid of concentrated urban residential segregation, specialized employment and labor union involvement, and a shared sense of ethnic identification – all elements of a particular historical and political context shaped in substantial ways by the political parties of the time. Although distinctive in many ways, African Americans have exhibited a similar degree of political unity in terms of their support of the Democratic Party since the formation of the New Deal coalition. Alternatively, however, it is not at all clear that today's immigrant and ethnic communities will act as monolithically as their early-twentieth-century migrant counterparts or contemporary African Americans. Indeed, there is a good deal of evidence suggesting a relatively high degree of political heterogeneity within panethnic racial categories.

A third theme running through the chapters in the book questions the degree to which traditional models of political behavior, developed in the mid-twentieth century to explain voting and political attitudes among the Anglo white population, are applicable to U.S. minority populations. There is a degree of skepticism well reflected in the data analyzed in the chapters of this volume that the conventional wisdom focusing on individual-level social and economic resources drive voting and public opinion for African Americans, Latinos, and Asian Americans in the same ways as they influence behavior and attitudes among the dominant white population. Although a good deal of weight may still reside in traditional measures of socioeconomic status (SES) to explain voting, the authors in this volume endeavor to go beyond SES in explanations of minority political behavior. Indeed, a critical reexamination of many of the assumptions driving individual-level behavioral research is undertaken in order to advance understanding of how and why African Americans, Latinos, and Asian Americans participate in politics.

Finally, and in a related theme, we highlight the significance of political context, broadly conceived, to the study of minority politics in the United States. The imperative to account for the significance of differences in state-level electoral structures, competitiveness of elections, macro-level conditions in the economy, and variations in perceptions of status by minority groups all signal a strong recognition of the importance of political context. Similarly, the substantial growth in new immigrant populations in regions of the United States that have not traditionally been immigrant gateways creates a new multiracial context with important political consequences for opinion formation and multiracial political coalitions.

## UNDERSTANDING NEW RACE POLITICS: OUTLINE OF CHAPTERS

One of the central concerns regarding the large influx of immigrants into the United States is their assimilation into the democratic system. Kristi Andersen addresses this question in the second chapter, "In Who's Interest: Context and the Political Incorporation of Immigrants." Andersen examines how immigrants have been integrated into the political system in the past and under what conditions such integration might occur today. Specifically, she explains the role of political parties in incorporating immigrants into American democracy as well as the increasing importance of organizations such as local nonprofit groups and ethnic organizations in bringing America's newest citizens into the political process. Andersen argues that certain political and institutional factors need to be satisfied, such as a large concentration of immigrants in electorally important states, in order for immigrants to be integrated fully into America's political system.

Dennis Chong and Dukhong Kim in Chapter 3 discuss the importance of racial consciousness in the political opinions of America's newest voters. In their chapter, "Beyond Black and White: Latino and Asian American Social Status and Racial Consciousness," Chong and Kim analyze the extent to which Latinos and Asians conceptualize politics along racial lines, and argue that their perceptions of social status and experience with discrimination and economic opportunity are critical determinants in the development of racial consciousness. In comparing these dynamics with perceptions among African Americans, the authors conclude that the degree of discrimination one faces when improving his or her status affects his or her propensity to think about politics in racial terms.

In Chapter 4, Wong, Lien, and Conway make use of the first-ever multi-city, multilingual, multiethnic survey to analyze the political partic- ipation of Asian Americans. The data in "Activity Amidst Diversity: Asian American Political Participation" allow the authors to examine the extent and nature of political participation among Asian Americans as well as the factors influencing their behavior. They find traditional socioeconomic predictors of voter turnout, such as education and church attendance, suc- cessfully explain voting behavior but may not explain adequately political participation beyond voting. Their analysis suggests ethnic group origin and minority group status play an important role in explaining the behav- ior of Asian Americans and also may be important in predicting the civic participation of Asian Americans in the future.

The fifth and sixth chapters explore the factors influencing the voting behavior of Latinos, the largest minority group in the United States. In "Get Me to the Polls on Time: Co-Ethnic Mobilization and Latino Turnout," de la Garza, Abrajano, and Cortina analyze the effect of several factors on Latino voter turnout. They find the political participation of Latinos can not be understood in the same way as Anglo participation is understood. Like Anglos, mobilization is an important predictor of Latino turnout. The influence of various demographic and political factors, such as strength of partisanship, varies from state to state for Latino voters. Their analysis of a five-state study of Latino voting behavior in the 2000 election distin- guishes between the influence of direct and indirect mobilization, and iso- lates the significance of coethnic mobilization for Latino voters. In the fifth chapter, "*Se Habla Espanol*: Ethnic Campaign Strategies and Latino Voting Behavior," DeFrancesco Soto and Merolla analyze the effects Spanish lan- guage and targeted political advertisements on Latino voting turnout in the 2000 election. Analyzing a unique set of data marrying individual-level data from the U.S. Census with aggregate-level data on actual campaign advertisements aired during the campaign, Soto and Merolla find political advertisements play an important role in influencing Latino turnout. The influence this form of mobilization has on Latino voters is mediated, how- ever, by the voter's dominant language as well as the party sponsoring the political advertisement.

Chapters 7 and 8 focus upon African Americans and the role race plays in politics. In "Structuring Group Activism: A Macro Model of Black

Participation," Harris, Sinclair-Chapman, and McKenzie forward an important model of black participation that takes analysts beyond the individual level. Instead, they focus on structural forces influencing African American activism, and analyze the mobilizing significance of black social networks and political entrepreneurs for black activism over a twenty-year period. Using black respondents from the Roper Social and Political Trends data set, the authors examine trends in black civic activity between 1973 and 1994. They argue that black political involvement is stimulated by factors that enhance the political empowerment of African Americans and is depressed by downward turns in the social and economic fortunes of black communities. In addition, the authors draw on current research on black political life to support their claims about changes in black activism in the post–Civil Rights era.

In Chapter 8, "Black Elites and Latino Immigrant Relations in a Southern City: Do Black Elites and the Black Masses Agree?" Paula McClain and colleagues undertake a unique study of the influence of black elite perspectives on new Latino immigrants in Durham, North Carolina. This state has experienced the highest rate of increase in Latino immigration of any in the nation, and the authors investigate what blacks in Durham think about these newly arrived immigrants. In particular, they analyze the extent to which black elites and black citizens of the city have corresponding views on the significance of new Latino immigrants, and the implications for race relations. The chapter raises important questions about the potential for multiracial coalitions in the South.

Taken together, the chapters in *New Race Politics* introduce readers to the complexity of the relationship between race and ethnicity and electoral politics in the United States. Emphasizing the significance of institutional and organizational mobilization, the authors focus on the impact of these groups to encourage immigrant and minority voters to become active in politics. The extent to which that group-based activity is rooted in a sense of racial and ethnic identity is also analyzed in detail in these chapters. Acknowledging the unique circumstances of immigrants and minorities today, the authors consider the role of group consciousness in activating political engagement among Americans. Finally, and given the substantial changes in the demographic composition of the U.S. population over the last two decades, the chapters in the book reexamine the extent to which traditional models developed in political science to study voting in the mass public are applicable to the newest entrants to the American political system. Grounding this analysis is the recognition that contextual difference across states, electoral systems, economic conditions among other structural elements, drives much of the dynamism we witness in the practice of electoral politics in the United States. Although the exact shape of American democracy in the midst of a new race politics remains to be seen, these chapters take us a long way toward understanding the contours of minority and immigrant voting.

## 2   In Whose Interest?

## Political Parties, Context, and the Incorporation of Immigrants

The inclusion of immigrants in the American political system has been a subject of contention throughout American history. In the mid-nineteenth century, the anti-immigrant, anti-Catholic Know-Nothing party became popular for its support of nativist policies, such as prohibiting immigrants from holding public office and increasing the length of the waiting period before U.S. citizenship could be obtained. Although there is no direct contemporary analog to the "Know-Nothings," the questions of how immigrants are included or excluded, the definition of their roles in the political system, and the potential for political change from the addition of large new groups of citizens remain salient today as the size of the immigrant population in the United States continues to grow. Indeed, contemporary debate on issues such as guest worker programs, access of immigrants to social services, and voting rights for non-citizens in New York City and elsewhere testifies to the persistent importance of issues surrounding immigration and naturalization.

Political parties are often identified as the driving force behind immigrant political incorporation in the United States, a perception fortified by the widespread image of early-twentieth-century machine politicians trading food baskets and patronage for votes in Irish and Italian immigrant communities. An important function of political parties is to mobilize mass publics, but their overriding goal is to win elections, and parties will attempt to activate voters only when it is in their interest to do so. Such an imperative creates incentives for political parties to concentrate mobilization efforts on their most reliable and predictable voters, and spend fewer resources activating political independents, episodic voters, and new entrants to the U.S. political system. This strategy produces a "rich get richer" situation for habitual voters already endowed with resources, and for whom political participation is less costly. Meanwhile, targeted mobilization by parties deprives citizens who are either new to American politics or who do not take part in elections regularly of an important stream of information and other resources that encourage voting. Nevertheless, there are clearly times when parties need to go to previously untapped voters to expand their base, head off an electoral threat, or increase the size and strength of their coalition.[1] In this chapter, I analyze the role of political parties and political context in the political incorporation of immigrant Americans.

To help contextualize immigrant participation in the United States today, I begin by outlining some of the roles parties have undertaken historically in structuring the opportunities and costs of political incorporation. Next, I consider what symbolic and concrete efforts are being made by contemporary political parties and other organizations to mobilize new members of the electorate, and in so doing, evaluate the conditions under which political parties will be most likely to reach out to immigrant communities on the local level. I address these questions by examining U.S. Current Population Survey data on naturalization patterns in the United States, along with data from a case study of Syracuse, New York, that includes interviews with local political officials. A central theoretical argument of the chapter is that political and institutional contexts have substantial importance for the pace and contours of immigrant political incorporation. Although becoming a naturalized citizen and voting in elections – the two most common indicators of political incorporation – are clearly influenced by individual-level factors such as socioeconomic resources, political institutions responding to their own strategic imperatives have a powerful influence in structuring the opportunities and costs of political activity for immigrants. Thus, to understand variations in the ways immigrants contribute to political change past, present, and future, we must begin by asking this question: In whose interest is it to expand the electorate by mobilizing immigrant communities?

## IMMIGRANT POLITICAL INCORPORATION
## IN THE EARLY TWENTIETH CENTURY

In the late nineteenth century and early twentieth century, concerns about the impact of immigration on American society produced not only anti-immigrant spokesmen and initiatives but also generated a number of

---

[1] For example, Oregon Republicans in the early 1920s successfully mobilized women to counter the Klu Klux Klan's support of Democratic candidates (see Andersen 1994).

institutional programs to "Americanize" immigrants. Efforts were made to acculturate, assimilate, and incorporate immigrants into American society and politics through public education, citizenship, and voter training programs. Urban party organizations served as important intermediaries between foreign immigrants and political and governmental institutions.[2] Although there are many examples of party organizations dominated by a particular group (usually white Anglo Saxon Protestant or Irish Catholic) that ignored immigrants' interests, these organizations' desire to increase electoral strength pushed parties to make some accommodation to newer groups. In this regard, organizations located in areas where immigrants settled typically recruited precinct leaders and other party workers who matched constituents in terms of race, religion, and national origin (Allswang 1977). New immigrants thus became involved in politics through coethnic mobilization sponsored by the local parties.[3]

By the late 1920s, the heavy flow of immigration had been effectively restricted to a trickle by federal legislation imposing national quotas. At that time, most of the immigrant-stock population had either been in the United States long enough to pursue naturalization, or were the second generation offspring of immigrant parents. These developments supported the efforts of urban machines to both enfranchise and organize Italians, Jews, and Poles in their local communities, and also presented the opportunity to expand the "ethnic" electorate at the national level. It was the Democratic Party, firmly in the minority at the end of the 1920s, that capitalized on the potential of foreign-stock voters. After the 1928 election, in which Republican Herbert Hoover defeated Democratic nominee Alfred E. Smith in a landslide, Franklin Roosevelt sent letters to Democratic state and county chairmen, convention delegates and alternates, and congressional candidates, asking for their analysis of the political situation and suggestions to strengthen the party. Many of his correspondents urged the effective organization of women, young voters, and immigrants. Where there had been active organizations of women (in Washington, Kansas, and Kentucky) or young people (in Indiana and Iowa), the impact of

---

[2] The extent to which political parties in the late nineteenth and early twentieth centuries helped or hindered the political incorporation of immigrants remains an issue open to debate. For interesting arguments on these issues, see the work of Gamm (1990) and Erie (1990).

[3] The machines did not value diversity for its own sake, and came only later to the habit of balanced slate-making, but Allswang 1977 points out that while Tammany Hall "... did not really try very hard to get representatives of the new immigrant groups into elective office, its opponents went so far in the other direction as to make the Hall look good by comparison" (p. 75).

mobilizing new voters had been positive. Many correspondents urged stronger emphasis on these groups, indicating that the Republicans had done a better job, particularly among women, during the 1928 campaign. Several correspondents, including officials from New Jersey, Pennsylvania, and Rhode Island, recommended educating and organizing immigrants.[4]

Although the common understanding of the New Deal realignment includes the near-unanimous movement of immigrant voters to the Democratic column, this process was neither quick nor simple. In 1932, the *New York Times* examined the foreign-language press and found it split evenly in support of FDR and Hoover. Of over one thousand publications, they found 163 explicitly backing Roosevelt and 152 supporting Hoover. A few supported Norman Thomas or other candidates, a couple hundred were "independent" politically and many were nonpolitical. The lack of a clear majority for either the Democratic or Republican Party persisted within specific ethnic groups; German, Italian, Hungarian, and Russian papers, for example, were evenly split, although some groups were more consensual, such as Czechs for Roosevelt and Scandinavians for Hoover.[5]

In 1932 the Democratic National Committee (DNC) distributed more than three million pieces of foreign language literature throughout the United States – in Italian, German, Polish, Russian, French, Yiddish, Hungarian, Slovene, Czech, Norwegian, and Swedish.[6] Four years later, the DNC created a naturalized citizens' bureau with eighteen units, each targeting a different nationality group. An Italian American "caravan" toured the state of New York during the 1936 presidential campaign, staging rallies and speeches, aided and organized by state and local Democratic leaders.[7] They worked through groups such as the American Labor Party, which provided a mobilization channel for particular categories of voters, including "radical political groups whose foreign born members were not attracted to any of the major parties" (Spencer 1976, 142). The Progressive National Committee included naturalized citizens' bureaus in many states, and conducted a good deal of activity among foreign voters by advertising in foreign language newspapers and sending out appropriate speakers.[8] Nationality clubs provided another linkage between party

[4] "National Political Digest" in papers of Democratic National Committee, FDR Library.
[5] *New York Times*, 7 Nov. 1932, 11.
[6] *New York Times*, 7 Aug. 1936, 6; Letters to Jim Farley DNC Library and Research Bureau Papers, 1932 campaign, box 866, FDR Library.
[7] *Rochester Daily Chronicle*, 19 Oct. 1936, 1; *Buffalo Evening News* 16 Oct. 1936, 37.
[8] Ibid., p. 224.

elites and elected officials and immigrant groups.[9] Ethnic-group organizations helped with registration and get-out-the-vote drives and provided key endorsements and support. For example, the organizational and geographic density of Chicago's ethnic groups allowed Anton Cermak's Democratic organization to more easily educate and mobilize foreign-born citizens in Chicago.[10] Thus the movement of immigrant communities toward the Democratic coalition after 1928 was a result of a number of factors, including the Depression, but also was significantly shaped by intentional behavior on the part of national, state, and local Democratic leaders who saw the addition of these groups to their electoral coalition as, on balance, advantageous.

## PARTIES AND IMMIGRANTS IN THE EARLY
## TWENTY-FIRST CENTURY

At the beginning of the twenty-first century, the foreign-born population numbered over thirty-two million people, or 11.5 percent of the U.S. population. Immigrants combined with second-generation Americans totaled almost fifty-six million and accounted for roughly 20 percent of the population.[11] This composition is in stark contrast to earlier decades between 1940 and 1970 when the American electorate changed only as a function of generational replacement – the process by which young adults replenish the loss of older voters from the electorate. In contrast, since 1990, millions of potential new voters have been added and will continue to increase the size of the electorate *via* naturalization.

There is an emerging consensus among scholars of immigrant politics that political parties no longer serve the important role that they once

[9] Ibid., p. 162. Peel's 1935 study of political organizations in New York City found that even those groups that were not explicitly political (they were social, fraternal, recreational, or civic), "gradually, almost unconsciously, acquire political interests and attitudes reinforcing a common nationality as a bond of union.... These groups then become relevant to political leaders" (Peel 1935).

[10] In contrast, in Buffalo, New York, the Democratic Party had a difficult time forging cross-ethnic coalitions in part because of the failure of Buffalo's divided Italian population to support community-wide institutions, both political and nonpolitical (Yans-McClaughlin 1977, Ch. 4).

[11] *Profile of the Foreign-Born Population in the United States: 2000.* Current Population Reports: Special Studies. U.S. Census Bureau, issued December 2001 (p. 23). Although the combined immigrant and second-generation population is large, it is smaller in proportion compared with the earlier era, when in 1920 over a third (34.7 percent) of Americans were foreign-born or the children of immigrants.

did either in naturalizing immigrants or including new citizens in political activities. In contrast to the situation a century ago, parties at all levels have fewer incentives to offer immigrants in return for their votes. The patronage jobs at the disposal of most local parties are severely constrained, and to the extent that institutions provide for immigrants' material needs, these are likely to be a combination of state and local welfare systems and nonprofit service providers. Although the extent to which political parties in the United States have "declined" over time is hotly debated among political scientists, there is consensus that the level of partisan identification among ordinary citizens has decreased and that election campaigns and voter decision making are increasingly candidate-centered. Parties derive more power from the services and funds they provide to candidates rather than from their grassroots organizational vigor.

The modest attention given to immigrant voters by political parties is reflected in differences in partisan affiliation between immigrants and native-born Americans. Twenty-nine percent of immigrants consider themselves "independent," rather than Republicans or Democrats, whereas only 18 percent of those born in the United States identify as independents. These data from the 2002 General Social Survey also show that immigrants are more likely to affiliate with the Democratic Party (33 percent) than the Republican Party (18 percent) as either "weak" or "strong" identifiers. Conversely, native-born Americans are more evenly split between Republican (29 percent) and Democratic (34 percent) supporters.

Similar patterns are repeated in racial and ethnic groups with large immigrant populations. An October 2002 Pew Hispanic Center/Kaiser Family Foundation survey found 49 percent of Latinos aligned themselves with the Democratic Party, compared with 20 percent who claimed a Republican Party affiliation. In a California study of Latino registered voters, Democrats outnumbered Republicans by a ratio of 3.4 to 1 in 1992, and 3.9 to 1 in 1998.[12] Echoing the General Social Survey data, unregistered Latinos, who are most likely to be recent immigrants, were overwhelmingly identified as independents.[13] Although Latino voters are most often characterized as leaning toward Democratic candidates, their weakness in party loyalty and volatility in party vote choice is widely recognized. As the director of voter mobilization for the National Council of La Raza noted in early 2004, "What has emerged very strongly in the last

---

[12] Barreto and Woods 2003.
[13] *Washington Post*, 4 Oct. 2003, A08.

election and, then, for this election, is the fact that Latinos are very strong swing voters."[14]

The absence of strong partisan ties is in a function of both the strength of mobilization efforts made by the political parties themselves and the relatively brief exposure most immigrant voters have had to American elections. Politicians thus are faced with some uncertainty – anathema to campaign strategists – in dealing with the votes of these new groups. Rather than groups of voters with a history of registration, consistent voting patterns, and predictable preferences, politicians and parties now contend with new voters who have neither crystallized political preferences nor strong partisan affiliations.

At the national level, political parties are not silent on either questions of interest to immigrants and new citizens or on issues of immigration and citizenship. Both national parties discuss immigration in their platforms. The Democratic and Republican Party stances on issues related to immigration, and the resulting rhetorical choices are similar, welcoming the "newest Americans," endorsing family reunification, and stressing the importance of English as a common language. Party platform differences include a commitment by Democrats to restore welfare benefits to legal immigrants and Republicans' endorsement of more funding for border control. The Democrats broadcast a weekly radio address in Spanish, and their Web site includes a voter outreach page listing leaders and contact information for African Americans, Asian Pacific Americans, Latino/Hispanic Americans, and "Ethnic Americans." The Republicans launched a monthly Spanish-language television show in May 2002. The first show focused on ways to reduce the school dropout rate amount Latinos and increase the number of Latinos in college. The GOP also has a Hispanic Training Program for recruiting and training candidates. George Bush's 2000 campaign targeted Latinos, and he was able to increase the Republican share of the vote from 21 percent in 1996 to 35 percent in 2000. His early 2004 proposal to institute a "guest worker" program for undocumented immigrants was widely seen as an effort to appeal to Latino voters, and some exit polls suggested that the Latino Bush vote was as high as 44 percent in 2004.[15] Examination of the websites of the parties in states with significant numbers of recent immigrants, including

[14] Syracuse *Post-Standard*, 2 Jan. 2004, A-13.
[15] Leal, Barreto, Lee, and de la Garza 2005 cast some doubt on the 44 percent figure, estimating the Latino vote in 2004 at about 39 percent.

California, Texas, Florida, Illinois, New Jersey, New York, Arizona, and New Mexico, suggests both symbolic and material efforts to reach out to immigrant groups, and suggests also that there may be a good deal of variation among states and state parties.

Despite these indications that political parties do exert some efforts to appeal to immigrants, there is also much evidence that parties are opting out of more systematic work of this sort. Focusing not on immigrants *per se* but on Latino voters in the eight states with the largest Hispanic populations, de la Garza finds that both parties ignored Latinos. "With the exception of Democratic efforts in California in 1996, during these years [1988 through 1996] neither party systematically implemented GOTV campaigns targeting Latinos" (de la Garza 2004, 101). Michael Jones-Correa's study of Latin American immigrants in Queens takes this position, arguing that neither major party in New York City has mechanisms to integrate non-citizens into the political process. "For those who *are* citizens, voter registration is rarely encouraged by local machine politicians. Party-sponsored registration at any time other than the quadrennial presidential election years is practically nonexistent" (Jones-Correa 1998, 70).

Although small, ad hoc groups do sometimes conduct voter registrations, Jones-Correa explains, "If actors are at the margins of electoral politics, as immigrants are, then they are ignored; if political players rise to challenge the machine, they are thwarted. Only if the new political actors succeed in mobilizing themselves on their own does the party organization attempt to bring them into its cycle" (Jones-Correa 1998, 70). In comparative work on community organizations in New York City and Los Angeles, Janelle S. Wong concludes that mainstream political parties do not mobilize immigrant communities. "In contrast to earlier immigrants, those of today, who hail mostly from Asia and Latin America, find themselves on the periphery of the American political system.... Unless the mainstream political parties modify the mobilization strategies ..., other civic organizations may become the most viable institutions for encouraging immigrant involvement in American politics" (Wong 2006, 3).

## NONPARTY GROUPS AND IMMIGRANT INCORPORATION

These other organizations include unions, religious groups, ethnic associations, and a variety of nonprofit groups. All of these groups, at various times, may encourage naturalization or registration, for example, by providing registration materials or sponsoring citizenship classes; churches may have voter-registration tables after services, service-providing groups may set out literature about government programs or voter registration processes, and so forth. Labor unions, following years of ignoring immigrants or supporting anti-immigrant legislation through their desire to protect the jobs of their members, have recently begun to shift their position. The American Federation of Labor and Congress of Industrial Organizations (AFL-CIO) decided several years ago to begin making efforts to organize immigrants, and SEIU (Service Employees International Union), with its "Justice for Janitors" movement in particular, has organized large numbers of immigrant workers and in so doing has encouraged political participation.

Religious organizations have historically provided and now currently provide immigrants with social services, mechanisms for maintaining ethnic ties, and opportunities to develop civic skills. At the same time, churches vary dramatically in the extent to which they take explicitly political positions or even encourage political participation on the part of their members. Recent work by Foley and Hoge (2003) analyzes the explicit and implicit inculcation of civic skills by a range of Washington, DC, congregations that serve immigrants, although de la Garza argues that in general, "religious institutions are not linking Hispanics to electoral activities" (de la Garza 2004, 100).

There are at least three other types of organizations that are important features in the landscape of current immigrant politics and political involvement: local nonprofit (largely service-providing) organizations, ethnic voluntary organizations, and groups explicitly organized to mobilize immigrant or ethnic voters. Chi-kan Richard Hung's research (2002) documents the substantial growth of Asian American nonprofit groups (including religious, cultural, service agencies, and activist associations) in eight metropolitan areas over the last ten years. Janelle Wong's work illustrates the reach of some of these groups – a Los Angeles organization that provides legal education (including help with citizenship applications) to over forty thousand immigrants annually, for example. Wong says, "While not every community-based organization has an explicitly political agenda, many leaders see their organizations as having a political role in immigrant communities" (Wong 2002, 24). In Syracuse (see later) we found that agencies such as the Refugee Resettlement Program and Catholic Charities conducted ESL and citizenship classes, help people through the naturalization process, and offer voter registration materials. Certainly in providing assistance with finding jobs, obtaining social services, and naturalizing, groups such as these are playing an important role in the process of civic, if not political incorporation.

Ethnic voluntary organizations play many roles in immigrant communities, from maintaining home country ties – often at the town or village level – to raising money for political causes related to homeland politics, preserving cultural traditions, and protecting the civil rights of group members. The Chinese Consolidated Benevolent Association (CCBA) in New York City, for example, has provided housing and job assistance to immigrants, assistance with the naturalization process, and has been involved in local politics in Chinatown, including hiring Asian contractors and workers (Lin 1998).

Finally, voter education groups often target immigrants, sometimes in response to particular threats such as Proposition 187 in California. Ramakrishnan's recent research investigates the mobilizing activity in 1994 and 1998 of groups such as the Southwest Voter Research and Education Project (SVREP), the Mexican American Legal Defense and Education Fund, and the Salvadoran American Legal and Education Fund, all of which targeted newly registered voters, many of them first generation (Ramakrishnan 2005, Ch. 6). In late 2003 the Houston Coalition for Immigrant Rights began a campaign to persuade immigrants to register in time for the 2004 election, and the organizers pointed out that they may have an easier time now that Mexico allows dual citizenship. The coalition included the SEIU, three Central American immigrant rights group, and a youth group.[16] SVREP dispatches organizers to work with church and civic groups to register and activate Latino voters, and is attempting to mobilize four hundred thousand Latino voters in fifteen states in the South, the Southwest, and the West. "The hope is to work with these people through three election cycles, eventually turning them into habitual voters." It is hard to imagine a clearer statement of incorporativist intentions. "We do what political parties used to do two generations ago," says Antonio Gonzalez, president of SVREP (Freedman and Johnson, 2002, 10–11).

Although the contemporary portrait of immigrant political incorporation remains a work in progress, the emerging picture is one including a large and growing immigrant and immigrant-stock population for whom parties are neither a vital nor the only mechanism of political incorporation. In the early twentieth century, political parties played a critical role as intermediary between immigrant communities and the political system, aiding in naturalization, voter registration, and voting. But parties today have not developed strategies to bring new immigrants into politics. They appear to be leaving these functions to nonparty groups. Although

[16] *Houston Chronicle*, 16 Oct. 2003, A21. Attention to immigrants' rights was an issue in the mayoralty election in Houston during November and December 2003.

some of these groups may promote naturalization and registration as part of their general mission, and others may want to mobilize immigrants to increase their leverage on particular issues, votes of immigrant groups (or other groups) are not central to their mission and goals, as they are for political parties.

## PARTIES OPTING OUT: A CASE STUDY OF LOCAL POLITICS IN SYRACUSE

A brief case study of Syracuse, New York, provides a concrete example of how even local political parties have abandoned their traditional role with regard to new groups (Andersen and Wintringham 2003). Syracuse, like many mid-sized U.S. cities, has seen steady streams of immigrants over the last decade. In 2000, the foreign-born constituted 7.6 percent of the city's population. Of these eleven thousand immigrants, almost 60 percent had entered the country between 1990 and 2000. The Syracuse foreign-born included significant numbers from Eastern Europe (particularly Poland, Ukraine, and the former Yugoslavia); Italy; a scattering of Caribbean and Latin Americans; significant numbers from China, Korea, and India as well as almost seventeen hundred Vietnamese.[17] For the most part, immigrant groups in Syracuse are not highly visible to local politicians and party leaders, although state-level shifts in this regard may be percolating down to the local level. A local Republican leader, while acknowledging that the party had not taken any initiatives to help immigrants naturalize, pointed to Governor Pataki's efforts to create a good relationship with the Latino community and talked about first efforts to reach out to the Latino community in Syracuse. This experience was important, and in the next campaign, one Republican Party official said he intended to have Spanish-language materials ready.

The party leaders we talked to were aware of the Spanish Action League and the Southeast Asian Center in Syracuse, as well as the various other agencies providing assistance to immigrants. They sometimes attended citizenship classes or visited the organizations' headquarters, but these visits were made with the intention of making some initial contact with new voters rather than urging people to naturalize, register, or vote.[18] Party officials mentioned no ongoing programs or initiatives in this regard. Republicans described the Vietnamese as "probably Republican" in philosophy, but party leaders admitted that they had not done a very good

---

[17] U.S. Census, 2000. Summary File 3. PCT19, Place of Birth for the Foreign-Born Population.
[18] Vice Chair, Onondaga County Democratic Party, interview 2-26-03.

job with voter registration, suggesting tables in malls, for example, but acknowledging that their get-out-the-vote efforts were limited to regular voters.[19]

A Democratic county legislator agreed that politicians reach out to voters who have voted for them in the past: "I guess when a politician says 'a constituency,' our constituency that we have embedded in our mind are those people who are out there voting."[20] The registration and voting rates of the areas with significant concentrations of immigrants are lower than those of the city as a whole. In 2000, Onondaga County Board of Elections data show that the rate of voter registration (percentage of those over eighteen registered) for the city of Syracuse was 53.7 percent, compared with 39.4 percent for people residing in census tracts with a high concentration of immigrants. Similarly, over the elections from 1994 to 2000, the average percentage of registrants who voted was lower for those residing in heavily immigrant areas (36.5 percent) as compared with Syracuse as a whole (44.7 percent).

Another local Republican officeholder told us that when the local party conducted voter registration drives aimed at registering new voters, it introduced a great deal of uncertainty into the outcome. Indeed, as a result of some losses in those areas, party leaders have retreated from registration and mobilization strategies. In this regard, party organizations do not casually reach out to new voters. Rather, they calculate the contribution that potential new voters are likely to make to a victory by the party's candidate, relative to the costs of attempted mobilization. Building up a long-term relationship with a community requires substantial time and effort, and may not be deemed worthwhile. Speaking particularly of the Vietnamese community, a leader of one of the nonprofits we spoke with said,

> Political parties don't try as hard as they should, in my opinion to get to this community. There are almost 5000 people here, many of them are citizens, many of them feel very grateful to this country for allowing them to come here, and so would vote. But candidates don't stop around here. It's an untapped population, in terms of politics.[21]

In this case, the language barrier adds to the challenge: "I think there are a lot of potential voters, and it's easier to go after ones that speak English if you speak English."[22]

---

[19] Ibid.

[20] Democratic County Legislator, interview 2-26-03.

[21] Interview with the director of the Refugee Resettlement Program of IRC, October 7, 2002.

[22] Ibid.

Immigrants are not particularly visible to local party leaders and politicians, because party leaders are accustomed to dealing with established groups; because their overall numbers are not great and, perhaps more important, because they are so heterogeneous. The situation might be different in a city with a similar proportion of immigrants but with less diversity among the new arrivals. But in Syracuse, those people we talked with who are associated with immigrant communities believe that the parties almost completely ignore the immigrants and refugees.

## CONTEXTUAL FACTORS AND POLITICAL INCORPORATION

Although research probably supports the general claim that parties have opted out more than they have reached out to immigrant voters, there are certainly variations in the contours of immigrant incorporation. To understand these variations it is important to go beyond the national level and consider the state and local political contexts. Political incorporation is most often treated as an individual decision – a calculation of the costs and benefits of naturalization, membership in a political organization, voting, or participating in some other way. But individuals do not live in isolation from one another, whether they live and work among fellow coethnic immigrants or are more integrated with native-born Americans. Instead, people are embedded in a social and political context that structures the opportunities and incentives for making political decisions. In this section, I discuss several dimensions of political context that are relevant to immigrant political incorporation, reviewing what we know about the factors that influence political incorporation, and analyzing state-level differences in naturalization.[23]

The decision to naturalize as a U.S. citizen, to register, and to vote are influenced by a myriad of factors. It is most common for analysts to identify predictors of political incorporation that are based in individual-level resources such as income and education. In the most comprehensive study of immigrant political incorporation to date, Ramakrishnan finds resources have an effect on voting across all the racial groups and immigrant generations he studied. " . . . [R]eturns to voting from SES factors are weaker for first-generation immigrants than for those in later immigrant generations, but these effects are still positive and significant" (Ramakrishnan

---

[23] Irene Bloemraad 2006 has analyzed historical data from the United States that illustrates nicely the substantial variation in naturalization rates across states in the early twentieth century, variations that were somewhat reduced when immigration laws were nationalized in 1906.

2005, 52). Earlier studies such as Junn (1999) and Cho (1999) present findings bearing inconsistencies across groups, although some of this may be a result of a difference in sampling frames and time of data collection. Similarly, length of stay in the United States, and respondent's age have been found to influence naturalization and voting behavior (Bass and Kasper 2001). Other recent studies conclude that both individual characteristics including property ownership matter for voting but contextual factors such as living in a relatively wealthy community also contribute to political incorporation among immigrants (Minnite and Mollenkopf 2001).

These studies underscore the importance of individual-level traits for political participation. Nevertheless, understanding variation in immigrant political behavior requires a consideration of the context of local political and institutional factors. In particular, Michael Jones-Correa argues that patterns of settlement among immigrants to the United States is uneven, varying substantially by geographic region, and between rural and metropolitan areas. "The nature of this variation is still largely unexplored. Does it make a difference if immigrants reside in areas where there are already large immigrant populations versus those where they are only one of a few? Does it make a difference if immigrants live in the sprawl of suburbia versus compact central cities? Does it make a difference if immigrants live in key 'battleground' states which are fought over in national elections rather than living in a relative electoral backwater which is taken for granted by one party or another?" (Jones-Correa 2005, 92).

Among the most important set of contextual factors influencing immigrant political incorporation is state of residence (DeSipio 2001, 12). State-level variations reflect differences in political culture as well as election-specific factors. For example, DeSipio notes that Texas had a low level of campaigning in 2000, as the presidential race was "largely uncontested and there were not competitive state-wide or Congressional races" (De-Sipio 2001, 13). Similarly, other research demonstrates that political context makes a difference for newly naturalized Latino citizens in California, who in the 1990s registered and voted at higher rates than native-born citizens, longer-term naturalized citizens, and Latinos in other states (Pantoja, Ramirez, and Segura 2001). Pantoja and his colleagues argue this higher degree of mobilization was the result of perceived threats to their interests presented by California ballot propositions during that period.[24]

---

[24] DeSipio 2002 also points to a particular effect of California politics in the 1990s: "California Latinos who naturalized between 1992 and 1996 were approximately 23 percent *more* likely to vote than all other respondents (a mixed category of earlier naturalizer and the

The distribution of immigrants is not even across the nation, and areas with high concentrations of immigrants – and perhaps especially those places with high concentrations of naturalized immigrants – will be particularly interesting as indicators of the ways new voters are entering and having an impact on the political system.[25] The national party organizations may put up Spanish Web pages, but it is at the local level where new voters are registered, contacted by candidates, and where they vote. Six states currently have foreign-born populations of one million or more, including California, New York, Texas, Illinois, Florida, and New Jersey. These six states alone account for more than two-thirds (68 percent) of the foreign-born population in the United States. Large metropolitan areas within this set of states, including New York City, Los Angeles, Houston, and Chicago are home to large concentrations of immigrants and their children.

Other states such as Arkansas, Georgia, Nevada, and North Carolina have seen dramatic increases in immigrant populations, on the order of 200 percent increases between 1990 and 2000. Although the proportion of immigrants has grown substantially, their arrival has been recent, and relatively few are naturalized citizens, compared to California, New York, and Texas. This clearly dampens the immediate electoral impact of immigrants in the Southern, Western, and border states, but their potential power in elections remains to be seen. In this regard, the timing of immigration is important in shaping how newcomers are incorporated politically, and the extent to which they have a political impact. Immigrants must reside in the United States for five years before they can gain citizenship, one reason why states with high levels of recent immigration still have relatively low naturalization rates. Only a few states with more well-established immigrant populations saw an increase in naturalized citizens as a proportion of the total foreign-born population between 1990 and 2000. These include California, Florida, Hawaii, Maryland, Virginia, and New York.

The density and concentration of immigrant and ethnic communities, the presence of organizational networks, the existence of political entrepreneurs in the new communities, the incentives to create cross-group coalitions, and the receptiveness of local political parties will shape the ways that immigrants are involved in politics. Barreto et al. (2004)

---

U.S. born). Latinos who naturalized recently in Florida, on the other hand, were less likely to vote than the blended residual category" (8). Thus the unique political situation in California mobilized naturalized immigrants to vote. See also de la Garza et al. 2002.

[25] Money (1999) makes an extended (and cross-nationally comparative) argument to this effect.

examined the effects of minority-majority districts on Latino turnout. Waldinger (1996) argues the institutional structures of Los Angeles and New York including the at-large political representation in Los Angeles versus district level representation in New York as well as the tradition of ethnically balanced slate-making have meant that immigrants to New York are more easily incorporated into politics than new citizens who settle in Los Angeles.

These observations are consistent with the more general claim among political scientists such as Rosenstone and Hansen (1993) that patterns of participation can be traced largely "to the strategic choices of politicians, political parties, interest groups, and activists. People participate in politics not so much because of who they are but because of the political choices and incentives they are offered" (Rosenstone and Hansen 1993, 5). Theda Skocpol has made similar arguments about the structuring of opportunities to participate in voluntary organizations (Skocpol 1993). Jeremy Weinstein (1999) examined state-level variables measuring party competition and party mobilization efforts to explain levels of "social capital" such as political engagement and index of community organizational life. He found that "inter-state differences in party mobilization are a powerful correlate of levels of political and community engagement" (18). These perspectives dovetail with the long tradition in political science recognizing the impact of unique state political cultures on political participation.

Before candidates and parties can either court them as potential voters or opt out of mobilization, immigrants must become citizens. As with patterns of international migration to particular locales in the United States, there is substantial variation in the extent to which immigrants have naturalized by state. Rates of citizenship are heavily dependent on the average length of time immigrants have been in United States. Table 2.1 categorizes states according to rates of immigrant naturalization, and compares that proportion to the recency of arrival of immigrants. The first column lists the states from lowest to highest in terms of percent of foreign-born who are naturalized. This proportion varies from the low of 26–32 percent to the high of 50–60 percent naturalized citizens. The third column of the table provides the average percentage of immigrants who entered the United States between 1990 and 2000. The data in Table 2.1 show a clear pattern of an inverse relationship between proportion who are naturalized citizens, and recency of immigration. The higher the proportion of foreign-born arriving in the United States between 1990 and 2000, the lower the level of naturalization.

**TABLE 2.1.** Naturalization and Time in United States by States

| State | Percentage of immigrants who are naturalized | Average percentage of immigrants entering after 1990 |
|---|---|---|
| NC, GA, AZ, AK, DC, UT, TX, CO, NE | 26–32 | 54.7 |
| IA, ID, KS, TN, OR, KY, OK, NM AL, NV, SC MN, IN, CA, WI | 33–39 | 50.6 |
| IL, MS, SD, VA, MO, WA, DE, ND, MA | 40–44 | 47.8 |
| FL, MD, WY, MI, NY, NJ, RI, NH, LA, CT | 45–49 | 39.6 |
| OH, PA, VT, AK, WV, ME, MT, HI | 50–60 | 35.7 |

*Source:* U.S. Census 2000, Summary File 3, Tables QT P14 and P21.

Although this relationship is obvious, there are other factors at work influencing the process by which immigrants become American voters. For example, even in states with very similar patterns of recent immigration, naturalization rates vary substantially. For example, in the category where more than 50 percent of the foreign-born arrived recently, rates vary from 26 percent in North Carolina to 43 percent in North Dakota. Conversely, in states with more settled immigrant populations – where fewer than 40 percent of immigrants arrived after 1990 – California has a 39 percent naturalization rate, Rhode Island 47 percent, and in Hawaii 60 percent of immigrants are naturalized citizens.

In this regard, recency of immigration tells only part of the story about how many immigrants will naturalize to U.S. citizenship and become potential voters. Variation in political institutional conditions among states may help to account for some of the differences in the naturalization rates. The analysis that follows in Table 2.2 represents a brief and preliminary attempt to examine the impact of state institutional variation on rates of naturalization. The independent variables in this model include the level of statewide party competition in the 1990s; average presidential turnout in 1988 and 1992; and average state turnout in House of Representatives elections between 1989 and 1994. Together, these variables provide information about the extent to which parties structure the political context in a particular state. Higher turnout may be an indicator of the extent of party mobilization activity in a particular state, and parties in competitive situations presumably have a stronger interest in mobilizing

TABLE 2.2. State Institutional Factors and Rate of Naturalization

| Factor | Coefficient (and standard error) | Standardized coefficient, Beta |
|---|---|---|
| Average time in United States | .015** (.003) | .604** |
| Presence of civic and social organizations | .616** (.172) | .527** |
| Presidential election voting turnout | .345 (.213) | .284 |
| U.S. House election voting turnout | −.006** (.002) | −.580** |
| Party competition (Ranney index) | −.024 (.068) | −.034 |
| Percent immigrants in metro areas | .001 (.00) | .139 |
| N | 50 | |
| Constant | .094 (.099) | |
| Adjusted R-squared | .629 | |

Significance levels: ** p <.01.
*Sources:* Naturalization Rate: Census 2000, Summary File 3, P21. Average time in US: Census CPS Voting & Registration Supplements, 1994–2000 (pooled); Turnout variables and Ranney index of party competition: Gray, Hanson and Jacobs 1999; Civic organizations per 1000: bowlingalone.com.

new groups. Because the research on immigrant political incorporation suggests that parties are no longer very active in incorporating immigrant groups and that to some extent other groups and organizations have taken on that role, I also include a variable that measures the density of civic organizations in the state. Another important aspect of the political context for immigrants is their spatial concentration; thus another independent variable is the percentage of the immigrant population living in metropolitan areas. Finally, because time in the United States is such an important correlate of naturalization, I include average time in the United States as reported by immigrant respondents in the Census supplemental surveys. The dependent variable in this analysis is the percentage of a state's foreign-born residents who are citizens, as reported in the 2000 Census.

This analysis shows clearly that the average length of time a state's immigrants have resided in the United States has a significant positive impact on the state's rate of naturalization, even when controlling for other variables. The other major factor that is associated with high rates of naturalization is the density of civic organizations. Turnout in House elections has a negative impact on naturalization rate, whereas party competition is not significant. This supports the notion that nonparty organizations are involved – perhaps more than parties in many places – in encouraging immigrants to naturalize. That the existence of competitive party systems, situations in which it should be in the parties' interest to attract new voters, seems to have no impact on naturalization rates further supports the argument that parties are not actively reaching out to immigrant voters. Another possibility, of course, is that states are not really the appropriate units of analysis, and that we should be characterizing local parties and looking at naturalization rates by city or county. And, of course, an aggregate-level model like this cannot take into account the influence of individual-level factors such as education and income among immigrants. What it can do is highlight the significance of state and local contextual factors in establishing a mobilizing network for new immigrant voters. Similarly, although naturalization does not necessarily signify political activity such as voting, becoming a U.S. citizen is the first and most important step, both symbolically and legally for political incorporation. And the ability to vote puts individual citizens and organized groups of citizens in a much different position with regard to political leaders and political parties, an argument made repeatedly by advocates of woman suffrage in the early twentieth century.

## IN WHOSE INTEREST? THE FUTURE OF IMMIGRANT POLITICAL INCORPORATION

I have been discussing the "political incorporation" of immigrants as if this was analytically distinct from other forms of incorporation – in particular economic incorporation. There are numerous examples of states and localities eager to incorporate immigrants into the local economies. The city of Pittsburgh, one of the few large cities without recent Latino immigrants, has a grant-supported program to recruit immigrants to supply labor to the city in jobs as diverse as landscapers and nurses.[26] Some states that have seen recent increases in immigration have created legislation designed to make it possible for even the undocumented to participate in the economy. These measures include liberalizing driver's license standards and college tuition requirements, allowing banks to offer home loans to undocumented immigrants, and wide acceptance of a controversial Mexican identification card for many purposes. It should be noted that, at the same time, other states are acting to restrict the access of undocumented immigrants to a whole range of public services – thus, like political incorporation, economic incorporation varies across space.

[26] *Wall Street Journal*, 28 May 2003, B1.

But, in general, incentives to accommodate new employees and con-
sumers are stronger than the incentives for political parties and elected
officials to incorporate new citizens. Immigrants as new citizens are
"nonimmunized" voters, with no track record of partisan affiliation or voting record in the United States. Established political mobilizing institutions,
most notably political parties, develop electoral strategies to maximize
winning the election rather than to bring in new voters. Effective local
parties have traditionally had excellent information about their prospects,
down to very specific political geographies. A potentially volatile electorate
only creates uncertainty for strategic actors, and therefore discourages
parties from undertaking efforts to mobilize immigrants. For this reason
and others, it is an unusual local political party these days that engages
in much political education and community organizing in immigrant
communities.[27]

Nonetheless, if modern American parties at all levels of government
are correctly seen as organizations fundamentally geared toward winning
elections, they might be expected – at least occasionally – to welcome
the opportunity to create new groups of supporters and add to their constituency base. For this to happen, several conditions need to be met.
First, the parties must be in a competitive situation; a party with a consistent majority will have no incentive to invest resources in cultivating
new supporters, and a party in a consistent minority position may be too
demoralized and disorganized to engage in this activity. The increasing
geographical polarization of the parties and decreasing competitiveness of
House seats may thus be partially responsible for the parties' unwillingness
to reach out to immigrants.

Second, the new groups have to be visible to the parties, either as a
function of large and growing numbers, or because community leaders
fight for access to government and make their demands known to party
leaders and government officials. This is increasingly true in New York City,
where by some estimates, foreign-born voters now constitute as much
as a fifth of the city's electorate, and where over a dozen foreign-born
citizens ran in the City Council elections in 2001.[28] Third, the leaders of
political parties must perceive the immigrant group as being sympathetic
to the party philosophy. Finally, the party must see the advantages of

---

[27] See Vallely 2005 for a good theoretical discussion of the costs and benefits of incorporating
new groups into party coalitions and an attempt to apply these ideas historically in the
United States.
[28] *New York Times*, 8 Jan. 2001, 37.

attaching the group to its coalition, and calculate that those advantages outweigh potentially negative reactions of its core constituency to the new group. Only under these conditions – when it is in the interest of the political parties – does the potential for large-scale political incorporation of immigrants become possible.

Returning to the example of Syracuse for a moment, the first condition is met. The Central New York area is reasonably competitive in partisan terms, although the city is more consistently Democratic than the rest of the county. The backlash possibility seems remote in Syracuse. As argued earlier, however, immigrant groups – in part because they are not large, although they are fairly concentrated geographically – are not very visible to politicians and party leaders. Because these communities are not well known, the parties and politicians are probably unable to make informed judgments about the new groups' political preferences.

Politicians in immigrant-rich locations from New York, California, and Texas are far more conscious of the potential political impact of immigrant groups, taking both symbolic and material steps to accommodate the interests of local immigrant communities in their areas. But even in high-immigrant states and cities, today's parties see less of a role in educating and mobilizing the mass public. Compared to the national parties of one hundred or even seventy years ago, today's Democrats and Republicans derive their power increasingly from their roles as providers of services and funds to candidates, and less from their ability to organize at the grassroots level. Though American parties have always been primarily motivated by the desire to win elections, and in that context have always had the incentive to avoid the uncertainty associated with mobilizing new voters, shifts in the nature of parties particularly at the state and local level mean these organizations are not playing a central role in the political incorporation of immigrants. Other groups and organizations such as unions, churches, nonprofits, and neighborhood organizations may be filling this gap, but the patterns are distinctive by locale and more research is needed to specify the conditions under which the traditional role of political incorporation has been replaced by social organizations.

Among the most interesting cases for future study include states and metropolitan areas either where there are large numbers of naturalized citizens, or where the growth in immigrant populations has undergone recent increases. Some proportion of new citizens eventually turn into voters, and to the extent they are organized around appeals made to immigrants, these voters can have a measurable political impact. It is a risky strategy for parties to continue to ignore new voting populations, and the chances are greater that efforts at political incorporation will begin to increase.[29] At present, we know surprisingly little about the relationship between increases in the foreign-born population, changes in the level of votes cast, and changes in party control at the congressional and state legislative levels.

As first- and second-generation immigrants move from gateway cities and ethnic enclaves to suburbs and smaller towns and cities in the South and Midwest, it is unlikely to be sheer numbers that will capture the attention of parties and politicians. Electorally competitive seats are also rare, with less than 10 percent of U.S. congressional districts truly competitive. Given this, organization and leadership within immigrant communities become critical. What carries the greatest potential for political impact is the situation in which an immigrant community, once it has reached a certain numerical threshold, develops strong organizational capacity. Under these circumstances, leaders can be easily identified, and can gain the reputation of being able to mobilize the community; there are associations or clubs that politicians can visit; there are "obvious" people or organizations that elected officials feel they need to consult about local issues. In this situation, parties begin to reach out to the community even if some of the other conditions are not met: This is one way that ethnic organizations, unions, religious organizations, and other groups become important politically, as they produce leaders who are visible to politicians and parties.

---

[29] Although, as we have seen, naturalization rates among first-generation immigrants are low, parties themselves are not generally encouraging naturalization, and other groups and organizations often have other priorities. As a result, it is not surprising to find legislative districts in California with large Latino populations represented by long-term Republican incumbents.

# 3  Beyond Black and White

## The Experiences and Effects of Economic Status among Racial and Ethnic Minorities

As the size of the black middle class has grown in the post–Civil Rights era, scholars have debated whether improved living standards and conditions of political equality have caused racial consciousness to be supplanted by class consciousness among African Americans. Wilson (1980) argued that the salience of race among African Americans would diminish with the decline of racial discrimination on the assumption that, as the life prospects of African Americans became more dependent on their economic status, their attitudes would be guided less by racial considerations and more by social class concerns.

Dawson (1994), however, found that identification with racial group interests was not weaker among higher status African Americans. On the contrary, income and education were positively correlated with the feeling among African Americans that they shared a common fate with other blacks. According to Dawson and other scholars (Cose 1995; Hochschild 1993, 1995), racial consciousness persists because racial discrimination remains sufficiently pervasive that individuals believe their personal advancement is tied to improvements in the status of the entire group. Middle-class African Americans continue to focus on economic disparities between blacks and whites and to equate their self-interest with the interests of the group despite their personal achievements.

The socioeconomic barriers created by racial prejudice and discrimination have led scholars to question whether the most recent immigrants to the United States from Latin America and Asia will follow the classic pattern of assimilation exhibited by earlier generations of European immigrants in which ethnic identities faded as individuals were structurally assimilated in American society (e.g., Alba and Nee 1997; Portes and Rumbaut 1996; Rumbaut 1997). Socioeconomic mobility creates opportunities for "equal status contacts across ethnic lines in workplaces and

39

neighborhoods" (Alba and Nee 1997, 831), but minorities may discover that their economic achievements do not erase racial and ethnic boundaries that limit their opportunities. If Asian Americans and Latinos face more formidable barriers to social acceptance by the majority population than did previous European immigrants, will they react to discrimination and impediments to mobility in the same way as African Americans?

## GROUP CONSCIOUSNESS AMONG AFRICAN AMERICANS, LATINOS, AND ASIAN AMERICANS

Most of what we know about the sources and effects of racial and ethnic group consciousness in U.S. politics derives from studies of African Americans (e.g., Chong and Rogers 2005; Dawson 1994; Gurin, Hatchett, and Jackson 1989). Only recently with the collection of representative survey data on Latinos and Asian Americans have researchers begun to explore whether racial and ethnic consciousness affects the political attitudes and behavior of other minority groups in the same degree as consciousness affects African Americans. This work largely follows the approach taken in research on African Americans by examining perceptions of shared interests among individuals and the potential for group consciousness to foster political participation (e.g., de la Garza et al. 1992; Jones-Correa and Leal 1996; Lien, Conway, and Wong 2004).

These studies have just begun to examine whether Latinos and Asian Americans will place the same priority as African Americans on racial and ethnic group interests over economic considerations in their political attitudes and policy preferences. To explain similarities and differences in the political attitudes of African Americans, Latinos, and Asian Americans, we need a theory flexible enough to accommodate variations among minority groups in their socioeconomic status and their evaluations of opportunities and conditions in American society. It is a reasonable first approximation to place these three groups into the general category of minorities and to contrast their structural position and subjective states to those of whites. But within the common outlook of minority populations are significant differences that are likely to have a bearing on their political attitudes and behavior.

An important source of variation among African Americans, Latinos, and Asian Americans that may influence the salience of race and ethnicity among them is their contrasting levels of socioeconomic success. Compared to African Americans, Asian Americans have achieved greater levels of economic success, although the group averages calculated on the basis of this broad racial category masks significant variation among Asian Americans. In terms of education, income, and home ownership, Asian Americans appear to be rapidly integrating into American society and making the kind of progress that befits their disputed title as a "model minority" (Ong 2000; Alba and Nee 2003). Asian Americans also report experiencing discrimination significantly less frequently than do African Americans. They are more optimistic than other minorities about their prospects and believe they are doing well according to most conventional measures of success (Kaiser Family Foundation 1995).

Latinos face markedly different contemporary social and economic conditions compared to Asian Americans and African Americans (Hero 1992; Jones-Correa 1998; de la Garza 2004). In median income, housing, and education, Latinos have a status that is similar to, if not worse than, African Americans. Latinos themselves believe their socioeconomic status compares unfavorably to that of whites, but at the same time many Latinos came to this country because they believe the United States offers more economic opportunities than their home countries.[1] Latinos experience high rates of discrimination (second only to African Americans) that might foster group consciousness, but a majority do not attribute their socioeconomic difficulties to past and present discrimination (de la Garza et al. 1992).

Such differences in the economic circumstances of African Americans, Latinos, and Asian Americans, and in their interpretations of group conditions and economic opportunities, should affect the centrality of racial and ethnic group interests in their evaluations of political issues. In particular, we should not assume the political attitudes of Asian Americans and Latinos will be as impervious to changes in economic status as those of African Americans given their disparate assessments of prospects for success and varying experiences with discrimination. With these premises as our starting point, we examine the effects of economic status, opportunities, and perceptions of discrimination on the propensity of African Americans, Latinos, and Asian Americans to pursue racial and ethnic group interests. We use the variation among minorities on these dimensions to develop a theory of opportunities and group consciousness that explains how and when economic status will affect support for group interests.

From this theory, we derive two hypotheses relating support for group interests to the economic status and socioeconomic experiences and

[1] See the survey top lines from the *Washington Post*/Kaiser Family Foundation/Harvard University 1999 National Survey on Latinos in America, available at http://www.kff.org.

perceptions of individuals. We first examine variation among African Americans, Latinos, and Asian Americans in the extent to which economic status influences support for racial and ethnic group interests. We then test conditions when higher economic status is more likely to diminish support for group interests among members of all three groups. In our conclusion, we discuss the implications of these results for political assimilation and minority group politics.[2]

## A THEORY OF OPPORTUNITIES AND GROUP CONSCIOUSNESS

The persistence of racial consciousness among African Americans in reaction to unequal opportunities highlights a general relationship between group consciousness and discrimination that has been replayed through the course of American history. The assimilation of a minority group into American society depends not only on the actions of group members but also on the reception accorded that group by the majority population. An impediment to the assimilation of immigrants in different eras has been the reluctance of the majority to allow new groups equal access to the mainstream social and political institutions of society (Higham 1992). Whether the majority opens its doors to minorities – in its neighborhoods, schools, corporations and businesses, private clubs, and political institutions – affects the propensity of minorities to relinquish their identification with a racial or ethnic subculture (Gordon 1964). Immigrants who enjoy more extensive social and economic opportunities are more likely to assimilate to the mainstream and reduce their attachment to racial or ethnic groups as a means to improve their own life chances and those of their children (Dahl 1961; Alba and Nee 2003).[3]

---

[2] We maintain a distinction between perceptions of a group interest and support for policies that promote group interests. We refer to these perceptions as "racial group consciousness" (in the case of African Americans and Asian Americans) and "ethnic group consciousness" (in the case of Latinos), and to the policy preferences as "support for racial and ethnic group interests." The conceptual distinction is blurred because the two concepts are closely related and significantly correlated empirically. Some researchers (e.g., Verba, Schlozman, and Brady 1995) have ignored the distinction between identification with group interests and support for them by including indicators of both in a measure of racial consciousness. The theory we develop in this paper is meant to account for variation in both group consciousness and support for group interests, and in discussing the dynamics of that theory we will often refer interchangeably to both perceptions and support. Our empirical tests of the theory focus on support for group interests in public policy.

[3] An important qualification of this dynamic is the idea of segmented assimilation proposed by Portes and Zhou (1993), which raises the possibility that upward mobility does not weaken group values among those immigrant groups that possess strong social networks based on race or ethnicity.

These social psychological dynamics conform readily to the general theory of social identity developed by Henri Tajfel and his associates (Tajfel and Turner 1979; Tajfel 1981; Hogg and Abrams 1988). According to this theory, dissatisfaction with one's social status can motivate efforts to improve one's position through either individual or collective means. The choice between these strategies depends on whether one believes society provides individuals with an equal opportunity to advance. Individuals who believe that social mobility is possible are less likely to identify with their current group because they feel the boundaries between groups are permeable and that hard work, education, and other investments will allow them to move to a higher status group. A belief in the possibility of social mobility therefore tends to be associated with individualist strategies that work within the status quo.

On the other hand, if socioeconomic boundaries are less permeable and opportunities for mobility are blocked, individuals will become more conscious of their group memberships, especially if those group affiliations are responsible for restricting their mobility. One avenue for individuals to improve their personal status is by working with fellow group members to advance the group's status, because their individual interests are tied to the fortunes of the group as a whole. This basic dynamic between mobility and group identification lies at the center of our theory of opportunities. We expect the effect of economic status on support for group interests will depend significantly on the degree to which individuals perceive opportunities for social mobility. Whether middle-class minorities experience equal opportunity or encounter prejudice and discrimination in their daily lives will affect the extent to which they remain conscious of their minority status and support policies that address racial and ethnic inequality. Variation across minority groups in the effect of economic status on racial and ethnic consciousness and support for group interests can therefore be explained by systematic differences in the perceptions and experiences of group members rather than by contrasting psychological processes.

The theory of opportunities suggests two hypotheses about the relationship between economic status and group consciousness among African Americans, Latinos, and Asian Americans. Our first hypothesis is that African Americans' support for group interests, relative to that of Latinos and Asian Americans, will be the least responsive to changes in economic circumstances because African Americans face more daunting economic and social barriers than other racial and ethnic minorities. When African Americans achieve higher economic status, they continue to experience discrimination and to evaluate their life prospects in racial terms.

Our second hypothesis tests whether the same factors that explain inter-group differences can also explain intragroup variation. As Gay (2004) recently demonstrated, greater satisfaction among African Americans with the quality of their residential neighborhoods tends to weaken their belief that they share a common fate with other African Americans. We examine more generally whether the effect of economic status on support for group interests is conditioned by individual experiences of status among all minorities. If prejudice and discrimination reinforce the tendency of minorities to think in group terms, then the effect of improvements in economic status on group consciousness will depend on the socioeconomic experiences of individuals. Individuals who experience social and economic integration alongside their higher economic status should attribute less importance to race or ethnicity as a determinant of life circumstances. Economic security in such cases should reduce support for group interests.

By contrast, individuals who achieve nominal material success but continue to feel excluded on racial or ethnic grounds from the economic and social institutions that normally accompany higher status should be more likely to retain their group consciousness. They will be more inclined to view politics in racial or ethnic terms and to support policies designed to remove structural and institutional barriers to equality. This specification of the circumstances in which economic status will moderate group consciousness should account for differences *across* racial and ethnic groups as well as *within* them.

There are, of course, other factors that influence development of group consciousness beyond the socioeconomic elements examined here, but they fall outside the scope of the data analyzed in this chapter. A comprehensive model also would take account of various agents of socialization, patterns of social interaction, and the racial composition and quality of neighborhoods – among other life experiences and contextual factors – to explain similarities and differences in consciousness across racial and ethnic groups (e.g., Demo and Hughes 1990; Welch et al. 2001; Gay 2004). We develop a central component of this comprehensive model with our theory of opportunities, by offering general propositions about the effect of economic status and socioeconomic experiences on racial and ethnic consciousness that are applicable across minority groups.

Our analysis uses data gathered in a national survey conducted jointly by the *Washington Post*, the Kaiser Family Foundation, and Harvard University (*Post*/Kaiser/Harvard) in 2001. This survey allows us to study how minority groups regard their own position in society, and how their perceptions of social conditions combine with their material life circumstances and experiences to influence their support for racial and ethnic group interests. Unlike typical national surveys, this survey included an oversample of 696 minority respondents (230 African Americans, 237 Latinos, and 229 Asian Americans) in addition to a regular national random sample of 1,013 respondents. This resulted in a nationally representative sample of 1,709 randomly selected respondents aged eighteen and older consisting of 779 whites, 323 African Americans, 315 Latinos, and 254 Asian Americans. Sampling bias was reduced by conducting interviews with Latinos in either English or Spanish, and with Asian Americans in English, Korean, Cantonese, Mandarin, Vietnamese, or Japanese depending on the respondent's preference. The descriptive statistics and model estimations reported here are weighted to reflect the actual racial and ethnic distribution in the nation.[4]

## TESTING THE THEORY OF OPPORTUNITIES

The *Post*/Kaiser/Harvard survey contains extensive data on the material quality of life of racial and ethnic minorities, and their assessments of opportunities for advancement in American society. In addition, the survey contains self-report data on the amount of prejudice and discrimination experienced by respondents in everyday life. These data allow us to test how variations in economic status and socioeconomic experiences and perceptions affect support for group interests among African Americans, Latinos, and Asian Americans.

We estimate two statistical models corresponding to our two hypotheses. Our first model examines the relative influence of economic status, perceptions of life opportunities, and direct experiences with discrimination on support for racial and ethnic group interests. Our second model examines the effect of economic status conditional on perceptions of opportunities and experiences of discrimination. In the second model, we use interaction terms to test whether improvements in economic circumstances are more likely to weaken support for group interests among African Americans, Latinos, and Asian Americans who experience equal treatment in society than among individuals who continue to face discrimination. The key comparison for our purposes is between those individuals who have had positive experiences (i.e., those who perceive equal

---

[4] The margin of sampling error for the whole sample is ±3 percent; for non-Hispanic Whites – ±4 percent; for African Americans – ±6 percent; for Latinos – ±7 percent; and for Asian Americans – ±9 percent.

opportunity *and* encounter little discrimination) and those who have had negative experiences (i.e., those who perceive unequal opportunities *and* encounter frequent discrimination). Higher economic status should significantly reduce support for group interests among those in the former category, but have a negligible effect among those in the latter. We will pay less attention to respondents in the hybrid mixed category (i.e., those who *either* perceive equal opportunity *or* encounter little discrimination) because our theory does not offer a definite prediction about how these individuals will respond to their conflicting perceptions and experiences.

## RACIAL AND ETHNIC GROUP INTERESTS

In previous research, racial and ethnic consciousness has been most commonly measured with items probing feelings of shared interests and closeness with other individuals of the same race or ethnicity. The *Post*/Kaiser/ Harvard survey does not contain these traditional consciousness items, but it contains several questions assessing whether racial or ethnic group interests are central to how one thinks about politics. We use three of these indicators of support for group interests on political issues as our dependent variables.[5] Our first measure is a question asking respondents whether more attention or less attention should be paid to racial issues in this country (or if just the right amount of attention is currently being paid to race). Our two other measures of group interests are based on preferences toward affirmative action and government policies to ensure equality between minorities and whites in health care, education, jobs, and the administration of the law. The affirmative action question asks whether special efforts should be made by colleges and businesses to recruit qualified minorities. The four questions about government's role in ensuring equality, which we aggregated into a scale, present a trade-off between group interests and individual economic costs by asking respondents if they support government action in each policy domain even if it leads to higher taxes.

Each of these measures probes the extent to which one thinks about public affairs along racial or ethnic lines and gives priority to group benefits when evaluating public policy. In recognition of the difference between these items and conventional measures of racial consciousness, we will generally refer to our dependent variables as measures of support for racial

---

[5] See the appendix for the question wordings and additional information about the survey data.

and ethnic group interests.[6] However, we assume that minority group members who call for more attention to race and support government policies aimed at redressing inequality are also more conscious of their own racial or ethnic identity and more likely to associate their group's interest on these issues with their individual interest.

This assumption is substantiated in Dawson's (1994) analysis of the predictors of support among African Americans for government racial policies similar to those used in our analysis, including affirmative action, aid to blacks, programs to improve the quality of education for blacks, and government efforts to improve the economic position of blacks. Dawson found that perceptions of a "linked fate" with other African Americans "played the greatest role in predicting support for government racial policies.... On the whole, the expectation that the perception of linkage between individual and group interest would dominate in policy areas where race is clearly salient is supported by this analysis" (194).[7]

The marginal distributions of opinion on our three indicators of group interests confirm that African Americans place more emphasis on racial considerations than do Latinos and Asian Americans. Sixty-four percent of African Americans believe that too little attention is paid to race, compared to 41 percent of Latinos and 33 percent of Asian Americans. Similarly, 77 percent of African Americans endorse extra efforts by employers and colleges to recruit qualified minorities versus 63 percent of Asian Americans and 62 percent of Latinos.

African Americans are also more likely to believe the federal government is responsible for ensuring equality in the areas of employment, education, health care, and law. Seventy-two percent of African Americans believe the government is responsible for ensuring that minorities have jobs of equal quality as whites. Identical proportions (89 percent) of African Americans believe the government should make sure that schools are of equal quality; guarantee that minorities and whites receive equal

[6] The three indicators of group interest are significantly correlated with one another and together form a scale with a reliability coefficient of .57. In the analysis to follow, we disaggregate the scale and examine how individuals respond to its separate components, because there is some variation across the measures, but we also report our findings when we use the scale as our dependent variable in the same models.

[7] We returned to the 1984–1988 NBES Panel Study and built a scale using the four racial policy attitude items described in the text to calculate the correlation between this scale and the measure of linked fate. The Pearson's r between the two measures is .21 and is statistically significant at the .001 level. Because the policy items in the NBES are similar in substance to the *Post*/Kaiser/Harvard items, we interpret this result as further evidence that the racial policy attitudes reflect racial consciousness.

health care services; and ensure that minorities and whites are treated equally by the courts and police. Majorities of Latinos and Asian Americans also feel the federal government is responsible for enforcing equality in these areas, but there is greater division of opinion within these two groups. The average level of support for government action across the four domains is 77 percent among Latinos and 71 percent among Asian Americans, compared to 85 percent among African Americans.

## ECONOMIC STATUS

Economic status is a composite measure that combines annual family income and ownership of stocks and bonds with subjective assessments of financial well-being and reports of past financial problems with rent and mortgage payments, medical care, and saving money for the future.[8] There is considerable group variation on these indicators of living standards. In objective terms, Asian Americans enjoy significant material advantages over Latinos and African Americans. Although a majority of African Americans (66 percent) and Latinos (63 percent) report annual family incomes of less than $40,000, a majority of Asian Americans (52 percent) indicate yearly family incomes greater than $40,000. A majority of Asian Americans (51 percent) own stocks, bonds, or mutual funds, whereas a majority of African Americans (66 percent) and Latinos (67 percent) do not.[9]

When asked to describe their personal financial situations, 64 percent of Asian Americans, and 53 percent of Latinos report that their financial state is either excellent or good, but a majority (51 percent) of African Americans say their financial situation is either poor or "not so good." African Americans and Latinos are also more likely than Asian Americans to report they have experienced difficulty paying mortgages or rents, getting medical care, or saving money for future needs.[10]

---

[8] The Cronbach's alpha measure of reliability for this scale is .72. The scale reliability declines to .68 if we omit the item measuring respondents' subjective perceptions of their personal economic situations. Subjective and objective indicators of well-being prove to be closely related. The simple correlation between subjective perceptions and the economic status scale constructed without this item is .51.

[9] According to the 2000 U.S. Census, the median incomes of African American, Latino, and Asian families were $33,255, $34,394, and $59,394, respectively. By comparison, the median income of white (non-Hispanic) families was $53,356.

[10] In the analysis to follow, we sometimes refer to the effect of "improvements" or "changes" in economic status, even though we are analyzing cross-sectional data. This phrasing is in keeping with the conventional interpretation of a regression coefficient as the change in the dependent variable produced by a unit change in the independent variable. Panel data would be needed to assess the effect of changes in economic status in the same individuals.

## PERCEPTION OF OPPORTUNITIES

Individuals were asked to evaluate their life opportunities relative to those enjoyed by whites. African Americans offer the most negative evaluations of their own group's chances in society. Seventy-four percent of African Americans feel they have fewer opportunities than whites, compared to 45 percent of Latinos and 34 percent of Asian Americans. Only 24 percent of African Americans think they have as many opportunities as whites. Asian Americans are more positive about their own group's opportunities than are Latinos. Sixty percent of Asian Americans feel they have either the same or better opportunities than whites, whereas 53 percent of Latinos believe they have at least as much opportunity as whites.

## PERSONAL EXPERIENCE OF DISCRIMINATION

Respondents were asked a series of seven questions about whether they had experienced racial or ethnic prejudice and discrimination in the workplace and in their daily lives. Answers to these questions were summed and converted to a scale measure. As in the case of economic status and perceived opportunities, there are systematic differences among minority groups, with African Americans suffering the indignities of racial discrimination to a significantly greater extent than other minorities. Latinos and Asian Americans also report being subjected to intolerance, but they are not exposed to prejudice as extensively and routinely as African Americans.

One out of every two African Americans report personal experiences with discrimination during the past ten years, compared to four in ten Latinos and Asian Americans. When asked about specific forms of discrimination, more than three out of every ten African Americans report having been unfairly stopped by the police. One in five Latinos and one in ten Asian Americans also report they have been subjected to racial profiling by the police. African Americans feel the slights and insults of prejudice and discrimination on a regular basis. A majority of African Americans report they have at least occasionally been treated with disrespect, received poor service, or encountered people who acted fearfully toward them because of their race. By contrast, a majority of Latinos and Asian Americans say they have never experienced discrimination in these ways.

The two models estimated also include statistical controls for education and ideology. We control for education, a component of socioeconomic status, to isolate the effects of *economic* status that are captured by our measure. We control for the respondent's political ideology to test whether the effects of economic status hold across all ideological groups.[11] Education is based on the respondent's highest grade or class completed, ranging from no education to a graduate degree. The majority of Asian Americans (64 percent) have at least some college education, whereas only 41 percent of African Americans and 26 percent of Latinos have attended college. Ideology is measured with a self-classification question on a seven-point scale ranging from very liberal to very conservative. In this survey, Asian Americans have the highest proportion of self-identified liberals, and Latinos have the highest percentage of conservatives, but moderates constitute the largest category within each of the three minority groups.[12]

## THE EFFECT OF ECONOMIC STATUS ON SUPPORT FOR GROUP INTERESTS

The *Post*/Kaiser/Harvard survey reveals a consistent pattern of Asian Americans' enjoying more economic security than Latinos and African Americans as well as having a more positive outlook on the opportunities and status of their group in American society. African Americans experience the

---

[11] We estimated models in which we included additional controls for age and gender on the assumption that younger respondents and men may be more likely to experience discrimination. For Asian Americans, neither age nor gender is significantly correlated with reports of discrimination; but for African Americans and Latinos both variables are moderately correlated in the expected direction (Pearson's r's range between .13 and .18). However, in the multivariate models predicting African Americans' and Latinos' racial attitudes, age and gender have a weak and inconsistent effect. Among African Americans, women are more likely than are men to support government action to address racial inequality. Among Latinos, younger individuals and women are more likely to call for greater attention to race. Otherwise, age and gender are statistically insignificant factors. With respect to the two main hypotheses tested in this paper, controlling for age and gender does not affect our findings and conclusions about the interaction between economic status and perceptions of opportunities and discrimination. Given the inconsistent and usually insignificant effects of age and gender, we favored the more parsimonious model reported here that excludes these variables.

We also tested (and rejected), using a form of Hausman specification test, the hypothesis of a reciprocal relationship between support for group interests and perceptions of economic opportunities and reported discrimination. See Chong and Kim (2006: 340–41) for details.

[12] In this survey, 22 percent of African Americans identify themselves as liberal, whereas 16 percent and 29 percent of Latinos and Asian Americans, respectively, say they are liberal. This marginal distribution differs from a 1995 *Washington Post* survey that was a precursor to the 2001 *Post*/Kaiser/Harvard survey. In the 1995 survey, the percentages of African Americans, Latinos, and Asian Americans who claimed liberal identification were 38 percent, 29 percent, and 25 percent, respectively. We do not have an explanation for this shift during the 6 years between surveys, although a potential source of variation may be the method used to over-sample minority respondents.

most discrimination and have the bleakest assessments of their opportunities relative to those of whites. Given the sharp contrast in the ways that African Americans, Latinos, and Asian Americans perceive their opportunities and standing in society, we expect a corresponding variation among these groups in the degree to which economic status will influence support for racial and ethnic group interests. Our first model therefore tests the hypothesis that economic status will have the least effect on the racial attitudes of African Americans compared to other minorities. We estimated this model separately for each of the three measures of group interest, and for each of the three minority groups.

## ATTENTION TO RACE

The results in Table 3.1 generally support our hypothesis that economic status has a weaker impact on the attitudes of African Americans than on the attitudes of Latinos and Asian Americans. Economic status has a statistically *insignificant* effect on the emphasis that African Americans place on race. Instead, their attitudes are highly dependent on their perceptions of group opportunities; individuals who believe they have fewer opportunities in life than whites want to increase the salience of race in public affairs. Political ideology, which has a significant impact among both Latinos and Asian Americans, has no effect on the degree to which African Americans call for attention to racial issues.

In contrast, economic status exerts a significant influence on the degree to which Asian Americans focus on race. Asian Americans who have a higher economic status are significantly more likely to downplay racial issues. Individuals who have a favorable assessment of Asian Americans' group opportunities also place less emphasis on race. But Asian Americans who have frequently experienced discrimination call for greater attention to be given to race.

Higher economic status also significantly diminishes the salience of race among Latinos, but the effect is somewhat weaker among Latinos than it is for Asian Americans. Latinos with a positive assessment of group opportunities assign a lower priority to racial issues. Higher education reduces attention to race only among Latinos. But conservative ideology in both Latinos and Asian Americans directs attention away from racial issues.

## AFFIRMATIVE ACTION

There is also no significant variation by economic status among African Americans in support for recruiting qualified minorities in education and

**TABLE 3.1.** Explaining Support for Racial and Ethnic Group Interests

| | Attention to Race | | | Recruiting Qualified Minorities | | | Support for Govt. Action to Ensure Equality | | |
|---|---|---|---|---|---|---|---|---|---|
| | African Americans | Latinos | Asian Americans | African Americans | Latinos | Asian Americans | African Americans | Latinos | Asian Americans |
| Economic Status | -.10 | -.23** | -.37** | -.14 | .67** | -2.38*** | -.03 | -.23** | -.31** |
| | (.10) | (.12) | (.16) | (.40) | (.40) | (.62) | (.06) | (.09) | (.12) |
| Perception of Opportunities (unequal – equal) | -.40*** | -.23*** | -.13* | -.60** | -.43* | -1.03*** | -.13** | -.13** | -.34*** |
| | (.10) | (.09) | (.10) | (.37) | (.28) | (.34) | (.06) | (.06) | (.07) |
| Experience of Discrimination (never – often) | .00 | .03 | .35** | .62* | 1.00** | -.66 | -.01 | .12+ | -.23* |
| | (.11) | (.13) | (.18) | (.47) | (.43) | (.61) | (.07) | (.09) | (.13) |
| Education | .00 | -.24*** | .10 | .83*** | -.47* | 1.50*** | -.02 | -.18** | .00 |
| | (.09) | (.10) | (.12) | (.38) | (.30) | (.41) | (.06) | (.07) | (.08) |
| Ideology (liberal – conservative) | -.05 | -.31*** | -.25*** | -.24 | -.29 | -.66** | -.08* | -.24*** | .01 |
| | (.08) | (.09) | (.08) | (.31) | (.28) | (.29) | (.05) | (.06) | (.06) |
| Constant | .87*** | .99*** | .80*** | .62** | .26 | 1.82*** | .97*** | 1.12*** | 1.13*** |
| | (.08) | (.10) | (.13) | (.33) | (.34) | (.47) | (.05) | (.08) | (.10) |
| N | 306 | 286 | 216 | 297 | 286 | 213 | 296 | 280 | 211 |
| $R^2$ | .06 | .11 | .12 | | | | .03 | .14 | .13 |
| Log Likelihood | | | | -136.92 | -176.39 | -123.02 | | | |
| Likelihood Ratio Chi$^2$ | | | | 13.78 | 13.96 | 33.22 | | | |

$^{***}p < .001$; $^{**}p < .01$; $^{*}p < .05$; $+ p < .1$; (one-tailed tests). OLS estimations for "attention to race" and "support for government action to ensure equality" and probit estimation for "support for recruiting qualified minorities." All variables are normalized between 0 and 1. Refer to Appendix for the exact questions. All coefficients are unstandardized with standard errors in parentheses.

employment. However, African Americans who have encountered discrimination or have a more negative assessment of the opportunities available to them are substantially more likely to support affirmative action.

Similarly, among Latinos, those who have faced discrimination are more inclined to support affirmative action, as are those who believe that opportunities are unequal. But, contrary to our expectations, higher economic status elevates support for affirmative action. We cannot account for this result, but suspect it is an anomaly because it is inconsistent with other national survey data we analyzed on Latino attitudes.[13] Economic status has the expected *negative* effect among Asian Americans; affluent Asian Americans are significantly more opposed to affirmative action than Asian Americans of lower economic status. But Asian Americans are no different from Latinos and African Americans in being more likely to support affirmative action if they perceive unequal opportunities. Asian Americans who identify themselves as political liberals place greater emphasis on recruiting minorities, whereas political ideology has no significant effect on African Americans and Latinos.

A puzzle in Table 3.1 is that better educated African Americans and Asian Americans are more supportive of affirmative action but better educated Latinos are significantly less supportive. The negative relationship between education and support for affirmative action among Latinos is confirmed by other data we analyzed, but we do not have an explanation for the varied effect of education across racial and ethnic groups.[14]

## GOVERNMENT PROGRAMS TO ENSURE EQUALITY

The findings in Table 3.1 on support for government action in health care, education, jobs, and the administration of the law reveal the expected divergence between African Americans, on the one hand, and Latinos and Asian Americans, on the other. For African Americans, higher economic

---

[13] In the absence of comparable studies that examine the sources of Latinos' support for affirmative action, we analyzed the influence of economic status using the 1989–1990 Latino National Political Survey. The simple correlation between income and "support for quotas in employment and college education" is $-.15$ ($p < .01$). In addition, a multivariate test of the effect of income, controlling for age, education, gender, ideology, and experiences with discrimination in daily life, yields a similar result. Those with higher income are significantly less likely ($p < .01$) to support quotas.

[14] The correlation between education and support for racial quotas in the 1989–90 Latino National Political Survey is $-.14$ ($p < .01$); the negative relationship remains statistically significant ($p < .01$) in a multivariate analysis controlling for age, income, gender, ideology, and experiences with discrimination in daily life.

status does *not* reduce support for government efforts to address racial and ethnic inequality. In contrast, higher economic status significantly reduces support for government action among both Latinos and Asian Americans. Perception of group opportunities has a significant effect in the expected direction on the policy preferences of individuals in all three groups. Among Latinos, education and conservatism increase opposition to government action. There is also a modest statistically significant relationship between conservatism and opposition to these measures among African Americans.[15]

The statistical estimates presented in Table 3.1 therefore confirm that support for group interests tends to be more strongly related to economic status among Latinos and Asian Americans than among African Americans even after controlling for education, ideology, perceptions of opportunities, and experiences with discrimination. As African Americans experience greater economic success, the salience of race for them tends not to decline. By contrast, Latinos and especially Asian Americans are more likely to extrapolate from their individual success in judging race-based policies and the attention that should be given to race.

Although we presented the results separately for each issue and minority group, we also conducted an explicit test on the total sample of the interaction between economic status and minority group, using the group interests scale as the dependent variable. This test shows that economic status is unconnected to support for group interests among African Americans, but that a higher economic status significantly reduces support for group interests among Latinos and Asian Americans. A statistical test of the interaction between economic status and each minority group confirms that the effect of economic status is significantly different among Latinos and Asian Americans, relative to African Americans, at the .10 and .05 levels, respectively.

---

[15] The goodness of fit statistics for these models are characteristically low in the case of explaining African Americans' racial attitudes. The marginal distributions of their attitudes on the attention to race and government action items are highly skewed in the direction of support. Because there is little variance to explain in the models of African American attitudes, the $R^2$ statistics for the estimations are low. Even if we control for additional variables (e.g., age, gender, and living in an integrated neighborhood) our $R^2$ statistics only marginally improve to .07 and .04 for the "attention to race" and "government action" equations. These results are in line with previous studies of African Americans' attitudes toward racial policies. For example, Dawson's (1994, 195) model of the determinants of racial policy attitudes shows a similar low $R^2$ of .07 despite using a four-item policy index for his dependent variable.

TABLE 3.2. Correlations Between Economic Status and
Opportunities and Discrimination

|  | Perception of Opportunities | Experience of Discrimination |
|---|---|---|
| *African Americans* | | |
| Economic Status | ns | ns |
| *Latinos* | | |
| Economic Status | .16** | −.26** |
| *Asian Americans* | | |
| Economic Status | ns | −.28** |

**$p < .01$; ns: not significant. Entries are Pearson's r coefficients. Refer to Appendix for exact questions.

## THE VARIED EXPERIENCES OF ECONOMIC STATUS

It appears from these results that support for racial and ethnic group interests is least responsive among African Americans to changes in personal economic status because of the broader consensus among African Americans that group opportunities and social conditions remain poor despite individual examples of success. This explanation can be tested more directly by tracing the experiences of higher status minorities that are relevant to their orientations toward political issues. A simple way to peer into the different experiences that accompany higher economic status among African Americans, Latinos, and Asian Americans is to explore the structure of correlations among economic status, reports of personal encounters with discrimination, and assessments of the opportunities enjoyed by group members. The correlation matrix in Table 3.2 for these variables illustrates the disparate experiences of higher status members of the three minority groups. As economic status increases among African Americans, there is *no* accompanying tendency for them to acquire a more positive outlook on American society. Higher status changes neither their appraisal of group opportunities nor the frequency of their personal encounters with discrimination.

Latinos and Asian Americans differ from African Americans in notable ways. Affluent Latinos provide a more positive assessment of group opportunities; they also report fewer personal experiences with discrimination. A similar pattern of correlations describes the experience of economic status among Asian Americans. A higher standard of living among

Asian Americans is unrelated to perceptions of opportunities, but is accompanied by a significant reduction in reports of personal discrimination. Therefore, improvements in living standards go hand in hand with more favorable assessments of social conditions among Latinos and Asian Americans, but they do not alter the generally negative outlook on society among African Americans.

## SPECIFYING THE EFFECTS OF ECONOMIC STATUS

The effect of economic status varies among minority groups because the experiences accompanying that status are generally different depending on whether one is African American, Latino, or Asian American. African Americans place greater emphasis on race than do Latinos and Asian Americans, because they are on the whole more pessimistic about their socioeconomic prospects in American society and more likely to experience prejudice and discrimination. It should follow generally that individuals *across minority groups* who have not had the same bracing encounters with discrimination and who believe that minorities have a fair chance to better themselves should be more willing to downplay racial or ethnic group concerns as their own economic status improves.

In this section, we test our second hypothesis that the effect of economic status depends on individual perceptions of opportunity and reports of discrimination. We expect that economic status will have an insignificant impact on the attitudes of those who frequently encounter discrimination and believe that equal opportunity is a fiction. But we also anticipate that higher economic status will reduce support for group interests among those who believe they are not limited by their racial or ethnic identity.

This hypothesis is once again tested on all minority groups for each of the three measures of group interest. The identical regression model is specified for each group. There are three coefficients corresponding to the effect of economic status: (1) the baseline coefficient estimates the effect of economic status among those who believe they face unequal opportunities and report high levels of discrimination; (2) the first multiplicative term ("mixed" experiences * economic status) reflects the incremental effect of economic status among those who either perceive equal opportunities or experience low levels of discrimination (but not both); and (3) the second multiplicative term ("positive" experiences * economic status) captures the incremental effect of economic status among those who both perceive equal opportunities and report experiencing low levels of dis-crimination.[16] Our analysis focuses on the contrast between the specified effects of positive and negative experiences.

The results of this test provide substantial support for the hypothe-sis that the effect of economic status is conditional on perceptions and experiences of social and economic equality. In most cases, as predicted, the baseline effect of economic status on racial attitudes among those with "negative" experiences is negligible; higher economic status does not diminish support for group interests among those who continue to feel social and economic discrimination. However, the interaction term com-bining economic status and "positive" perceptions of opportunities and discrimination tends to be negative and statistically significant.

Table 3.3 contains the statistical estimates for each of the three mea-sures of group interest, calculated separately for each minority group. In addition, we provide a graphical summary of the key coefficients in Figure 3.1.[17] The figure contains nine graphs (3 measures of group interest × 3 groups), with each graph representing the relationship bet-ween economic status and a measure of group interest conditional on the respondent's perception of opportunities and experiences with discrimi-nation. A negative sloping line, for example, means that support for group interests diminishes as economic status increases.

## ATTENTION TO RACE

Consider the first item regarding the emphasis that respondents place on race in public affairs. The pattern of responses to this item across minority groups provides a remarkably good fit to the theory. In all three groups, the effect of economic status on the amount of attention that respon-dents feel should be devoted to race is negligible among those who say

---

[16] The unweighted percentage and number of each minority group in the "negative," "mixed," and "positive" categories of the combined index of opportunities and discrimi-nation is as follows: among African Americans, 61 percent (193) are negative, 29 percent (92) are mixed, and 10 percent (33) are positive; the comparable figures for Latinos are 28 percent (88), 38 percent (117), and 34 percent (104); for Asian Americans, the com-parable figures are 30 percent (74), 41 percent (102), and 29 percent (70).

[17] In estimating model 2, we centered the continuous "economic status" variable by sub-tracting its mean from each observation to create a new variable with a mean of zero. Centering the variable in this manner reduces multi-collinearity between economic status and the measure of perceived opportunity and reported discrimination. See Aiken and West (1991) and Friedrich (1982) for discussions of the benefits of centering in models containing interaction terms.

TABLE 3.3. Interaction Between Economic Status and Experiences in Explaining Support for Group Interests

| | Attention to Race | | | Recruiting Qualified Minorities | | | Support for Govt. Action to Ensure Equality | | |
|---|---|---|---|---|---|---|---|---|---|
| | African Americans | Latinos | Asian Americans | African Americans | Latinos | Asian Americans | African Americans | Latinos | Asian Americans |
| Economic Status | .05 | .19 | −.03 | .01 | .73 | −1.70* | .01 | −.01 | −.07 |
| | (.13) | (.23) | (.26) | (.51) | (.75) | (.91) | (.08) | (.16) | (.19) |
| Mixed Experiences of Opportunities and Discrimination | −.09* | .04 | −.01 | −.19 | −.25 | −.23 | −.06* | .08* | −.13** |
| | (.05) | (.07) | (.07) | (.20) | (.22) | (.24) | (.03) | (.05) | (.05) |
| Positive Experiences of Opportunities and Discrimination | −.20** | −.19*** | −.24*** | −.42+ | −.55** | −.40* | −.03 | −.12** | −.13** |
| | (.08) | (.07) | (.07) | (.28) | (.22) | (.25) | (.05) | (.05) | (.05) |
| Mixed Experiences* Economic Status | −.21 | −.48* | −.43 | .28 | .06 | 1.79+ | −.06 | −.18 | .27 |
| | (.23) | (.30) | (.36) | (.86) | (.96) | (1.22) | (.14) | (.21) | (.26) |
| Positive Experiences* Economic Status | −.81* | −.63* | −.57* | −2.34+ | −.52 | −3.68** | −.17 | −.52* | −.69** |
| | (.38) | (.31) | (.32) | (1.44) | (1.02) | (1.53) | (.23) | (.22) | (.25) |
| Education | .00 | −.21* | .07 | .88* | −.41+ | 1.33*** | −.03 | −.16** | −.03 |
| | (.09) | (.09) | (.11) | (.38) | (.30) | (.41) | (.06) | (.07) | (.08) |
| Ideology (liberal – conservative) | −.04 | −.29*** | −.24** | −.27 | −.35 | −.59* | −.07+ | −.23*** | .05 |
| | (.08) | (.09) | (.08) | (.31) | (.28) | (.29) | (.05) | (.06) | (.06) |
| Constant | .82*** | .84*** | .65*** | .75** | 1.06*** | −.03 | .95*** | .97*** | .84*** |
| | (.07) | (.08) | (.10) | (.27) | (.26) | (.35) | (.04) | (.06) | (.07) |
| N | 306 | 286 | 216 | 297 | 286 | 213 | 296 | 280 | 211 |
| $R^2$ | .05 | .16 | .17 | | | | .02 | .21 | .14 |
| Log Likelihood | | | | −136.24 | −177.93 | −118.39 | | | |
| Likelihood Ratio Chi$^2$ | | | | 15.15 | 10.87 | 42.48 | | | |

*** $p < .001$; ** $p < .01$; * $p < .05$; + $p < .1$; (one-tailed tests). OLS estimations for "attention to race" and "support for government action to ensure equality" and probit estimation for "support for recruiting qualified minorities." All variables are normalized between 0 and 1. Refer to Appendix for the exact questions. All coefficients are unstandardized with standard errors in parentheses.

58

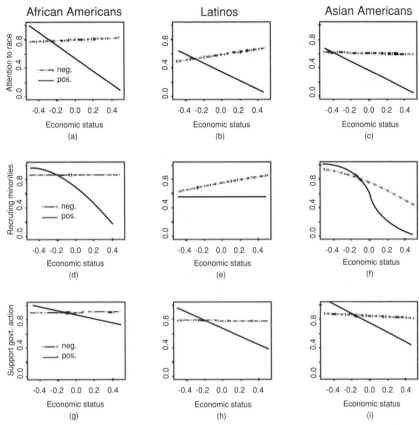

Figure 3.1. Predicted Support for Racial and Ethnic Group Interests by Economic Status. *Note*: The effect of economic status on group interests depends on whether perceptions and experiences of opportunities and discrimination are "negative" or "positive." Coding of these categories is explained in the Appendix. Predicted values for support for group interests are derived from the estimates in Table 3.3, holding constant all other variables at their mean values. Predicted values for the "mixed" category are not shown.

they are treated unequally. But among those who report more favorable experiences in society, the effect of economic status is consistently strong and statistically significant. As economic status increases in the latter group, there is a sharp decrease in the tendency to call for more attention to be paid to race. Moreover, the size of the coefficient is comparable across all three groups. This is indicated in Figure 3.1 (panels a–c) by the similarly angled, downward sloping line in all three groups among those who provide a positive assessment of their opportunities and treatment by others.

The significant interaction between economic status and evaluations of opportunity and discrimination also means that the effects of opportunity and discrimination increase in magnitude as economic status increases. There is little difference among those with an extremely low standard of living between individuals who perceive unequal conditions and individuals who perceive equal conditions. The tendency of practically all such individuals is to call for greater attention to race. But with the exception of this small group of respondents, reports of equal opportunity and treatment lead people to downplay racial considerations in public policy.

## AFFIRMATIVE ACTION

Similar findings emerge on the issue of recruiting minorities in education and employment. The baseline effect of economic status among those with negative evaluations of society is negligible among African Americans and Latinos. The interaction terms for those with positive experiences are also in the expected negative direction for these two groups, although it is statistically significant only among African Americans. Therefore, increased economic status significantly reduces support for affirmative action among African Americans who perceive equal opportunity and report few personal encounters with discrimination. The lack of confirmation among Latinos on this issue is consistent with the positive relationship between economic status and support for affirmative action presented earlier in Table 3.1.

By contrast, higher economic status tends to reduce support for affirmative action among Asian Americans, regardless of their perceptions of opportunities and experiences with discrimination. However, the negative effect of higher status is larger among those who have a positive appraisal of opportunities and discrimination. Figure 3.1(f) shows that as economic status increases among Asian Americans who report equal opportunity and treatment, support for affirmative action drops precipitously from overwhelming support to overwhelming opposition.

## GOVERNMENT PROGRAMS TO ENSURE EQUALITY

A similar specification by perceptions and experiences is observed among African Americans, Latinos, and Asian Americans on the index of questions about the responsibility of the federal government to ensure that minorities enjoy equality in their jobs, health care, schools, and treatment by the police and courts. In all three groups, among those who offer a negative assessment of opportunities and discrimination, higher economic status does not affect support for federal action to guarantee equality in these realms. But among those who provide a positive evaluation of opportunities and levels of discrimination, affluence is accompanied by greater reluctance to pay higher taxes for government programs to ensure equality.

Nevertheless, the magnitude of the interaction between economic status and positive experiences varies across groups. For Latinos and Asian Americans, the interaction is statistically significant and comparable in size, as reflected in the roughly parallel downward sloping solid lines in Figure 3.1 (panels h and i). The more gently sloped solid line in Figure 3.1(g) illustrates that the preferences of African Americans on the set of government action items deviate somewhat from those of Latinos and Asian Americans. For African Americans, the negative direction of the interaction between economic status and positive experiences is consistent with the prediction of the theory, but the size of the interaction effect is not statistically significant.

The regression model on this set of issues also provides little explanatory power in the case of African Americans ($R^2 = .02$) because aggregate support for government action is so high that it is difficult to differentiate among the preferences of African Americans. The government action items therefore prove "too easy" for black respondents, although this easiness can also be seen to reflect the stronger orientation of African Americans, compared to Latinos and Asian Americans, toward government efforts to address inequality. Some of these residual group differences may be attributable to unmeasured factors such as the intense socialization processes within the African American community that reinforce perceptions of a racial group interest (Allen, Dawson, and Brown 1989; Dawson 1994).

In sum, the effect of economic status on support for racial and ethnic group interests is statistically insignificant as predicted in eight out of nine tests (three measures of group interest by three groups) among individuals who face frequent discrimination and believe they do not enjoy equality of opportunity. The lone exception is that higher status leads to stronger opposition to affirmative action among Asian Americans even if they hold negative evaluations of society. When we combined the measures of opportunity and discrimination to identify those individuals who perceive *both* equal opportunities and report infrequent discrimination, the interaction between this measure of socioeconomic acceptance and economic status is negative and statistically significant, as predicted, in seven out of nine tests. The interactions are also negative in the remaining two cases, but do not achieve statistical significance.

The observed patterns are sufficiently consistent across racial and ethnic groups that a common model using the group interest scale as the dependent variable describes the dynamics of opinion in all three groups. We pooled together the three groups and constructed a saturated model that tested for two-way interactions between economic status and experiences, economic status and minority group, and experiences and minority group, and a three-way interaction among experiences, economic status, and minority group. The results show that economic status significantly weakens support for group interests among all individuals who perceive equal opportunities and report infrequent discrimination; but that the effect of economic status is reduced to insignificance among those who perceive unequal opportunities and report frequent discrimination. However, the three-way interaction among economic status, assessment of opportunities and discrimination, and minority group is *not* statistically significant, meaning there are no differences in the effects of changing economic status among the three minority groups once we take into account the conditional effects of the experiences of status.

Thus, the overall results provide strong evidence for the proposition that higher economic status diminishes support for racial and ethnic group interests only among those who believe they can be socially mobile in American society. On average, Latinos and especially Asian Americans are more sanguine than African Americans about the opportunities available to their own groups, a *distributional* difference that explains our earlier results (in Table 3.1) showing that economic status tends to have a larger impact on the attitudes of Latinos and Asian Americans than of African Americans. But these are only group tendencies; within each group, there are economically successful individuals who downplay the significance of race or ethnicity because they perceive social and economic boundaries to be fluid.

By contrast, African Americans, Latinos, and Asian Americans who attain material security but experience hostility toward their success and continuing discrimination are loath to relinquish racial or ethnic considerations in their political decisions. These results both corroborate and extend previous research on African American racial consciousness by identifying the general conditions under which support for group interests among all minorities will either be strengthened or weakened by changes in individual life circumstances.

## CONCLUSION

The study of racial politics in the United States can no longer be confined to analyzing contrasts between blacks and whites. Population changes in the last forty years resulting from the massive influx of immigrants from Latin America and Asia after the Immigration Act of 1965 have created a new demographic context for the politics of race and ethnicity. Although whites still constitute a numerical majority, minority groups now wield considerable potential power in electoral politics because of their high concentration in several parts of the country.

As we shift our attention to this new multiracial environment, an important question is whether *individuals* in these groups will share a political outlook and exercise political power as members of racial and ethnic *groups*. Our analysis shows that intergroup differences in attitudes toward racial and ethnic policies are explained by varying experiences among minority groups rather than by different theoretical processes. Vital differences between African Americans and other minority groups in their experiences of economic status affect their respective tendencies to embrace a racial or ethnic identity and pursue group interests in public policy. Among Latinos and Asian Americans, economic status is correlated with more favorable assessments of race relations. In contrast, middle-class African Americans retain negative assessments about group opportunities and report more personal discrimination than lower-status African Americans. Therefore, racial consciousness tends to remain stronger among affluent African Americans, whereas successful Latinos and Asian Americans place less emphasis on racial or ethnic considerations in their political attitudes and policy preferences.

But these findings also suggest the general proposition that the effect of economic status on the group consciousness of all minorities depends on the experiences accompanying that status. Indeed, we found that African Americans who have more positive experiences of middle-class status pay less attention to race and show less support for race-based public policies. In general, for all minority individuals who perceive equal opportunity and experience social acceptance, an improved standard of living tends to lead to a weaker focus on race and ethnicity. By contrast, higher economic status fails to diminish the salience of race and ethnicity among those who encounter frequent discrimination. Nonetheless, there remain residual differences across minority groups even after opportunities and discrimination are controlled, indicating that group identification is somewhat stronger among African Americans.

An important lesson from this analysis is that support for racial and ethnic group interests is *strengthened* by the failure of society to provide equality of opportunity and *weakened* by favorable experiences of economic status.[18] Critics of multiculturalism (e.g., Huntington 2004) who contend that strong racial and ethnic group identities inevitably weaken national identity sometimes underestimate the structural and socioeconomic conditions that influence identity formation (Rogers and Chong 2004). Structural barriers to individual advancement in the United States have reinforced the tendency of each generation of immigrants to build social and economic networks on the basis of their race and ethnicity in order to amass the collective resources needed to succeed economically and politically.

People emphasize or downplay their racial and ethnic group memberships partly depending on the utility of those identifications. When minority status carries a stigma and presents an obstacle to personal achievement, individual group members may try to differentiate themselves from the group by avoiding the attributes and behaviors associated with it. This is a form of exit from the group. When we speak of social mobility, we normally think of socioeconomic or class mobility, but we can also include mobility between ascriptive categories. People can take measures to heighten or conceal their racial and ethnic backgrounds or their sexual identities by modifying their behavior and appearance (Chong 2000).

But individuals cannot totally control how they are defined, for their social identities are affected by how others perceive them. Some individuals may prefer not to be categorized by their race or ethnicity, but others may treat them stereotypically and thereby increase the salience of these group identifications. If race and ethnicity restrict opportunities for social mobility, minority group members may not have the option to choose other forms of social identification. Instead of reducing their racial or ethnic ties, they may alternatively embrace their group and pursue various means to improve its status. These strategies may include collective action to achieve political goals; systematic efforts to increase the value of group attributes that have been underappreciated by the majority culture; and social comparisons with less (rather than more) powerful groups in society, a strategy that may heighten competition and conflict

---

[18] Alba and Nee (2003, 278) similarly argue that the assimilation of contemporary immigrants depends on creating democratic institutions that protect the civil rights of minorities, allow for socioeconomic mobility, and eliminate racial discrimination.

among socioeconomically disadvantaged groups (Hogg and Abrams 1988; Chong 2000).

In contrast, individuals who feel less constrained by their minority status are more likely to downplay racial or ethnic considerations when their economic situation improves. As their need for group identification diminishes, such individuals give greater weight to their own life circumstances as opposed to the group's condition, and are more inclined to evaluate government policies in terms of how those policies will impinge on themselves.[19]

Although we found considerable evidence of a common theoretical process affecting all minorities, there remain hints in the data that support for group interests is more robust among African Americans. Compared to higher-status Latinos and Asian Americans, economically secure African Americans were more likely to maintain support for government action to obtain racial equality in employment, education, health care, and the administration of the law even when they evaluated socioeconomic conditions favorably. As we noted earlier, such residual contrasts between African Americans and other minorities may reflect some of the unmeasured contextual factors not accounted for in our model. Racial consciousness among African Americans may be sustained, despite improvements in living standards, because African American communities, more so than Latino and Asian American communities, assign greater utility to collective action and contain institutions, such as African American churches and mass media, that promote perception of a racial group interest (Allen, Dawson, and Brown 1989; Tate 1993; Dawson 1994). Neither Latinos nor Asians have experienced a watershed event such as the Civil Rights Movement that fortified African Americans' belief in the instrumental value of group solidarity as a political resource (McAdam 1982; Morris, Hatchett, and Brown 1989; Chong 1991). Therefore, even middle-class African Americans who perceive progress toward racial equality and diminished prejudice against them may continue to draw lessons from recent political history and believe their individual interests are furthered through political solidarity with fellow African Americans.

Finally, we do not rule out the possibility that individualistically oriented minorities can be mobilized to adopt a group or collective frame

---

[19] Minority individuals may nevertheless retain racially or ethnically based identities and affiliations for social and cultural reasons that are not explicitly instrumental to economic and political outcomes (Alba 1990).

of reference. Those who are individualistic in some circumstances can be group oriented in others depending on the nature of the issues and the local political conditions and contexts in which they arise (e.g., Cohen and Dawson 1993; Junn 2003; Gay 2004). Although the material and educational successes of Asian Americans would seem to undermine their incentives to adhere to a racial group identity, both the record of discrimination against Asian Americans and their historical exclusion from politics and economic activities (e.g., Ancheta 1998; Chang 2001) remind Asian Americans that their life chances continue to be defined in part by their race. Asian Americans therefore are more ambivalent between individualist and collective approaches to politics and less likely than either African Americans or Latinos to pursue a political strategy built around racial identity. But the racial identity of Asian Americans nevertheless may be invoked effectively in specific contexts or on issues that directly address their collective interests.

Likewise, ethnic divisions and generational differences among Latinos may hinder political mobilization around ethnic identity, but contemporary political conflict on salient issues such as English-only legislation and immigration and social welfare reform may prove to be a unifying force (Cain, Citrin, and Wong 2000; de la Garza 2004).[20] Latinos who are affected by these issues have an interest in organizing around their group identity. Moreover, because of the dramatic increase of the Latino population and its concentration in large cities, political elites from both parties are eager to acquire Latino voters. With the major parties as suitors, Latino elites have an incentive to mobilize individual members *as Latinos*. A majority of Latinos already believe that Latinos are working together successfully to achieve common political goals. Furthermore, an overwhelming majority of Latinos are persuaded that political mobilization will improve the well-being of group members (Kaiser Family Foundation 1999). There would thus appear presently to be a greater potential for Latinos than Asian Americans to organize themselves around a common identity and to view their interests as being closely linked to the fate of the group. It remains a task of future research to disentangle further variation within the array of groups encompassed by the labels African American, Latino, and Asian American, and to broaden the analysis to understand how local contexts and political mobilization can augment the tendencies uncovered here.

---

[20] de la Garza et al. (1992) found that Mexicans, Puerto Ricans, and Cubans are more likely to identify with separate ethnic groups than with a common panethnic group.

## APPENDIX

The survey analyzed in this paper was sponsored by the *Washington Post*, Kaiser Family Foundation, and Harvard University, and conducted by International Communications Research during March 8–April 22 and May 16–20 in 2001. The data are available from the Roper Center for Public Opinion Research. The total sample size is 2,717. In the first round of the survey, 1,709 respondents were interviewed. Because White respondents were not asked about their direct experiences of discrimination in the first survey, a brief additional survey of 1,008 respondents was conducted to gather information on these questions (Q57, 58, 59(a–d), and 59a1(a–b)). In our research, we used only the respondents who answered the first survey. Thus, the sample size for our study is 1,709. We used Stata version 8.0 statistical software for our analysis.

### Dependent Variables

*Attention Paid to Race.* Q12_a. Is there too much, too little, or about the right amount of attention paid to race and racial issues these days? (Too little = 3, About the right amount = 2, Too much = 1)

*Recruiting Qualified Minorities.* Q51. Do you favor or oppose employers and colleges making an extra effort to find and recruit qualified minorities? (Favor = 1, Oppose = 0)

*Support for Government Action to Ensure Equality.* A 4-item scale was created from the following items: Q12a–d. Do you believe it is the responsibility or isn't the responsibility of the federal government to make sure minorities have equality with Whites in each of the following areas, even if it means you will have to pay more in taxes? Making sure minorities have:

a. Jobs equal in quality to Whites; b. Schools equal in quality to Whites; c. Health care services equal to Whites; d. Treatment by the courts and police equal to Whites
(Responsibility of the federal government = 1, Not the responsibility of the federal government = 0). Cronbach's alpha for the scale is .794.

### Independent Variables

*Economic Status.* A 6-item scale was created from the following items: Q3. Would you describe the state of your own personal finances these days as excellent, good, not so good, or poor?
(Excellent = 4, Good = 3, Not so good = 2, Poor = 1)

Q61a–c. For each of the following, please tell me whether or not it is something you and your family have had to deal with recently:

a. You have had problems paying the rent or mortgage for yourself or your family; b. You have delayed or had trouble getting medical care for yourself or your family; c. You have been unable to save money for future needs.
(Have had to deal with = 1, Have not had to deal with = 0)

Q62. Do you own stocks, bonds, or mutual funds – either directly or through a 401K plan? (Yes = 1, No = 0)
D11, D11 a–b. Your total annual household income from all sources and before taxes.
Cronbach's alpha for the scale is .732.

*Perception of Opportunities.* Q6a–c. Do you feel that [a. African Americans; b. Hispanic Americans; c. Asian Americans] have more, less, or about the same opportunities in life as Whites have? (More opportunity = 3, About the same = 2, Less opportunity = 1)

*Experience of Discrimination.* A 7-item scale was created from the following items: Q 58: During the last 10 years, have you experienced discrimination because of your racial or ethnic background, or not? (Yes = 1, No = 0)
Q59a–d. In your day-to-day life, how often do any of the following things happen to you because of your racial or ethnic background? Would you say very often, fairly often, once in a while, or never?

a. You are treated with less respect than other people; b. You receive poorer service than other people at restaurants or stores; c. People act as if they are afraid of you; d. You are called names or insulted.
(Very often = 4, Fairly often = 3, Once in a while = 2, Never = 1)

Q59ala–b. Have you ever been (items a, b) because of your racial and ethnic background?

a. Physically threatened or attacked; b. Unfairly stopped by police.
(Yes = 1, No = 0). Cronbach's alpha for the scale is .789.

*Perception of Opportunities and Experience of Discrimination.* "Perception of opportunities" was dichotomized by recoding "more opportunity" and "the same opportunity" to 1 = positive perception of opportunity; and "less opportunity" to 0 = negative perception of opportunity. Similarly, the scale variable "experience of discrimination" was dichotomized by dividing the scale at the 65th percentile for the population. The values below 65% of the distribution are recoded to 0 = low levels of discrimination, and above the cut point to 1 = high levels of discrimination. The cut point was adjusted to ensure a meaningful distribution of African Americans across high and low categories. There is still a skewed distribution of African Americans even after we use this cut point: about 28% of African Americans fall in the low category, whereas 72% fall in the high category. We combined the two dichotomized variables to create three ordered categories: "negative" experiences of opportunity and discrimination = 0, "mixed" experiences (i.e., either positive assessments of opportunities or infrequent encounters with discrimination, but not both) = 1, and "positive" experiences of opportunity and infrequent encounters with discrimination = 2.

*Education.* D09. What is the last grade or class that you completed in school? (Responses range from none to postgraduate training or professional school after college.)

*Ideology.* D02. Would you say your views in most political matters are liberal, moderate, conservative, something else, or haven't you given this much thought? (Liberal = 1, Moderate = 2, Conservative = 3, Something else = 4, Haven't given this much thought = 5). In the analysis, those who said "something else" or "haven't given this much thought" were recoded as "moderate" to reduce the number of missing cases.

JANELLE S. WONG, PEI-TE LIEN, AND
M. MARGARET CONWAY

# 4   Activity amid Diversity

## Asian American Political Participation

Despite the fact that Asian Americans have been in the United States for centuries, attention to their political behavior is a strikingly new phenomenon. Asian Americans have been overlooked until recently because of the relatively small size of the population compared with minority groups such as African Americans and Latinos, the residential concentration of Asian Americans in a handful of states, and the perception that Asian Americans are quiescent rather than active in politics. These reasons share common origins in U.S. immigration policy, in particular the Immigration Exclusion Act of 1882, the Immigration Acts of 1917, 1924, and the Tydings-McDuffie Act of 1934, all of which explicitly excluded immigrants from China, Japan, India, and the Philippines, and prohibited citizenship among Asian Americans. In addition, the Alien Land Laws of 1913, 1920, and 1923 barred Asian immigrants from owning land and other forms of property (Takaki 1989; Chan 1991; Ngai 2004; Tichenor 2001). Not until 1952 could Asian Americans become naturalized U.S. citizens.

Although these openly discriminatory statues no longer constitute federal law, immigration and citizenship policy favorable to Asian Americans came only with the reforms enumerated by the 1965 Immigration Act. Indeed, the rapid increase in the Asian American population in the United States is a product of immigration laws that no longer explicitly exclude Asians. Between 1990 and 2000, the Asian American population grew from 6.9 million to 11.9 million, an increase of 72 percent (Barnes and Bennett 2002).[1] As a result, the Asian American population in the United

---

[1] U.S. Census data on race in 1990 and 2000 are not directly comparable due to the change in the question allowing individuals to check more than one race. The statistics for 2000 are based on Asian and one or more races. Using the Asian alone category, the population in 2000 was 10.2 million, representing a 48 percent increase from 1990 to 2000.

States is heavily immigrant, with nearly two-thirds foreign-born. In addition, Asian Americans are highly diverse in terms of ethnic origin, and no single ethnic group is a majority. The 2000 U.S. Census estimates the composition of the Asian American population in terms of ethnic origin to be 23 percent Chinese (except Taiwanese), 18 percent Filipino, 17 percent Asian Indian, 11 percent Korean, 11 percent Vietnamese, 8 percent Japanese, and 12 percent of other Asian origin. The growth in the Asian American population and its dispersal in states across the United States have fueled a new interest in Asian American political participation.

Understanding political behavior among Asian Americans is challenging not only as a function of the diversity and relative newness of the population but also because explanatory models developed in political science to explain political participation may not account for many of the unique factors influencing Asian American political activity. In order to better understand political involvement among Asian Americans, we begin by examining factors that are likely to affect political participation of the general population, including resources, engagement, and institutional connections. However, the critical contribution of this work is to move beyond these traditional models to examine the influence of factors unique to the heavily-immigrant Asian American population, including minority group status, migration-related factors, and ethnic origin. We draw on research on Asian Americans in terms of education (Nakanishi 1998), demography (Hum and Zonta 1996; Sanjek 1998), and race relations (cf. Saito 1998; Kim 2000) to build our argument about Asian American political activity amidst ethnic diversity.

## APPLYING TRADITIONAL MODELS OF PARTICIPATION TO ASIAN AMERICANS

Traditional studies of political participation emphasize the importance of socioeconomic status in determining whether or not individuals will participate in politics (Verba and Nie 1972; Wolfinger and Rosenstone 1980; Conway 2000; Rosenstone and Hansen 1993; Verba, Schlozman, and Brady 1995). Researchers have attempted to refine the socioeconomic status model by focusing on specific resources such as money and civic skills (Verba, Schlozman, and Brady 1995). Having more money, for example, leads to more input into the political system through campaign donations and giving to other political causes. Another important resource for understanding participation is formal education (Wolfinger and Rosenstone 1980). Education is thought to facilitate participation because it fosters civic skills, by helping people learn to organize or communicate in ways that make it easier to take part in politics (Wolfinger and Rosenstone 1980; Verba, Schlozman, and Brady 1995; Nie, Junn, and Stehlik-Barry 1996).

Because the average household incomes of Asian Americans are higher than those of most Americans (Seelye 2001), traditional socioeconomic theories of political participation would predict high rates of political activity among Asian Americans. But recent research shows educational achievement and family income have either less effect on the participation of Asian Americans compared to either blacks or whites, or, according to some studies, no effect at all (Uhlaner, Cain, and Kiewiet 1989; Nakan-ishi 1991; Lien 1994, 1997, 2001b; Cho 1999; Junn 1999).[2] This is not to suggest that education and family income are unrelated completely to participation among Asian Americans. In fact, Lien (1998, 2000, 2001a, 2001b) finds education and family income to have positive and strong effects on the voting registration and turnout of eligible Asian American voters.

In addition to individual resources such as income and education, scholars also have identified a psychological orientation toward politics to be an important predictor of political participation. Verba, Schlozman, and Brady (1995) contend that political participation depends on resources and psychological engagement with politics. This is measured conven-tionally by political interest, information, efficacy, and partisan inten-sity. These components of psychological engagement provide people with the "desire, knowledge, and self-assurance" to become politically active (ibid., 354). In addition, Verba, Schlozman, and Brady (1995, 358) find individual measures of political interest, knowledge, and efficacy predict both voting and participation beyond voting in activities requiring time, such as working on a political campaign, contacting a public official, or working on a community problem.[3]

Involvement in civic institutions, such as churches and voluntary organizations, is also thought to increase political activity among the general population. Church attendance is a leading indicator of voting

---

[2] Also, see excellent discussions of the inappropriateness of using the average median house-hold income to gauge the socioeconomic achievement of Asian Americans in Fong 2002 and Cheng and Yang 1996. Although they are closely related, education and income are distinct from one another and their effects vary across different types of participation in the general population. Lien 2001b finds educational attainment, but not income, increases the probability that registered Asian Americans voted between 1994 and 1998.

[3] Strength of partisanship is a strong predictor of voting but not participation in time-based activities beyond voting.

participation across ethnic and racial groups (Verba, Schlozman, and Brady 1995; Houghland and Christenson 1983; Morris 1984; Dawson, Brown, and Allen 1990; Calhoun-Brown 1996; Harris 1999; Wilcox 1990; Assensoh 2001; Jones-Correa and Leal 2001).[4] Among Latinos, for example, Jones-Correa and Leal (2001) find church attendance is important for political participation because churches provide a space for sharing of political information and recruitment into political networks. Although scholars have begun to devote increasing attention to the role of religion and religious institutions in the lives of Asian Americans (e.g., Yoo 1999; Min and Kim 2002), research examining the link between religious activity and political participation among Asian Americans is scarce (see Lien 2003). Based on studies of other minority groups and research showing religious institutions occupy a central place in many immigrants' lives, we expect a strong relationship between church attendance and political involvement among Asian Americans. Note, however, that many Asian Americans practice non-Judeo-Christian religions, such as Buddhism, that may not be characterized by a tradition of regular attendance at a religious institution. Thus church attendance is best considered a measure of one's connection to a religious institution through participation at religious services, rather than a measure of religiosity per se.

Connections with community organizations may lead to increased political involvement because organizational involvement fosters civic skills (Putnam 2000; Verba, Schlozman, and Brady 1995). Organizations constitute important spaces for the exchange of political cues and information (Rosenstone and Hansen 1993). Similar to the church, nonreligious civic associations may be places where mobilization by community activists and leaders occurs (Schlozman, Verba, and Brady 1999). Thus, those Asian Americans who are members of such community organizations may be expected to be more politically active than those who are not involved in them.

In addition, institutional connections may matter for political participation because they are potential sources of mobilization.[5] Mobilization within Asian American communities has received little attention from

---

[4] The effect of church attendance varies according to type of political activity, and studies have found church attendance does not have a strong effect on political activities beyond voting, such as working on a campaign or contacting a public official (Houghland and Christenson 1983; Verba, Schlozman, and Brady 1995; Jones-Correa and Leal 2001).

[5] It is important to note that nonwhites appear to be targeted for political mobilization less often than whites (Frymer 1999; de la Garza, Menchaca, and DeSipio 1994; Hardy-Fanta 1993; Wong 2001; Leighley 2001).

scholars, though studies have devoted attention to the role of Asian American elected officials in generating interest and activity in elections (Nakanishi 1996; Lai 2000; Lai et al. 2001). Consistent with studies of the general population and racial minorities' political behavior (Leighley 2001), we expect mobilization to have a positive influence on the participation of Asian Americans.

Honolulu, Hawaii, is distinct from other metropolitan areas because Hawaii is the only majority-Asian American state in the union and Asian Americans constitute the majority of voters there. This demographic fact means that Asian American politics has developed differently on the islands compared to the continental United States. In addition, because past studies show Asian Americans in Hawaii tend to register and vote at higher rates in the aggregate than Asian Americans elsewhere, regional context may also play a role as a result of the greater political empowerment and mobilization infrastructure in Hawaii. The large population size and long historical presence of Asian Americans in Honolulu may lead to more participation there than in other cities, like Chicago, where Asians are by no means dominant in terms of size, history, or political representation (Lai 2000; Lien 2001b). We contend that Hawaiian Asians may be exposed to a political environment that is unique and not shared by Asians elsewhere and to control for the very unique population characteristics of Hawaii, we distinguish Honolulu from the other areas studied.[6]

## THE IMPACT OF MINORITY GROUP STATUS, IMMIGRATION, AND ETHNIC ORIGIN

Although the characteristics of individual and group-based mobilization resources enumerated by traditional models of political participation may be important to Asian American political participation, we expect a set of other factors related to racial minority group status, migration, and ethnic origin to have additional effects. To distinguish these factors from the traditional predictors of political participation outlined previously, we conceptualize them as Asian American–specific influences on political participation. It is clear from the literature, however, that many of the variables

---

[6] Although there are important regional distinctions among Asian Americans on the continental United States compared to Honolulu, the other metropolitan areas in our study – New York, Los Angeles, San Francisco, and Chicago – are similar in terms of Asian Americans constituting fast growing populations in places where they still represent a relatively small minority group.

described have been considered by researchers studying other minority and immigrant populations.

For historically disenfranchised racial and ethnic groups in the United States, racial minority status may play a critical role in mobilizing political participation (Miller, Gurin, Gurin, and Malanchuk 1981; Shingles 1981; Bobo and Gilliam 1990; Tate 1993; Harris 1994; Alex-Assensoh and Assensoh 2001). First, experience with racial discrimination may lead individuals to become active in politics in order to challenge racial inequality (Uhlaner 1991, 141).[7] Alternatively, victims of racial discrimination also might turn away from the political system, especially formal political participation, because they feel alienated from the political process (for related arguments, see Salamon and Van Evera 1973; Henig and Gale 1987). This study tests these competing predictions about the effects of racial discrimination on political involvement.

Group consciousness implies an awareness of "shared status as an unjustly deprived and oppressed group" and a strong sense of ethnic or panethnic community (Shingles 1981, 77; see also Bobo and Gilliam 1990, 377; Dawson 1994). Studies of African Americans have found that feelings of common fate contribute to the formation of group consciousness (Gurin, Hatchett, and Jackson 1989). Although scholars have made progress in terms of explaining group consciousness among Asian Americans (Espiritu 1992; Omi and Winant 1994), research on the relationship between having a shared sense of racial or ethnic community and political participation remains somewhat limited. Research on other communities suggests that those who have a strong sense of "linked-fate" (i.e., the belief that one's individual prospects are tied to the fate of the group as a whole) might be more involved with politics because they are motivated by racial group–related concerns to participate in political activities that will benefit their community in the United States. We hypothesize that those Asian Americans who are more group-oriented in their outlook may be active in politics in order to advance group interests.

Activity and support for Asian American political causes and candidates also has to do with minority status. Those who support issues related to the Asian American community also will be more interested in getting involved in politics in order to benefit in their community. In addition, membership in an Asian American organization or participation in

---

[7] Lee 2000 reports that "contrary to popular beliefs of an overachieving, thriving Asian Pacific American 'model minority,' the levels of perceived discrimination reported by APAs is quite extensive" (115).

activities that represent the interests and viewpoints of the respondent's ethnic group or other Asians in America are related to minority group status and identity. Involvement in an Asian American or ethnic organization may be an expression of identity or a way of pursuing group-related interests.

Because immigration plays a profound role in the growth and experience of contemporary Asian Americans, it is imperative to take migration-related factors into account when examining civic participation in a multiracial, multiethnic context (Cho 1999; Ramakrishnan and Espenshade 2001; Lien 2004; Ramakrishnan 2005). Past studies have shown that nativity is a strong determinant of political involvement among Asian Americans and Latinos. Although immigrants are less likely to participate in American politics than the native-born generally (Ong and Nakanishi 1996; Wong 2001), participation rates among immigrants also depend on length of residence in the United States, language skills, and whether or not one is naturalized (Cain, Kiewiet and Uhlaner 1991; Cho 1999; Uhlaner and Garcia 1999; Lien 2001b; Wong 2000). Specifically, as Asian American immigrants spend more time in the United States, they are more likely to naturalize, register, and become voters (Ong and Nakanishi 1996; Lien 2000; Nakanishi 2001).

Of course, citizenship is one of the first steps toward voting participation in the United States. Lien (2001b) observes that in the 1990s, approximately half of the Asian American population was barred from voting due to lack of citizenship. In November 2000, 41 percent of voting age Asian Americans were non-citizens, compared to 2 percent of non-Latino whites and 6 percent of black Americans (Jamieson, Shin and Day 2002). DeSipio and Jerit (1998, 2–3) assert that "while eligible immigrants and the recently naturalized often offer civic reasons to support their decisions to naturalize," the reasons for naturalization are also likely to be practical in nature. For many Asian Americans, naturalization may represent a legal means for many immigrants to bring to the United States relatives from their countries of origin. Asian Americans also might naturalize in order to protect themselves from laws aimed at those without legal documents. In contrast to these more practical considerations, some scholars contend naturalization represents a sense of commitment to becoming full-fledged members of the United States (Jones-Correa 1998). Based on this assumption, naturalization may lead to more participation in a number of types of mainstream political activities among immigrant Asian Americans.

Having strong English-language skills and being educated in the United States are also hypothesized to affect political participation in the United

States (Cho 1999; Wong 2001). Cho (1999) provides a thoughtful discussion of how political socialization is likely to be linked to English language skills and the country where most education takes place among immigrants. English proficiency is likely to have a profound affect on immigrants' abilities to receive English language political messages and information in the United States. In addition, we expect those who are educated outside of the United States to be less likely to participate in activities that require socialization toward mainstream political institutions in the United States.

Contrasting hypotheses are associated with another important aspect of immigration, the maintenance of transnational ties. On the one hand, immigrants who are involved in home country politics might be too preoccupied with politics outside of the United States to pay attention to American domestic politics (Harles 1993; Portes and Rumbaut 1996). On the other hand, because those who are politically active in one context may continue to be politicized in other contexts as well (Wong 2006), those who are active politically in their countries of origin may participate more in the United States than those who are not active in country of origin politics. Some individuals also might become involved in the United States political system in order to bring about change in their home countries (Basch et al. 1994; Karpathakis 1999; Smith 2000; Lien 2001b).

Finally, the category of "Asian American" is made up of people of diverse ethnic origins. Indeed, one of the central challenges for Asian Americans in the United States has been forging a cohesive political community among people who are divided along ethnic lines that coincide and intersect with class, language, religious, generational, and regional divisions. As a result, we expect political participation will vary by ethnic origin group.

## EXPLAINING ASIAN AMERICAN POLITICAL PARTICIPATION

The theories and literature reviewed here suggests that there are two key sets of variables to consider in an examination of political participation among Asian Americans. The first set of traditional factors having to do with socioeconomic resources, engagement, and institutional connections are those expected to be critical for predicting participation in the U.S. population, including Asian Americans. At the individual level, greater income and education, higher levels of psychological engagement, stronger institutional ties (organizational membership and religious attendance), and mobilization (contact by a party or individual encouraging the respondent to vote) are expected to be associated positively with political participation. Note that the variable used to measure organizational membership is "Do you belong to any organization or take part in any activities that represent the interests and viewpoints of [R'S ETHNIC GROUP] or other Asians in America?" This question taps into respondents' organizational ties, but because it asks about the organizations' activism around Asian American causes, it may also measure their sense of minority group status to some extent. Classic scholarship has also focused on regional differences in political behavior (see for instance, Key 1949) and we group a regional variable (Honolulu, Hawaii) with other "traditional predictors" of political participation.

The second set of variables includes those that may affect Asian Americans in particular, compared to the general population and we group these "Asian American-specific" variables together as well. We examine minority status through respondents' experiences with discrimination, their involvement in non-voting activities aimed at supporting Asian American issues or candidates, and their sense of linked fate with other Asian Americans ("Do you think what happens generally to other groups of Asians in this country will affect what happens in your life?").

We expect that U.S.-born status, length of residence in the United States, strong English-language skills, and high levels of political activity related to the country of origin will be associated positively with participation. Education outside of the United States is expected to be associated negatively with participation. Many schools in the United States require courses on U.S. government and may play a strong role in socializing students into U.S. politics. Those who do not receive formal schooling in the United States may therefore be less familiar with the U.S. political system and feel less comfortable taking part in U.S. politics as a result.

If citizenship denotes a desire on the part of migrants to become more integrated into the U.S. political system, we would expect citizens to participate more in U.S. politics. However, the naturalization process may be attractive to immigrants for a wide range of reasons, some having nothing to do with political participation. Furthermore, for many immigrants the ability to naturalize depends upon material resources. As such, the direct association between citizenship status and political participation is difficult to predict. However, we might expect that citizenship would be less critical for nonvoting political activities, since citizenship is not a formal requirement for most types of nonelectoral activities.

In order to test these hypotheses, we analyze data from a study of Asian American political participation, the Pilot National Asian American

Political Survey (PNAAPS). The PNAAPS is the first multicity, multiethnic, multilingual survey of Asian American political attitudes and behavior (Lien et al. 2001a, 2001b) ever conducted in the United States.[8] The PNAAPS included a total of 1,218 adults of Chinese, Korean, Vietnamese, Japanese, Filipino, and South Asian descent residing in the Los Angeles, New York, Honolulu, San Francisco, and Chicago metropolitan areas. These metropolitan areas are the major areas of concentration for Asian Americans in the United States. The telephone survey took place between November 16, 2000, and January 28, 2001. Respondents were randomly selected using random-digit dialing at targeted Asian zip code densities and listed-surname frames. Selection probability for each ethnic sample is approximate to the size of the 1990 Census figures for the ethnic population in each metropolitan area.[9] The sample consists of 308 Chinese, 168 Korean, 137 Vietnamese, 198 Japanese, 266 Filipino, and 141 South Asian respondents. When possible, the interviews were conducted in the language preferred by the respondent (English, Mandarin Chinese, Cantonese, Korean, or Vietnamese), except for those of Japanese, Filipino, and South Asian descent, who were interviewed in English.[10]

We measured political participation in two distinct ways, as voting and as participation in political activities beyond voting. We present two models of voting: (1) whether registered respondents cast a ballot in the 2000 election and (2) whether respondents report voting in the elections of 1998 and 2000. The 2000 election was one of the most competitive in recent history, accompanied by a relatively high level of turnout. Because we are interested in Asian Americans' general voting behavior (outside of the context of the 2000 election), we analyze turnout in both 1998 and 2000. It is important to acknowledge, however, that we did not validate turnout and that at the time they were surveyed, some respondents probably could not recall whether or not they voted in 1998. Nonetheless, we believe there are some interesting comparisons between the two models of voting.

---

[8] The original name of the PNAAPS was the Pilot National Asian American Political Survey or PNAPPS (see Lien et al. 2001a; 2001b). The PNAAPS is sponsored by a research grant from the National Science Foundation (SES-9973435), and Pei-te Lien is the principal investigator. KSCI-TV of Los Angeles donated funds to augment the Los Angeles portion of the project.

[9] The resulting distribution of ethnic origins is close to the 2000 results because of the oversampling of particular populations (see Lien et al. 2001a).

[10] See Lien et al. 2001b for baseline survey results for each Asian ethnic group included in the study. Additional descriptions of the survey methodology are detailed in Lien et al. 2001a.

Political participation beyond voting is measured by an index based on responses to questions asking whether respondents had taken part in a range of political activities in their communities during the past four years including writing or phoning a government official, donating money to a campaign, signing a petition for a political cause, taking part in a protest or demonstration, and other types of activities. In the subsequent analysis, we divide the sample to analyze the foreign-born sample separately, where we assess the effects of the various explanatory factors on participatory activities beyond voting. A description of the questions and variable coding is available from the authors upon request.

To predict voting and political participation, we include the following factors in the explanatory models: socioeconomic status, psychological engagement with politics, organizational affiliation and mobilization, minority group status, migration-related variables, and ethnic origin. Respondents were asked whether most of their education took place in the United States or outside of the United States. This question allows us to distinguish between educational level and educational context. The analyses also include a measure of family income.[11] Independent variables related to psychological engagement in politics include measures of political interest, political knowledge, and perceptions of influence over local government decisions. Partisan strength and ideology are also included as indicators of political engagement. The PNAAPS included a question about whether respondents had received any letter, e-mail, or telephone call from a political party or candidate organization or other political group about a political campaign, an important measure of group-based mobilization.[12] In addition, a measure of mobilization by an individual, like a boss or friend, and a measure of church attendance is included in the analysis.

Explanatory measures related to racial minority status, minority group consciousness, and identity include activity related to support for an Asian American cause or candidate, perceptions of linked fate, membership in an Asian American organization, and experience with personal discrimination. In addition, measures of English language-use, foreign-born status,

---

[11] We include a measure of income substituting the mean value for missing values. This procedure has no major effect on the results and allows us to reduce the incidence of missing data.

[12] Forty-one percent of respondents claimed that they had been contacted during the past four years. Sixty-one percent of respondents who answered yes to this question specified the Democrats had contacted them, 43 percent indicated that the Republicans had contacted them, and 21 percent were not sure which party had contacted them.

length of residence, and participation in activities dealing with politics in the country of origin are incorporated into the estimation equations. Finally, to account for differences in ethnic origin and region among the respondents, a set of measures is included for each ethnic group represented in the study. As mentioned earlier, a variable accounting for regional variation in place of residence among the respondents is also included. In particular, Honolulu is distinguished from other metropolitan areas because Hawaii is the only majority Asian American state in the union. For ease of interpretation and comparison, independent variables are rescaled in maximum likelihood procedures with scores varying between 0 and 1. Control variables in the model include age, whether the respondent is female, and length of time at current residence.

Before examining the results of the models, it is important to foreground the implications of the findings. If immigration-related variables influence political participation among Asian Americans, then we can interpret the role of Asian Americans in the U.S. political system as dynamic. As nonimmigrant generations of Asian Americans enter politics and as immigrant generations gain experience with the political system over time, participation could be enhanced, although such an effect would depend on the size of the Asian American population compared to the population as a whole. Alternatively, if variables related to racial minority group status and ethnic origin remain significant, factors related to minority group status will continue to complicate chances for greater participation among Asian Americans in the United States.

## THE CONTOURS OF ASIAN AMERICAN POLITICAL PARTICIPATION

Table 4.1 shows rates of participation across a range of activities among Asian Americans. In the first column of data in the table (all Asian Americans), registering (54 percent) and voting (44 percent) are the most commonly reported types of political activity.[13] Compared with voting, a smaller proportion of Asian Americans participated in activities such as working with others in the community to solve a problem (21 percent), donating to a campaign (12 percent), or writing or phoning a government official (11 percent). Although past research has emphasized donations

[13] Data from the U.S. Census Current Population Survey show that among voting age citizens, 43 percent of Asian Americans voted in the November 2000 election compared to 45 percent of Latinos, 57 percent of African Americans, and 62 percent of non-Latino whites. Among the registered, all four groups voted at fairly similar rates (Jamieson, Shin, and Day 2002).

**TABLE 4.1.** Political Participation among Asian Americans

| | All Asian Americans % | US-Born % | Rates of Political Participation Foreign-Born % | Naturalized Citizens % | Noncitizens % |
|---|---|---|---|---|---|
| Registered to vote | 54 | 79 | 46 | 77 | Not Eligible |
| Voted in 2000 | 44 | 63 | 38 | 64 | Not Eligible |
| Contacted government official | 11 | 18 | 9 | 11 | 6 |
| Donated to campaign | 12 | 17 | 10 | 12 | 6 |
| Worked with others in community | 21 | 30 | 18 | 20 | 14 |
| Served on a board | 2 | 1 | 2 | 3 | 1 |
| Protested | 7 | 10 | 7 | 8 | 5 |
| Worked for a political campaign | 2 | 5 | 1 | 2 | 0 |
| N | 1209–1218 | 302–305 | 907–913 | 536–540 | 371–373 |

*Source:* 2000–2001 Pilot National Asian American Political Survey

to political campaigns as an important aspect of Asian American political behavior (Nakanishi 1998), both non-Latino whites (25 percent) and blacks (22 percent) in the Verba, Schlozman, and Brady (1995) study report higher rates of campaign contributing than do the Asian Americans in the PNAAPS. Still fewer Asian Americans participate in politics by serving on a governmental board or commission (2 percent), protesting (7 percent), or working on a political campaign (2 percent).

The second and third columns of data in Table 4.1 compare the U.S.-born to the foreign-born. In most cases, those who were born in the United States are more likely to participate across all activities than those who are immigrants. For example, 79 percent of the U.S.-born sample claimed that they were registered to vote compared to just 46 percent of the foreign-born sample. Among the U.S.-born, 63 percent reported voting in the 2000 election compared to 38 percent of the foreign-born sample. Similarly, 30 percent of the U.S.-born sample stated that they had worked with others in their community to solve a problem versus 18 percent of the immigrant sample. In addition, a larger proportion of Asian Americans born in the United States report they contacted a government official (18 percent) than Asian American immigrants (9 percent). However, differences between the U.S.-born and immigrants are less pronounced for protest activity where the difference is 10 percent for U.S.-born Asian Americans and 7 percent for immigrants.

Recent research attributes low rates of voting participation among adult Asian Americans to structural barriers, including lack of availability of bilingual voter materials and the eligibility requirements for voting (Kwoh and Hui 1993; Nakanishi 2001; Lien 2001b; Lien et al 2001b). The PNAAPS data support these findings. The picture of Asian American participation changes greatly depending on whether one assesses the population as a whole or concentrates on those who have acquired citizenship. The fourth column in Table 4.1 shows the registration rate is 77 percent among foreign-born respondents who are naturalized citizens. Similarly, 64 percent of naturalized citizens claim to have voted in the November 2000 elections. These data reveal Asian Americans who have become naturalized citizens register and vote at rates nearly identical to their U.S.-born counterparts. Furthermore, though it remains true that Asian Americans as a group have low rates of registering and voting relative to African Americans and Anglo whites, among Asian Americans who are citizens through either birth or naturalization, voting participation rates are comparable to the general U.S. population. Voting participation among registered Asian Americans in the PNAAPS study was 82 percent.[14] The data clearly demonstrate it is critical to consider structural barriers, such as eligibility requirements, in order to fully understand participation patterns among Asian Americans.

The determinants of voting turnout among Asian Americans are examined in Table 4.2. The data reported in this table are estimates of the coefficients representing the effect of each of the explanatory factors on voting participation using a method of logistic regression. Two models were estimated for eligible Asian American voters using the PNAAPS data. The dependent variable in the first model was whether one voted in the 2000 election. The dependent variable in the second model was consistent vote turnout in 1998 and 2000.[15] In the first data column of Table 4.2, the results indicate the most important influences on whether an Asian American registered citizen turned out to vote in 2000 are many of the same factors that predict voting in the general U.S. population, including higher levels of education, attending religious services, political interest, and political knowledge. Differences between these findings and earlier studies may be attributable to differences in samples.[16] Contrary to the classic model of voting, our data suggest that family income is related negatively to vote turnout in 2000. This finding deserves further examination. For Asian Americans, family income may indicate that there are more workers in a family, rather than higher class status (Cheng and Yang 1996). In addition, Asian Americans in the PNAPPS sample are concentrated in urban, coastal areas characterized by higher costs of living than the national average. Higher incomes may therefore reflect wages areas with a high cost of living rather than more resources.[17] The fact that high levels of family income may not have the same benefits or implications

---

[14] These figures are consistent with data from the November 2000 Current Population Survey showing that 83 percent of Asian American registered citizens of voting age turned out in the November 2000 election (compared to 86 percent of non-Latino whites, 84 percent of blacks, and 79 percent of Latinos who were registered citizens of voting age) (Jamieson, Shin, and Day 2002).

[15] Control variables included in the model but not shown in the table are age, female, and length of time at current residence. Age was positive and statistically significant. Listwise deletion of missing data was used in the analysis.

[16] Note several previous studies of Asian American voting behavior (e.g., Uhlaner, Cain, and Kiewiet 1989; Lien 1994; Cho 1999) find education is not as important a predictor of voting among Asian Americans. These were based on data collected in 1984 in California from a survey conducted in English and Spanish only.

[17] See, for example, Ong and Hee 1994, who show that though Asian Americans earn higher median incomes than non-Latino whites within the nation, within the high density Asian American cities of Los Angeles, San Francisco, Oakland, and New York City, Asian Americans earned less than whites.

**TABLE 4.2.** Predicting Voting: Eligible Asian Americans (logit regression estimates)

|  | Vote in 2000 | Consistent Voting in 1998 and 2000 |
| --- | --- | --- |
|  | Coefficient (and standard error) | Coefficient (and standard error) |
| TRADITIONAL PREDICTORS |  |  |
| *Socioeconomic Status* |  |  |
| *Education* | 2.43*** (.66) | 1.53*** (.48) |
| Family Income | −1.10* (.63) | −1.29*** (.48) |
| **Psychological Engagement** |  |  |
| Political Interest | 1.12** (.50) | 0.58 (.38) |
| Political Knowledge | 1.37** (.71) | 0.91* (.53) |
| Political Influence | 1.04* (.58) | −0.01 (.42) |
| Strong Partisan | 0.58 (.41) | 0.22 (.31) |
| Liberal | −1.13** (.48) | −0.10 (.35) |
| **Institutional Affiliation and Mobilization** |  |  |
| Member of Community Organization | −0.06 (.42) | −0.55* (.30) |
| Mobilized by a Party | 0.44 (.31) | 0.78*** (.26) |
| Mobilized by Individual | −0.09 (.36) | 0.16 (.26) |
| Religious Attendance | 1.45*** (.45) | 0.95*** (.33) |
| **Region Variable** |  |  |
| Honolulu | −0.32 (.40) | 0.19 (.33) |
| ASIAN AMERICAN-SPECIFIC PREDICTORS |  |  |
| **Minority Group Status** |  |  |
| **Personal Discrimination** | −0.34 (.42) | 0.49 (.32) |
| Panethnic Linked Fate | −0.11 (.40) | −0.26 (.31) |
| Participation for Asian American Causes | 0.80 (1.49) | 2.95*** (1.06) |
| *Migration Status* |  |  |
| Foreign-Born | −0.29 (.42) | −0.46 (.33) |
| English Language Use | −0.46 (.82) | −1.05 (.65) |
| **Ethnic origin (comparison group is Chinese)** |  |  |
| Japanese | −0.24 (.67) | 1.34** (.56) |
| Filipino | −0.57 (.61) | 0.78 (.48) |
| Korean | −2.27*** (.59) | −0.48 (.46) |
| South Asian | 1.03 (.92) | 0.58 (.54) |
| Vietnamese | 1.33* (.81) | 0.60 (.51) |
| Constant | −1.16 (.84) | −2.96*** (.70) |
| N | 480 | 480 |

Significance Levels: *$p \leq .10$; **$p \leq .05$; ***$p \leq .01$

for Asian Americans compared to other groups sheds some light into the reasons why family income may not show the same relationship to voting among Asian Americans as among other populations.

Feeling more efficacious in influencing local political decisions increased turnout in 2000, but liberal ideology is a negative predictor. English-language use, minority group experience, region, and nativity have no impact on vote turnout in 2000 once other factors are taken into account. Equally important, mobilization and membership in an Asian American organization have no significant impact. These findings suggest Asian American voting behavior, although consistent with conventional models, also has its unique contours. In terms of ethnic distinctions, when compared to their Chinese American counterparts, Korean Americans were less likely to vote in 2000, while Vietnamese Americans were more likely.[18]

Consistent voting in the 1998 and 2000 elections is examined in the second column of data in Table 4.2. Similar to the results stated earlier, the analysis suggests education and attending religious services frequently are strong predictors of consistent voting participation. As predicted by traditional models of vote turnout, party mobilization appears to be a key determinant of consistent vote turnout. One important issue to keep in mind in this case is the uncertain causal direction of the relationship between mobilization and participation. Although it might be the case that mobilization precedes voting, it also may be that those who are the most likely to participate are also the most likely to be targeted for mobilization by parties and other political groups (for discussion of this topic, see Rosenstone and Hansen 1993; Verba, Schlozman, and Brady 1995; Leighley 2001). Although we must exercise great caution in interpreting the effects of mobilization by individuals, parties, or community organizations on participation, there is some evidence from field experiment research that contact precedes participation.[19] Unfortunately, our survey data do not allow

[18] Korean Americans are somewhat distinct from other Asian American ethnic groups in terms of reasons for migration to the United States (for family reunion) and beliefs about the importance of an ethnic enclave community (Lien 2001b). In addition, they are more likely than other groups to report high levels of attendance at religious services and to indicate church as the primary site for their organizational participation (Lien 2001b). However, Korean political behavior in Southern California does not reveal similar differences between Korean Americans and other Asian ethnic groups in political participation in activities beyond voting (Lien 1997).

[19] Recent attempts have been made to address the causality issue by conducting field experiments comparing a randomly selected treatment group of individuals who are contacted to a randomly selected control group who are not contacted. These studies have

us to distinguish between types of mobilization. In addition, being active around Asian American causes is a strong, positive predictor of frequent voting habits. However, neither perceived political influence, strength of political partisanship, ideology, nor membership in an Asian American organization has the expected effect among registered Asian Americans.

The results from both analyses presented in Table 4.2 underscore the importance of election context. In particular, political interest and knowledge are major factors in determining turnout among Asian Americans in the high-stimulus context of the 2000 election, characterized as one of the closest presidential elections in history. The controversy that marked the election generated unprecedented media coverage and attention to the details of the electoral process. However, psychological engagement appears to be a less critical determinant of consistent voting habits across the two elections of 1998 and 2000. It is also interesting to note that English language use and foreign-born status do not have a significant effect on voting turnout in 2000 or consistent vote turnout among Asian Americans once other variables of interest are taken into account. Other things being equal, among Asian American who have overcome the hurdles of citizenship and registration, those who mostly use English are not more likely to vote than those who do not use English frequently. Similarly, among registered Asian American citizens, those who are immigrants are not likely to turnout significantly less frequently than those who are born in the United States. Other factors that may not contribute uniquely to predicting voting include indicators of minority group status and regional culture (Honolulu). Although the current governor of Hawaii is Republican Linda Lingle, Democrats dominated state politics for most of the state's history. Democrats ruled for many years without having to actively compete for votes and this may partially explain why voter turnout on the island is no higher than in other places, all else being equal. The lack of significance of foreign-born status and personal experience of discrimination in predicting Asian American voting participation have been reported in the past (Lien 1997).

---

focused on non-partisan contacting and voter turnout (Green and Gerber 2001; Ramirez 2002). The results show some evidence that contacting leads to more participation, but mobilization varies according to type of contact and sample. For example, in contrast to a more mixed-age turnout effort, Green and Gerber 2001 show that phone contacting of youth by other young people increases turnout. Based on data collected using an experimental design, Ramirez 2002 finds that phone contact among Latinos in a Los Angeles sample only marginally increased turnout overall.

Among Asian American ethnic groups, Japanese Americans appear to be more consistent in their voting habits compared to Chinese Americans (the reference group in the analysis). In other words, even after controlling for socioeconomic status, psychological engagement, minority group status, and foreign-born status, some differences persist between ethnic groups in terms of their propensity to vote and vote consistently. Although we attempted to investigate a wide range of factors related to Asian American voting, the measures do not fully account for the differences between ethnic groups. Given the great ethnic diversity characterizing the Asian American community, understanding how ethnic origin is related to political participation remains an important task for future research.

Political participation encompasses many activities beyond voting, and the following analysis reports the results from models predicting participation beyond voting among Asian Americans. These activities include contacting a government official, donating to a political campaign, working with others in the community to solve a problem, and taking part in a protest or demonstration. The results of the estimations of the models are presented in Table 4.3, including the explanatory factors of socioeconomic status, psychological engagement, organizational affiliation, political mobilization, minority group status, language, region, and ethnic origin.[20]

The first column of data presents the results when all Asian Americans are analyzed together, whereas the second column of data in Table 4.3 include the results for model for immigrants only. There are important differences between factors affecting participation beyond voting and the data presented in Table 4.2 for voting. In particular, education is not significant in predicting participation beyond voting and family income, while significant, has the opposite sign. Factors that were insignificant in predicting voting, such as membership in an Asian American organization, mobilization by individuals, possessing a sense of linked fate with other Asian Americans, having personally experienced discrimination, and residing in Hawaii are all positive and statistically significant in predicting participation beyond voting, but attending religious services is not relevant. Being Korean American is also no longer statistically significant for political participation beyond voting, but being either of South Asian or Vietnamese

[20] Because this measure of participation is an interval-level scale, we estimated the models using a method of Ordinary Least Squares regression. Control variables included in the model but not shown in the table include age, gender, and length of time at current residence. The coefficient for age is positive and statistically significant only for the immigrant sample, and length of residence is positive and significant only for the full sample.

**TABLE 4.3.** Predicting Participation beyond Voting (Unstandardized Ordinary Least Squares regression coefficients)

|  | All Asian Americans | Immigrants |
|---|---|---|
|  | Coefficient (and standard error) | Coefficient (and standard error) |
| TRADITIONAL PREDICTORS |  |  |
| **Socioeconomic Status** |  |  |
| Education | 0.03 (.03) | 0.03 (.03) |
| Family Income | 0.07*** (.03) | 0.08*** (.03) |
| **Psychological Engagement** |  |  |
| Political Interest | 0.20*** (.05) | 0.18*** (.05) |
| Political Knowledge | 0.67*** (.19) | 0.41** (.20) |
| Political Influence | 0.12** (.05) | 0.14*** (.05) |
| Strong Partisan | 0.02 (.04) | 0.03 (.04) |
| Liberal | 0.02 (.04) | 0.03 (.05) |
| **Institutional Affiliation and Mobilization** |  |  |
| Member of Community Organization | 0.65*** (.12) | 0.50*** (.13) |
| Mobilized by a Party | 0.18* (.09) | −0.03 (.10) |
| Mobilized by Individual | 0.72*** (.11) | 0.57*** (.12) |
| Religious Attendance | 0.02 (.03) | 0.03 (.03) |
| **Region Variable** |  |  |
| Honolulu | 0.31*** (.13) | 0.33** (.17) |
| ASIAN AMERICAN-SPECIFIC PREDICTORS |  |  |
| **Minority Group Status** |  |  |
| Panethnic Linked Fate | 0.09** (.04) | 0.11*** (.04) |
| Personal Discrimination | 0.35*** (.12) | 0.30** (.13) |
| **Migration-Related** |  |  |
| Foreign-Born | −0.40*** (.13) | – |
| English Language Use | 0.00 (.08) | −0.01 (.08) |
| Citizenship Status | 0.04 (.07) | 0.07 (.08) |
| Years in the United States | – | −0.01 (.01) |
| Educated Outside U.S. | −0.30*** (.11) | −0.30*** (.11) |
| Active in Country of Origin Politics | – | 1.24*** (.19) |
| **Ethnic origin (comparison group Chinese)** |  |  |
| Japanese | 0.09 (.20) | −0.32 (.26) |
| Filipino | 0.17 (.17) | 0.07 (.18) |
| Korean | −0.08(.15) | −0.08 (.14) |
| South Asian | 0.40** (.18) | 0.30* (.18) |
| Vietnamese | 0.58*** (.17) | 0.27* (.16) |
| Constant | −0.92*** (.29) | −1.37*** (.29) |
| N | 850 | 627 |
| Adjusted R-square | .37 | .34 |

Control variables included in model, but not shown in table are age, female, and length of time at current residence. The coefficient for age is positive and statistically significant only for the foreign-born and that for length of residence at current address is positive and significant only for the full sample. Listwise deletion of missing cases was used in the analysis.

Levels of Significance: *$p \leq .10$; **$p \leq .05$; ***$p \leq .01$

origin is associated with higher participation. Moreover, being foreign-born is now significant in suppressing participation as is being educated mostly outside of the United States. Importantly, those immigrants who are active in home country politics are also more likely to participate in political activities beyond voting in the host country. Nevertheless, similar to voting, respondents who are more interested in politics, who possess more political knowledge, and who indicate more efficacy in influencing local government decisions are more likely to participate. Similar to the voting analysis, participation beyond voting does not seem to be related to one's political partisanship, ideology, or English language use among Asian Americans.

One interesting finding that deserves attention is that citizenship status does not have an effect on participation beyond voting once other factors are accounted for. These results have important implications for the meaning attributed to citizenship and the naturalization process. Citizenship status matters most for voting – the political activity for which citizenship is a legal requirement. But for political activities beyond voting that do not require citizenship, the results from this study show that once other factors such as socioeconomic status, mobilization, and minority group status are considered, foreign-born Asian Americans who are not citizens are no less likely to participate in politics than citizens. In terms of their participatory behavior outside the voting booth, noncitizens and citizens exhibit similar rates of involvement. Thus, lack of citizenship may not be an indicator of less interest in being part of the United States for Asian Americans; instead, citizenship is a legal hurdle to overcome in order to enter the voting booth.

In comparing the findings detailed in Tables 4.2 and 4.3, it is clear that factors related to minority group status, regional culture, and individual mobilization, which are not strong predictors of voting, are indeed critical determinants of participatory activities that do not require U.S. citizenship. Other conditions being equal, membership in an Asian American organization, feelings of linked fate with other Asian Americans, and experience with discrimination may encourage some Asian Americans, citizens or not, to get more involved in politics. The findings on the significance of Honolulu suggests that the large number and long historical presence of Asian Americans in Honolulu may facilitate more participation there than in other cities where Asian Americans do not have a significant presence in politics. Although party mobilization is likely to increase participation beyond voting for all Asian Americans, it does not do the same for the immigrant sample. Party mobilization is also much less potent than individual mobilization in influencing participation. It could be that because parties are in the business of elections, they are more invested in mobilizing people to register and vote rather than in getting them to participate in political activities beyond voting (Wong 2005). Individuals, such as an employer, program director, church leader, or friend, might be more likely to encourage people to become involved in a wider range of political activities.

In terms of ethnic origin, past research has shown that Japanese Americans tend to both vote and participate in activities beyond voting at higher rates than other Asian ethnic groups (Lien et al. 2001a). However, this analysis shows that compared to their Chinese American counterparts, both Vietnamese and South Asian American respondents are more likely to be active in politics beyond voting. This result suggests the propensity of Japanese Americans to participate in politics may be a function of their relatively high average scores in terms of education, socioeconomic resources, length of residence, citizenship rates, English language skills, and greater concentration in Hawaii.

Using the immigrant sample, we are able to test the effects of length of residence in the United States, place of education, and activity in country of origin politics on participation. Although past studies using U.S. Census data have suggested the importance of length of residence on Asian American immigrants' participation in politics (Lien 2000, 2001a; Ong and Nakanishi 1996), these effects are likely to be related to the acquisition of language skills and immigrants' becoming citizens over time (Wong 2000). Therefore, it is not surprising that once citizenship status and English language use are accounted for (in addition to organizational affiliation, mobilization, and other factors), length of residence in the United States does not appear to have an independent effect on participation. In addition, those who were educated mainly outside of the United States participate at lower rates than those who were educated mainly in the United States. These findings suggest place of education matters as much as degree of education in the United States. Consistent with Cho's (1999) hypothesis, the U.S.-born may experience political socialization through different channels than immigrants, and the education system may be one of the most important socialization environments.

Finally, there are several interesting findings related to transnational behavior and political activity among immigrant Asian Americans. Those who are active in politics related to their country of origin are some of the most likely to be involved in political activities beyond voting.[21] Contrary to those who believe strong ties to or involvement in the country of origin detract from political participation in the United States, these data clearly demonstrate that Asian Americans who participate in activities relevant to politics in their countries of origin also tend to get involved in political participation beyond voting in the United States. One explanation for this finding is that politically active people will participate in politics wherever the opportunity arises. Another explanation is that individuals get involved in politics in the United States in order to bring about change in their home countries.

## ASIAN AMERICAN ACTIVITY AMID DIVERSITY

The racial categorization of Asian Americans belies substantial internal diversity in terms of ethnic origin, and generation of immigration. Although the majority of Asian Americans are immigrants, many have long-standing roots in the United States as fifth-generation Americans with Chinese or Japanese ancestors. Today's Asian immigrants come to the United States from sending countries as distinctive as Vietnam, India, and South Korea, and together, they are grouped as Asian Americans. Until recently, little was known about the political behavior of Asian Americans in part because it is much more costly and difficult to gather systematic data on a multilingual population that is relatively small and geographically concentrated compared to the general U.S. population. The absence of systematic information reinforced the stereotype of Asian Americans as politically quiescent. Indeed, Asian Americans have been identified as anomalous in terms of the applicability of the standard socioeconomic status models of participation, which suggests higher levels of educational and income resources drive political activity. Asian Americans are exceptional inasmuch as they have relatively high levels of individual resources but low rates of voting.

This puzzle, accompanied by the surge in the size of the Asian American population and its subsequent and geographic dispersal away from traditional immigrant gateways has fueled a new interest in the dynamics of political participation among Asian Americans. We argue that to understand Asian American political activity, explanations must

---

[21] The relationship between the summary measure of participation beyond voting and the measure of political activity related to country of origin was .34 (Pearson Correlation Coefficient with one-tailed $p < .01$).

go beyond traditional models used to predict participation in the general U.S. population. Rather, a new focus on factors related to immigration, racial group concerns and status, and national origin reveal important insights about the ways in which Asian Americans contribute to political life in the United States.

Through our analysis of multicity data, we find Asian Americans' participation patterns are partly a reflection of the "usual suspects" that drive political behavior among white Americans. At the same time, we uncover features and sources of Asian American participation that suggest that political activity may be more dynamic and exhibit more potential for mobilization than the American population more generally. Traditional indicators of political participation including socioeconomic status, psychological engagement with politics, attendance at religious services, and mobilization emerge as important predictors of Asian American political involvement. Yet these factors alone do not adequately explain activity among Asian Americans, particularly for participation beyond voting. Instead, it is important to consider the effects of immigration-related factors, minority group status, as well as ethnic group membership on Asian Americans' political participation.

One of our most important findings is that being foreign-born or being educated mostly outside of the United States is negatively associated with some types of participation beyond voting. This implies that participation patterns among Asian Americans are not likely to be static. Rather, as generations of Asian Americans continue to grow in the United States, we can expect participation rates to be dynamic, perhaps even contributing to higher overall rates of participation in the country as the portion of foreign-born and non-U.S.-educated changes among Asian Americans over time. Such a scenario is limited by the fact that Asian Americans currently constitute a relatively small proportion of the population. However, the Asian American population is one of the fastest growing minority groups in the country, and their potential political impact may mirror their rapid growth in the population.

Furthermore, some factors related to migration and minority group status may represent a source of participation not available to nonminority immigrant populations, such as being a member of an Asian American organization, having feelings of linked fate with others of the same racial background, and experience with racial discrimination. We found these to all be positive and statistically significant predictors of political participation beyond voting, reinforcing the notion that connection to a racial group may motivate political participation. Moreover, the findings presented here suggest that rather than encouraging Asian Americans to retreat into ethnic enclaves, a sense of linked fate with other Asian Americans, membership in Asian American organizations, and even activism related to the politics in the home country may spur political participation in the United States, leading to more, not less, political integration for Asian Americans. These unique features provide new insight into a future of activity amidst diversity for Asian Americans in the decades to come.

RODOLFO O. DE LA GARZA, MARISA A. ABRAJANO,
AND JERONIMO CORTINA

# 5 Get Me to the Polls on Time

## Coethnic Mobilization and Latino Turnout

Until recently, Latinos were nearly invisible on the national political scene, garnering little attention from political parties, candidates, and scholars alike. Much has changed in the last several decades, and Latinos are now the largest minority group in the country, making up more than 12 percent of the U.S. population. With a steady stream of immigrants from Mexico and Latin America, the proportion of Latinos is expected to more than double by mid-century to a quarter of the population. Once small and geographically concentrated in states in the American west and southwest, new patterns of settlement among immigrants to nontraditional gateway metropolitan areas in the United States has resulted in a highly diverse Latino population that is increasingly dispersed across states in the United States. Nevertheless, substantial populations of Latinos reside in five of the most electorally rich states in the United States – California, New York, Texas, Florida, and Illinois – and the dynamics of elections in those states and across the nation simply cannot be understood without accounting for Latino voters (Leighley 2001; Shaw et al. 2000).

Despite the momentous demographic changes and the resulting imperative to understand Latino electoral behavior, surprisingly little is known about how Latino voters are mobilized, and what impact that mobilization has on their voting behavior. In general, political scientists have focused their attention on developing models to explain voting among Anglos and African Americans. Patterns of electoral participation by new groups of voters such as Latinos have been analyzed with the assumption that Latino turnout is shaped by the same factors that influence voting in these traditional models. But the unique experiences of Latinos in terms of discrimination, racialization, immigration, national origin, ethnic ties, and political context all lead us to expect that explaining Latino voting turnout requires going beyond the effects of demographic and political characteristics identified as central factors in traditional models of Anglo voting behavior. We focus on the significance of coethnic mobilization among Latinos, and investigate the extent to which ethnicity and the interaction of ethnic factors, as well as mobilization within particular political contexts have an impact on Latino turnout. Analysis of electoral behavior also must account for variation in the particular political contexts of states, and we emphasize the significance of structural and compositional differences between states with large Latino populations in our analysis.

## DOES THE SHOE FIT? TRADITIONAL MODELS AND LATINO VOTING

There is a venerable tradition in studies of American voting behavior focusing on the individual characteristics of voters as the primary explanation for why people choose to vote. The most enduring of these findings is the propensity of high social and economic status individuals to cast a ballot and participate in politics more generally (Campbell et al. 1960; Verba and Nie 1972; Wolfinger and Rosenstone 1980; Verba, Schlozman, and Brady 1995). High-status individuals have more resources such as time, money, and skills that facilitate political activity. But as Verba and Nie (1972) show in their analysis of the importance of civic attitudes in explaining voting, individual level social and economic indicators alone cannot fully explain political participation. Also, Verba et al. (1995) highlight the significance of racial group membership for political participation, showing Anglos are far more likely to report being asked to participate than either African-Americans or Latinos.[1] Another explanation of turnout focuses on voter mobilization, and acknowledges that although socioeconomic status remains the primary determinant of political mobilization, high-status individuals are also more likely to participate because they are more likely to be recruited (Verba et al., 1995). Rosenstone and Hansen (1993) argue mass participation levels reflect the mobilizing activities of political elites and suggest much of the decline in voter turnout since the 1960s reflects changes in mobilization patterns.

The effect of individual resources and mobilization for voter turnout may be systematically different for Anglos than for African Americans

---

[1] Once the resource differences are accounted for, Latinos and blacks are no less likely to be asked to participate than are Anglos. Get-out-the-vote (GOTV) campaigns targeting African Americans and Latinos differ in that African Americans are most likely to report being recruited by other African Americans, whereas Latinos are most likely to report being contacted by Anglos (CITE).

and Latinos. Mobilization takes many different forms; among the most common in minority populations is through groups such as unions and ethnic institutions. These groups are especially salient for the mobilization of Latinos. Hero (1992) notes that various groups such as the League of United Latino Citizens (LULAC), Southwest Voter Registration and Education Project (SWVREP), farm workers unions, as well as local neighborhood associations played substantial roles in the Chicano movement of the 1970s. Tate (1993) and Gurin et al. (1989) find that even after accounting for resources and political attitudes, self-reported church membership and group membership has a positive effect on African American electoral turnout. Similarly, Diaz (1996) and de la Garza and Lu (1999) find reported memberships in voluntary groups or organizations among Latinos are also related to higher levels of voter registration and turnout. Nonetheless, despite mobilization's potential importance, most of the empirical evidence regarding how it affects African American and Latino voters is indirect. This is because the unit of analysis related to reaching out to voters from these groups is the mobilizing institution, whereas systematic data on the actual behavior of the individuals who are the targets of mobilizing campaigns is rare.

Verba et al. (1995) provide the most comprehensive approach to test the importance of group mobilization on minority participation among African Americans and Latinos. They suggest civic groups mobilize participation by directly asking individuals to vote and also by fostering skills that can be useful in political activity. They conclude that mobilization patterns are quite consistent across the three racial groups, including Anglos. Regardless of the form mobilization takes, after accounting for social and economic characteristics, African Americans and Latinos generally report being asked to participate at about the same rate as Anglos. How this affects turnout for Latinos as a group rather than as individuals is unclear because as a group, Latinos have relatively low levels of social and economic resources and status. Groups that are resource-poor are precisely the ones least likely to be mobilized to vote. In this regard, it is difficult to estimate how outreach influences the Latino vote overall.

Leighley (2001) addresses the political mobilization of racial and ethnic minorities by analyzing the relationship between group size and mobilization, and political empowerment and mobilization. As the size of a minority group increases, its potential for electoral influence also rises, and group size has an independent positive role on political participation. Political empowerment refers to increased political involvement by minorities as a result of having minorities elected to public office.

Leighley's analysis demonstrates that although Latino empowerment does not stimulate higher voter turnout, Latino population size is a strong and significant predictor of turnout in both presidential and local elections as well as overall participation. Further evidence that Latino turnout may be influenced by group size is suggested by Uhlaner's (1989) "relational goods" argument suggesting that increases in minority group participation are related to group interaction. In this regard, Latinos should be more likely to vote when they reside in homogenous ethnic environments as opposed to heterogeneous locales.

Although Leighley and Uhlaner argue group concentration positively affects Latino participation, other researchers disagree. Empirical evidence from de la Garza and DeSipio (1997) suggests group size depresses mobilization, largely as a function of the fact that areas with high concentrations of Latinos typically include a large number of non-citizens who cannot vote. Political elites have little incentive to target these ethnic pockets, and group size does not predict greater mobilization efforts. Furthermore, de la Garza et al. (2002) find Latino voters in Harris County, Texas, who reside in precincts with a low density of Latinos participate at higher rates than those who live in high-density Latino precincts. This trend was consistent across elections between 1992 and 1998, and provides further evidence that residential concentration among Latinos does not increase voting turnout.

Taken together, the conventional wisdom regarding voting behavior, and Latino turnout in particular, addresses the significance of mobilization, but the findings remain inconclusive. Indeed, nearly all of the studies measure and address mobilization indirectly, focusing on environments that may or may not be conducive to mobilization campaigns. Individual level data measuring whether people have been directly contacted and encouraged to vote, and by whom, is rarely gathered. In the following section, we analyze the effects of such mobilization efforts with particular attention to the effects mobilization by coethnics has on Latino voting turnout.

## LATINOS AND THE 2000 ELECTION

The rapid expansion of the Latino population in the United States, and its increasing diversity in terms of national origin, requires the development of creative strategies to study Latino mobilization in elections. Although the majority of Latinos across the United States have origins in Mexico, there is substantial variation across states with large Latino populations. For example, the majority of Latinos in Florida are of Cuban descent, whereas 50 percent of Latinos in New York are Puerto Rican. Alternatively, Latinos in California, Illinois, and Texas are overwhelmingly of Mexican origin. In order to capture this diversity and assess the impact of coethnic mobilization strategies on Latino voting turnout, we analyze data from a 2000 postelection survey of 2,011 Latinos citizens.[2] Data from about four hundred respondents was collected in each of the five states of California, Florida, Illinois, New York, and Texas.

In Texas, eight out of ten Latinos identify their national origin as Mexican, and a slightly smaller proportion does so in California (79 percent) and Illinois (71 percent). Illinois has a relatively large Puerto Rican population (17 percent) compared with both California and Texas, which have a very small proportion of Puerto Ricans. In Texas and California, the second largest group in terms of national origin for Latinos is the category of "other," representing a range of Latin American countries such as Honduras, El Salvador, Guatemala, and Ecuador. Florida and New York are quite distinct from their Western and Mid-Western counterparts, with relatively small populations of Mexicans – only 5 percent in Florida and an even smaller 2 percent in New York. In Florida, Cubans dominate, and are followed by Latinos with national origins from other Latin American countries. Twelve percent of Latinos in Florida are Puerto Rican. New York is unique in that it has a bare majority of Puerto Ricans as the largest Latino population, followed closely by 45 percent in the "other" category, in this case, representing large numbers of Latinos from the Dominican Republic as well as other Latin American countries.

In addition to the important variation in national origin among Latinos in the five states, Texas, California, Illinois, Florida, and New York, they also differ in terms of institutional characteristics and political context. We expect Latino mobilization to interact with the institutional characteristics of the state in which a respondent resides to affect voting turnout. Because each state varies in terms of the party structures, existence of political machines, competitiveness, union mobilization and other issues, which varies the efforts to mobilize Latinos within these diverse institutional structures, we expect the impact of coethnic mobilization to also vary across the states. Table 5.1 provides information on relevant characteristics of each of the five states in the TRPI survey.

---

[2] The telephone survey was conducted by the Tomas Rivera Policy Institute (TRPI) and the Public Policy Clinic in the Department of Government at the University of Texas at Austin. The total sample size is 2,011 Latino citizens. The sample has a margin of error of $+/-3$ points. Further details of the data collection are available at http://www:trpi.org.

**TABLE 5.1.** Characteristics of States

| State Characteristic | California | Florida | Illinois | New York | Texas |
|---|---|---|---|---|---|
| Median household income | $39,595 | $32,877 | $41,179 | $36,369 | $34,478 |
| Latinos in state legislature | 18.3% | 7.5% | 3.3% | 18.9% | 18% |
| Latinos in U.S. Congress | 11.5% | 8.6% | 5% | 9.5% | 20% |
| Competitiveness in presidential election | 11 | 0 | 12 | 25 | −21 |
| Number of Electoral College votes (in 2002) | 54 | 25 | 22 | 33 | 32 |
| Competitive state races | yes | yes | no | yes | no |
| Controversial issues | no | yes | no | yes | no |
| Mobilization by unions %Dem-%Rep in 2000 election | yes | no | no | yes | no |

Table 5.1 includes information on median household income, the proportion of Latinos in the state legislature and the U.S. Congress, the degree of competitiveness in presidential elections, the number of Electoral College votes each state holds, whether state races are competitive, if there were controversial issues present during the 2000 campaign, and the extent to which there was mobilization by unions during the election. Each of these characteristics constrains as well as provides opportunities for mobilization among Latinos, and as a result, produces different stories of the 2000 election in each of the five states. According to the U.S. Census, Latino turnout increased in the 2000 general election to over five million, representing growth of 20.4 percent over the 1996 election, compared to an increase of 16.9 percent among nonvoting Latinos. This was the first time in decades that the increase in Latino voters exceeded the increase among Latino nonvoters. Additionally, their average growth rate in our five states was 27.5 percent, with Texas showing the greatest increase (30 percent) and California the smallest (25 percent).

### California

California exhibited several of the key factors affecting Latino turnout, including competitive state races, mobilization by unions, and the perception that the state was a battleground state because of the "swing vote" potential of Latinos. Latinos make up 33 percent of the population of the state of California, and comprise 16 percent of registered voters. Although a substantial majority of Latinos in California are Democrats, George W. Bush and his campaign strategists believed they could make inroads into this group. According to one observer, the Republican National Committee in January 2000 announced a multimillion-dollar bilingual ad campaign aimed at Latino voters that included "an unprecedented Latino-aimed television and print advertising campaign in California before the March 7 primary" (Marinucci 2000). Lionel Sosa, one of Bush's campaign strategists went so far as to say "whoever wins the Hispanic vote in California will win the presidency. And make no mistake about it – we will win the Hispanic vote here" (Marinucci 2000). In addition to these primary efforts, in the final weeks of the campaign, Bush also spent an additional $8 million in California, with a considerable percentage of these funds devoted to Latino media (Novak 2000). Alternatively, Gore was more confident in his Latino base, and he limited his Latino-specific campaign to Spanish radio while failing to counter Bush's television advertisements. Despite the minimal campaign effort, Gore successfully won 68 percent of all Latino votes, whereas Bush received 29 percent. Latino voters also contributed to Democratic congressional victories by playing pivotal roles in four of the five seats in which Democrats unseated Republicans.[3]

Mobilization efforts by labor unions statewide also helped Latino turnout in California. The San Diego Labor/Neighbor program began in September of 2000 and conducted phone banking, neighborhood walks, and mailings every weekend before the election. Their primary target was the ten thousand union members in the San Diego area, many of whom were Latinos. A similar effort was implemented in the Los Angeles area by the AFL-CIO. They worked with Latino community based organizations and Catholic parishes to get new citizens to vote. In Northern California, union efforts were undertaken by the Labor/Neighbor Program in San Francisco. This effort also began in September and was conducted in collaboration with the Labor Council for Latin American Advancement, the A. Philip Randolph Institute, and the Asian Pacific American Labor Alliance (Tomás Rivera Policy Institute, 2002). These conditions created high levels of Latino turnout relative to previous presidential races as well as compared to Latino turnout in other states. In addition, the median income among Latinos in California is also relatively high, second only to income levels for Latinos in Illinois. Taken together, these patterns suggest Latino turnout in California would be higher than that of the other states in our analysis.

---

[3] See Rodolfo O. de la Garza and Louis DeSipio, eds. (2004), *Muted Voices: Latinos and the 2000 Election*, Rowman and Littlefield for further details on Latino voters and the campaigns in the five states.

## Florida

Although Miami's Cuban American community constitutes less than five percent of the nation's total Latino population, Cubans have been able to exert an inordinate amount of influence on national politics as a function of the competitive nature of elections in Florida. In the 2000 election, Florida was considered to be a "battleground state" despite the fact that Republican candidates have won the state in all elections since 1952 except 1964, 1976, and 1996.

Because it was considered a competitive state, both Bush and Gore campaigned heavily in Florida. Both candidates also targeted Latinos. Conventional wisdom predicted a decidedly pro-Republican base in Miami's Cuban community, but Latinos with national origins other than Cuban were not similarly oriented. Bush's dependence on Miami's Cuban vote is partially a result of his unpopularity with the state's other important minority constituencies, specifically African-Americans and Jews (Hill and Moreno, 2002). Thus, Bush poured significant resources into Miami's Spanish language media and also ran an extensive campaign both on radio and television to mobilize his Cuban American base. In contrast, the Gore campaign concentrated on non-Cuban Latinos in Central Florida, which explains why almost all of Gore's media time was purchased in the Tampa and Orlando markets. In addition to the funds spent on media, both Gore and Bush spent the last weekend of their presidential campaigns in Florida, with Bush ending his in a rally targeting Miami's Cuban community and Gore targeting Jewish voters.

Despite the significant advances made by Clinton in gaining Cuban support, these efforts were reversed by the Clinton administration's actions in the Elian Gonzalez case. Before this, Clinton was the first Democratic presidential candidate to campaign in Miami's Cuban community, and although he received 25 percent of the Cuban vote in 1992, he increased his support among Miami Cubans to 40 percent by 1996. Many Cuban Americans were outraged by the administration's decision to send Elian Gonzalez back to Cuba, and the 2000 election provided the opportunity to punish the Democratic candidate for the Clinton administration's handling of the Elian Gonzales case. This controversial issue served to both energize and mobilize Cuban voters who voted overwhelmingly for the Republican candidate.

In addition to the presidential contest, the mayoral race in Miami mobilized Latinos, particularly Cubans in Miami. Alex Penelas, Miami-Dade's Cuban American Mayor, was running for reelection. Penelas was a highly visible and popular Latino leader in Florida, and a strong supporter of

Clinton. In the wake of the Elian Gonzalez issue, Penelas remained critical of the Clinton administration in order to retain his base of Cuban voters. Penelas even went so far as to state that any violence resulting from the seizure of the boy would be the fault of the Clinton administration. This race not only mobilized the Cuban community to vote against the Democratic presidential candidate, but it also mobilized Cubans to support Penelas. Finally, despite their low median income, the fact that both parties targeted the Latinos and the saliency of the Elian Gonzalez issue angering the Cuban American voters suggested that Latino turnout would be quite high in Florida.

### Texas

Although Gore promised to fight for this important Electoral College state, it was widely acknowledged that this commitment was mostly rhetorical. No significant appeals were made to Latinos in Texas by the Democrats. In a similar vein, Bush took Latino votes for granted in his home state, knowing he already had the support of the Texas electorate. Texas was not considered to be a competitive state, and in 2000, there were no other contested races on the ballot, nor were there any polarizing issues stimulating voter interest. Furthermore, Latinos in Texas have the lowest median income compared to the other four states. Thus, even though there is a solid bloc of Latino Democratic elected officials in the state who could have led a GOTV effort, there was no reason to expect high turnout among Latinos in the Lone Star State.

### Illinois

As was the case in Texas, Illinois Latinos were not pivotal in the 2000 presidential election. In neither the primaries nor the general election did presidential candidates or political parties actively seek their votes. Illinois was not central to either candidate's strategy, and the state was neglected by both parties until the last two weeks of the election. Gore's safe margin of victory of 12 percent, and the fact that Illinois offered the smallest number of electoral votes compared to the other four states with the largest Latino populations, further explains the lack of attention that Latinos received in Illinois during the 2000 election.

Other structural conditions necessary to mobilize Latino turnout in Ilinois also were noticeably absent, such as no competitive statewide or local races with Latino candidates; nor were there controversial issues that could mobilize Latinos in 2000. Although there were a number of contested congressional races, in only one was the Latino population larger than 5 percent. The Bush campaign did run some commercials in selected media markets after Labor Day, but the advertising lasted less than a month. Moreover, when it was clear Illinois had become noncompetitive, both campaigns removed their Latino campaign staffs in early September and transferred them to Wisconsin. These factors more than countered the state's high median Latino income and indicate why there were few reasons to expect high Latino turnout in Illinois.

**New York**
New York was not a competitive state in terms of Electoral College votes, and this is evident from Gore's 21 percent margin of victory in the state. Although Latino turnout may have been depressed because of this Democratic advantage, it was counterbalanced by the mobilization of Latino voters by strong union efforts, controversial issues directly affecting Latinos, and competitive statewide races. The largest union in the state, the health care union led by Dennis Rivera, facilitated high rates of Latino turnout because not only do Latinos comprise a substantial portion of its members, but also because Rivera is of Puerto Rican descent. These union efforts helped mobilize Latinos in New York and complemented the standard party or community based organizations' initiatives, producing a pattern not visible in Texas or Illinois.

A number of issues also mobilized New York Latinos, who are primarily comprised of Puerto Ricans. Similar to the effects of the Elian Gonzalez issue in Florida, actions taken by the Clinton administration regarding the island of Vieques had detrimental effects for Vice President Gore. The administration's decision to allow Navy bombing exercises on Vieques caused a great deal of resentment among the Puerto Rican community. This action, however, may have been counterbalanced by President Clinton's offer of clemency to sixteen Puerto Rican nationalists who had participated in the assaults on the U.S. House of Representatives in 1953. Regardless of whether these issues had a positive or negative effect on Gore, they motivated New York Latinos to go to the polls, either to punish Gore for the actions taken by the Clinton administration or to provide their traditional support for the Democratic candidate. Another factor fueling turnout in New York was the U.S. Senate race between Hillary Clinton and Rick Lazio. Clinton's reliance on a strong Democratic turnout resulted in significant get-out-the-vote efforts in both black and Latino areas (Liff 2000). Such efforts further mobilized New York Latinos to vote, a phenomenon that was noticeably absent in both Illinois and Texas.

## LATINO COETHNIC MOBILIZATION IN THE 2000 ELECTION

In this section, we test the effect of Latino outreach on Latino voter turnout in the 2000 presidential election in the five states of California, Texas, Illinois, Florida, and New York.

The five-state TRPI survey of Latino citizens included questions on presidential vote choice and issues for the 2000 elections, opinions on a variety of issues, level of political attentiveness and interest, questions on who asked the respondents to participate, as well as demographic information. To get an accurate record of Latino voting rates, we used official turnout records to validate self-reported turnout. Validating turnout was necessary in light of evidence from Shaw et al. (2000) revealing over-reporting among Latinos in their level of turnout during the 1996 presidential election at a rate of 20 percent.

In order to test our hypothesis regarding the effect that coethnic mobilization has on turnout, we designed three models incorporating various factors that impact voter turnout. We predict whether or not an individual voted in the 2000 presidential election, and in so doing use a binary logit model to estimate the influence of mobilization and other factors affecting voting behavior. In the first model, we do not take into account the differences that may exist between and within states, that is, we fit a complete pooling logit regression. In the second model, we let the intercept and the mobilization variables (slopes) vary by state in order to capture each state's structural intricacies as discussed previously. In the third and last model we allow the mobilization and ethnicity variables to vary by state so we can gauge the interactions that may exist between ethnic groups and each state's institutional arrangements. Explanatory measures include demographic characteristics, political attitudes and behaviors, nonethnic and coethnic mobilization efforts.

In our models, we include the standard socioeconomic variables known to influence turnout including age, income, education, and nativity. To those we add another set of indicators that political participation literature has suggested plays a positive role in voter turnout; these include partisanship, strength of political interest, and strength of party identification (Verba et al. 1995). We also include other factors that could potentially increasing turnout such as whether one attends political meetings (Tate 1993; Gurin et al. 1989; Diaz 1996). In addition, we include measures of mobilization by any group or organization, contact by an ethnic group, and/or a political party. Because respondents were asked several questions regarding various types of mobilization, we created an overall mobilization

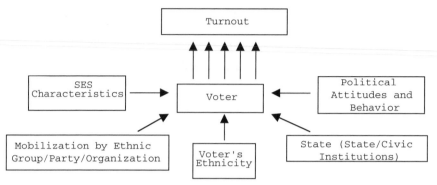

**Figure 5.1.** Model of Factors Influencing Voter Turnout.

measure coded as "1" if the respondent was mobilized by a Latino (group, person, or organization), "2" if the respondent was mobilized by a non-Latino entity, and "3" if the respondent was mobilized by either a Latino or a non-Latino regardless of the type of group. The baseline category is whether the respondent was mobilized by a Latino regardless of the type of group responsible for the mobilizing campaign. Finally, ethnicity or national origin was coded as a categorical variable consisting of Mexicans, Puerto Ricans, Cubans, and others.

State in this chapter is used as an aggregate indirect measure of a variety of factors that we group as Type I (exogenous) and Type II (endogenous) variables (Guerra and Fraga, 1996). Type I factors include variables that Latinos cannot control or directly influence in any given election, while the Type II factors include variables Latinos can control or directly influence. Type I factors include median family income, the presence of controversial issues either on the ballot or affecting the political climate at election time, state level partisan competitiveness, and the size of the state's electoral college vote. Type II factors are factors that Latinos can influence such as the extent of Latino representation within the state legislature, their percentage within the congressional delegation, and the extent to which Latinos initiated or implemented targeted Latino get-out-the-vote campaigns.

Figure 5.1 maps the direct mobilization model of how ethnic mobilization and other explanatory measures influence turnout.

However, the impact of ethnic mobilization and ethnicity on voter turnout may not be as direct as the path in Figure 5.1 specifies. Rather, mobilization can also be viewed in an alternative indirect manner, as shown in Figure 5.2. The decision to vote may be dependent on contact

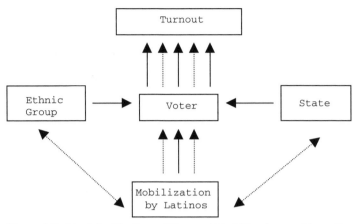

Figure 5.2. Model of Indirect Effects of Mobilization on Voter Turnout.

from a Latino, the state he or she comes from, and on the voter's ethnic group. Mobilization can occur based on ties to one's ethnic group as well as because of outreach by Latinos who are not coethnics. Likewise, when state institutions interact with mobilization by a Latino, they may affect an individual's decision to vote. We represent these indirect effects of mobilization by the dashed lines in Figure 5.2, and the arrows also indicate the causal path that can occur in either direction. In order to capture all the possible effects of mobilization, we include these interactive terms in the estimation of our model with interaction effects. The results from these estimates indicate whether indirect mobilization influences turnout. Given that we are dealing with ethnic groups that have had a tenuous relationship with political institutions, these indirect effects may be more relevant to these sets of voters because they have not been traditionally targeted by mainstream campaigns, and mobilization may be more successful when implemented by a coethnic.

### Direct Effects of Ethnic Mobilization
We first consider the direct effects of ethnic mobilization on the pooled sample of all Latinos in the five states. Table 5.2 presents the estimated coefficients from the direct mobilization model. In terms of the demographic factors, both age and income have positive but not significant effects on turnout among Latinos in the pooled national sample. The other traditional measures of individual social and economic status have a mixed influence on turnout; education, in particular, reveals no relationship to

**TABLE 5.2.** Complete Pooling

|  | Coefficient (and standard error) |
| --- | --- |
| Intercept | −1.76 (1.26) |
| Age | .01 (.0001) |
| Income | .13 (.09) |
| Some HS | 1.14 (.77) |
| HS Graduate | .13 (.63) |
| Some College | .28 (.63) |
| College Graduate | −.14 (.68) |
| Graduate School | .11 (.78) |
| U.S.-born | −.48 (.37) |
| Cuban | .22 (.88) |
| Puerto Rican | .61 (.50) |
| Mexican | .05 (.38) |
| Democrat | −.73 (.48) |
| Strong Partisanship | .58* (.31) |
| Campaign Interest | .56*** (.21) |
| Attends Political meetings | .26 (.48) |
| Female | .06 (.31) |
| Non-Latino Mobilization | .92** (.43) |
| Latino + Non-Latino Mobilization | .98** (.38) |

N = 333
Significance levels: ***$p < .001$; **$p < .01$; *$p < .05$
*Source:* 2000 TRPI Latino survey

one's likelihood of voting in the pooled national sample. Similarly, nativity is also non-significant, meaning that Latinos born in the United States were no more likely to vote than were immigrant Latinos, all else being equal. Being a Democrat is not a significant predictor of Latino voting in the 2000 election, however, those who identify as strong partisans and who express a strong interest in the campaign also are more likely to vote. Likewise, Latinos mobilized either by non-Latinos or by Latinos are also more likely to vote than those who are not personally encouraged to vote. Somewhat surprisingly, we find no turnout differences associated with national origin. In other words, the effect of national origin on turnout is not statistically significant.

When we turn to the estimation of the direct effects model by individual states, the results are almost identical regarding the sociodemographic and political variables. However, the impacts of our mobilization variables are somewhat different. Table 5.3 presents the state intercepts and the

**TABLE 5.3.** Direct Mobilization: Varying Intercepts – Varying Slopes (Mobilization)

| Fixed Effects | Coefficient (and standard error) |
|---|---|
| Intercept | −1.92 (1.28) |
| Age | .01 (.01) |
| Income | .12 (.09) |
| Some HS | 1.22 (.78) |
| HS Graduate | .18 (.64) |
| Some College | .41 (.64) |
| College Graduate | .03 (.68) |
| Graduate School | .23 (.79) |
| U.S.-born | −.41 (.38) |
| Cuban | .06 (.93) |
| Puerto Rican | .47 (.52) |
| Mexican | −.03 (.40) |
| Democrat | −.73 (.49) |
| Strong Partisanship | .54* (.32) |
| Campaign Interest | .58*** (.21) |
| Attends Political meetings | .24 (.49) |
| Female | −.01 (.32) |
| Non-Latino Mobilization | .93** (.44) |
| Latino + Non-Latino Mobilization | 1.00** (.40) |

| Random Effects | Intercept | Non-Latino | Latino + non-Latino |
|---|---|---|---|
| California | 0.07 (0.17) | −0.04 (0.09) | 0.06 (.15) |
| Florida | 0.09 (0.22) | −0.05 (0.12) | 0.08 (0.19) |
| Illinois | 0.27 (0.17) | −0.15 (0.09) | 0.24 (0.16) |
| New York | −0.13 (0.18) | 0.07 (0.09) | −0.12 (0.16) |
| Texas | −0.29 (0.17) | 0.16 (0.09) | −0.26 (0.16) |

N = 333
Significance levels: ***$p < .001$; **$p < .01$; *$p < .05$
*Source:* 2000 TRPI Latino survey

coefficients for our mobilization variables for California, Florida, Illinois, New York, and Texas. Most noteworthy is that the model indicates that no state effects have a statistically significant impact on mobilization (see Random Effects in Table 5.3).

*Indirect mobilization of Latino voters: Specifying interaction effects.* The results from the direct mobilization model estimated for individual states presents some contradictory findings, which lead us to estimate the impact of indirect mobilization of Latino voters. It is possible that there are interaction effects between coethnic mobilization and national origin, and that there are distinctive effects in specific states. To test this hypothesis, we allow ethnicity and our mobilization variables to vary by state. In addition, these models include all of the other measures specified in the direct mobilization models discussed earlier.

Overall, we find that the effect of mobilization increased from previous models and have a strong and significant effect on turnout among Latinos in the United States. Although the influences of the mobilization measures remain strong and robust, we need to test if the results support the argument that ethnic factors or interactive terms involving ethnicity and specific states stimulate turnout. In order to test the extent to which the institutional arrangements of individual states interact with ethnicity and coethnic mobilization, we estimated the indirect mobilization model allowing the mobilization variables and ethnicity to interact and vary by state. The effect of ethnicity and being contacted by both a Latino and a non-Latino is mixed. For instance, if a Cuban in Illinois was contacted by both a Latino and a non-Latino to vote, she was less likely to vote. However, in Texas, we find the opposite effect; if one is Cuban and contacted by a Latino or non-Latino to vote, she was more likely to vote. Thus, although our empirical results from Texas support our hypothesis that certain ethnic groups are more responsive to mobilization efforts from either their own ethnic group or from individuals who share a panethnic identity with them, we are puzzled as to why Latino mobilization sometimes plays a negative role. Nonetheless, being contacted by a noncoethnic and/or by a coethnic Latino has a systematic effect on turnout among the Latino groups included in this study.

## GETTING LATINOS TO THE POLLS

Our analysis reveals mobilization is an important predictor of turnout on a nationwide scale. These findings reaffirm the current participation literature that points to the importance of mobilization efforts to help increase voter turnout. More specifically, our findings demonstrate that Latinos who are asked to vote are more likely to vote. Another important insight from our analysis is the small amount of variation that exists across states regarding the factors that influence turnout for Latinos. Although different factors, from demographic characteristics to those concerning political attitudes and behavior, are more salient in turnout in some states that

**TABLE 5.4.** Indirect Mobilization: Varying Intercepts – Varying Slopes (Mobilization + Ethnicity)

| Fixed Effects | Coefficient and (standard error) | Fixed Effects | Coefficient and (standard error) | Fixed Effects | Coefficient and (standard error) |
|---|---|---|---|---|---|
| Intercept | -1.92 (1.38) | Graduate School | 0.37 (.80) | Campaign Interest | 0.59*** (.22) |
| Age | 0.01 (.01) | U.S.-born | -0.36 (.39) | Attends Political meetings | 0.17 (.50) |
| Income | 0.13 (.09) | Cuban | -0.20 (.97) | Female | -0.06 (.33) |
| Some HS | 1.19 (.78) | Puerto Rican | 0.52 (.67) | Non-Latino Mobilization | 1.00** (.46) |
| HS Graduate | 0.16 (.64) | Mexican | -0.28 (.53) | Latino + Non-Latino Mobilization | 1.14*** (.43) |
| Some College | 0.42 (.64) | Democrat | -0.74 (.50) | | |
| College Graduate | 0.11 (.69) | Strong Partisanship | 0.54* (.32) | | |

| Random Effects | Intercept | Non-Latino | Latino/ Non-Latino | Cuban | Puerto Rican | Mexican | Non-Latino/ Cuban | Latino/ Non-Latino/ Cuban | Non-Latino/ Puerto Rican | Latino/ Non-Latino/ Puerto Rican | Non-Latino/ Mexican | Latino/ Non-Latino/ Mexican |
|---|---|---|---|---|---|---|---|---|---|---|---|---|
| California | 0.22 | -0.13 | 0.27 | -0.07 | 0.06 | -0.18 | 0.00 | -0.33 | -0.04 | -0.54 | 0.09 | -0.17 |
| | (0.43) | (0.46) | (0.6) | (0.21) | (0.24) | (0.38) | (0.52) | (0.65) | (1.24) | (1.09) | (0.53) | (0.58) |
| Florida | -0.02 | 0.00 | -0.01 | 0.00 | -0.01 | 0.02 | 0.02 | 0.03 | 0.06 | 0.06 | 0.01 | -0.01 |
| | (0.49) | (0.44) | (0.58) | (0.2) | (0.31) | (0.47) | (0.59) | (0.73) | (1.42) | (1.3) | (0.54) | (0.56) |
| Illinois | 1.07 | -0.36 | 1.13 | -0.24 | 0.44 | -0.95 | -0.37 | -1.61 | -1.02 | -2.78 | 0.09 | -0.49 |
| | (0.54) | (0.41) | (0.66) | (0.2) | (0.26) | (0.48) | (0.45) | (0.81) | (1.09) | (1.39) | (0.44) | (0.52) |
| New York | -0.21 | 0.71 | -0.72 | 0.31 | 0.23 | 0.01 | -0.76 | 0.35 | -1.76 | 0.28 | -0.83 | 0.90 |
| | (0.27) | (0.27) | (0.31) | (0.12) | (0.19) | (0.26) | (0.38) | (0.39) | (0.92) | (0.71) | (0.35) | (0.34) |
| Texas | -1.14 | 0.44 | -1.24 | 0.27 | -0.44 | 0.99 | 0.31 | 1.71 | 0.89 | 2.92 | -0.17 | 0.59 |
| | (0.33) | (0.41) | (0.45) | (0.18) | (0.25) | (0.32) | (0.53) | (0.5) | (1.27) | (0.88) | (0.51) | (0.52) |

N = 333

Significance levels: ***p < .001; **p < .01; *p < .05

Source: 2000 TRPI Latino survey

in others their variation and impact is minimal. This suggests that Latino turnout cannot be explained by a single set of variables. We are therefore unable to arrive at any overarching conclusions with respect to how ethnic outreach affects Latino voting in 2000. Moreover, although the failure of ethnicity to directly influence turnout was surprising, the finding is consistent with findings from other scholars (Uhlaner et al. 1989; Graves and Lee 2000) who report ethnicity has a direct effect on partisan identification and issue positions, but only indirectly affects candidate evaluation and voting preference. Ethnicity is nonetheless directly linked to important voting considerations such as policy preferences and hence plays a major role in shaping voting preferences suggesting the role of ethnicity in determining voter turnout may also follow indirect paths other than those tested here.

Overall, mobilization plays a large role in influencing voter participation among Latinos. A noteworthy finding here is that Latinos who were mobilized by both Latino and non-Latino groups were more likely to vote than those contacted only by a Latino. Because our measure does not capture the number of times that an individual was contacted, we do not know whether those who responded "both" were contacted on a more frequent basis than those who were only contacted by a Latino. So perhaps this indicates that Latinos benefit from the frequency with which they are contacted and not just from being contacted by coethnics.

The institutional arrangements in Texas seem better able to mobilize and turn out some Latino group's vote than they are in California, Illinois, Florida, and New York. Thus, in order to fully capitalize on their everburgeoning Latino populations, states must create institutional arrangements that cater to their particular Latino communities. Our findings are consistent to some extent with those of Shaw et al. (2000) who conclude that mobilization efforts as well as institutional arrangements and campaign circumstances significantly affect Latino turnout.

From a normative perspective, our findings suggest the value of asking the broader question posed at the beginning of this chapter, "Are Latino turnout dynamics similar to turnout among Anglos?" Our answer is a qualified no. The well established relationship between individual-level demographic, social, and economic status indicators such as age, income, and education is inconsistent among Latinos. However, standard political variables such as strong partisanship and political interest have consistent positive effects. Furthermore, mobilization has a positive impact on Latino turnout nationally just as it does among Anglos, but not in each state. More than ever these patterns indicate the need for further research because the questions we are asking concern how the nation's largest minority population of Latinos will engage the polity. Such knowledge transcends pure scientific interests and instead highlights the importance these electoral dynamics will have on democratic representation and political equality in a nation of growing racial and ethnic diversity.

VICTORIA M. DeFRANCESCO SOTO AND
JENNIFER L. MEROLLA

# 6  *Se Habla Espanol*

## Ethnic Campaign Strategies and Latino Voting Behavior

Latinos in the United States have been described as a sleeping giant in electoral politics because of their relatively low voting rates compared to their share of the population. The electoral significance of this diverse group of Americans is a function not only of its size, but also its concentration in states with large U.S. congressional delegations and correspondingly hefty Electoral College votes. If the giant awakens, the Latino electorate has the potential to become a major influence in national electoral politics. The major parties have taken notice of the demographic trends, and in recent presidential elections they have started to make efforts to court the "Latino vote" (Garcia 2003). Political campaigns utilize a variety of voter outreach strategies, but television advertising has become the most important and ubiquitous technique of political communications in modern political campaigns. Latinos are beginning to figure more prominently in national campaign media strategies (Buehler 1977; Doherty and Cully Anderson 2003; Subervi-Velez and Connaughton 1999), and in the 2000 presidential election over three thousand political advertisements were aired in Spanish.

The development of strategies aimed at Latino voters is still in its infancy, complicated by the newness and diversity of the Latino population in the United States. Indeed, nearly half of Latinos are immigrants whose first language is most likely not English. Furthermore, there is substantial internal ethnic diversity within the Latino category in terms of country of origin. Although the largest proportion of Latinos in the United States has Mexican origins, most of whom are immigrants, smaller and long-established groups of Puerto Ricans and Cubans have been U.S. voters for generations. Conversely, the rapid rise in immigration from a host of countries in Latin America introduces still more uncertainty in the mix of the

Latino electorate. No longer are these groups of Latinos as geographically distinct as they once were. Until fairly recently, Puerto Ricans dominated the Northeast, whereas Cubans characterized Florida politics, and Mexicans distinguished Latino politics in California and the Southwest. But new patterns of international migration are bringing Mexicans and immigrants from Latin America to all parts of the United States, particularly the South. Movement within the United States, from state to state, and from urban metropolitan areas to small towns, brings further diversity to the geographic distribution of the Latino population. Taken together, these realities render ethnic campaign strategies targeting Latinos complex indeed.

Studies of Latino voter mobilization have considered the effects of direct mobilization efforts through personal contacts, door-to-door canvassing, and direct mail (de la Garza and Abrajano this volume; de la Garza and Lee 2000). The logic behind this type of mobilization is that direct contact increases the likelihood of voting by creating opportunities for citizens to participate by reducing the costs of acquiring information (Rosenstone and Hansen 1993). With the exception of direct mail contacts, personal mobilization efforts can reach only a fraction of the Latino voting public. Alternatively, mass political communications in the form of campaign advertisements have the potential to reach many more Latino voters. Yet very little is known about the extent to which political campaigns attempt to court the Latino vote through Spanish-language or targeted advertisements, and, furthermore, what the impact of those communications is on the voting behavior of Latinos.

We address these questions by analyzing a unique data collection of televised political campaign advertisements during the 2000 presidential election. We know where these advertisements were broadcast as well as the nature of their content and the language in which they were delivered. We examine the effects of these political advertisements on Latino turnout and analyze the impact of Spanish-language and targeted advertisements on Latino voters across the United States. Similarly, we investigate the efficacy of campaign messages expressly designed for Latinos either through language or thematic content versus campaign commercials aimed at the general population. Finally, we consider how these effects might vary depending on one's process of acculturation. In so doing, we tease out the variation among Latinos in terms of voting as a function of television campaign advertisement and highlight the significance of factors including language, length of residence in the United States, and national origin.

## TARGETING LATINO VOTERS

Voter mobilization takes many forms, and we focus on the effect of political communications through television advertisements for electoral behavior. During earlier generations when there were a large number of immigrant voters who did not speak English, political campaigns targeted ethnic voters with advertisements in their native languages in foreign-language newspapers. Half a century has passed since political parties and candidates targeted ethnic voters on a national scale, and only recently have advertisements for presidential candidates been produced in Spanish and designed for Latino voters. In recent campaigns, both the Democrats and the Republicans embarked on ethnically targeted campaigns that relied on messages delivered in Spanish, or that contained Latino cultural symbolism. One prominent example is an advertisement for George W. Bush featuring his relationship to his Latino nephew.

During the 2000 presidential election, political advertisements were tracked by the Campaign Media Analysis Group (CMAG) using satellite technology. The "Polaris Ad Detector" is an independent satellite tracking system that monitors political advertising activity throughout the year in the top seventy-five media markets on the national networks (ABC, CBS, NBC, and Fox) as well as twenty-five national cable networks (CNN, ESPN, TNT, etc).[1] The resulting database provides information on the content, timing, and geographic location of every commercial aired in these media markets.[2] Two types of advertisements were used in the 2000 presidential election to appeal to Latinos. First, Spanish language commercials, advertisements in which Spanish is the spoken language, accounted for 1.4 percent of all televised political advertisements. A second type of commercial is a targeted advertisement in English that utilizes themes or Latino subjects. Advertisements were coded as targeted from the storyboards if they mentioned Latinos, had a Latino narrator, or had a Latino pictured in the commercial.[3] About 18 percent of ads aired during the 2000 presidential campaign were targeted.

---

[1] Freedman and Goldstein (1999).

[2] The data was obtained from a joint project of the Brennan Center for Justice at New York University School of Law and Professor Kenneth Goldstein of the University of Wisconsin-Madison, and included media tracking data from the Campaign Media Analysis Group in Washington, DC.

[3] There were fifteen unique targeted advertisements, eight of which dealt exclusively with Latinos. Out of the remaining seven, five had Latinos as part of a crowd, including other minority groups.

**TABLE 6.1.** Distribution of Political Advertisements Across Media Markets in 2000

| Type of Advertisement | Number of Media Markets Exposed to Advertisement | Mean Advertisements in Exposed Market (standard deviation) | Range of Number of Advertisements in Exposed Market |
|---|---|---|---|
| Spanish | 9 | 217.1 (219.1) | 3–1017 |
| Target | 30 | 508.9 (584.7) | 1–2169 |
| General | 35 | 1966.0 (2592.7) | 1–8422 |

*Source:* Campaign Media Analysis Group

Table 6.1 details the CMAG data on the distribution of political advertisements across media markets. There were many more general political advertisements than either Spanish or targeted advertisements aired during the 2000 election campaign. The average number of general political advertisements, those without specific language or content-based appeals to Latinos, was 1,966; with the number of ads in the exposed market ranging from 1 to 8,422. General advertisements were aired in thirty-five media markets. In contrast, Spanish commercials were aired in only nine of the forty-four media markets included in the CMAG data. Targeted advertisements were aired in many more locations, with a total of thirty media markets being exposed.

The geographic distribution of Spanish political advertising during the 2000 election is presented in Table 6.2. The vast majority of Spanish commercials were aired in Las Vegas (1,017). Markets in California including San Diego, Sacramento-Stockton-Modesto, and Fresno-Visalia, were exposed to Spanish language ads, but no where near the numbers seen by Las Vegas residents. Los Angeles and Miami, two cities with the largest Latino populations, saw a total of 289 and 316 Spanish language ads, respectively. However, Miami was exposed to 1,742 targeted advertisements in English. Although many markets were not exposed to Spanish-language advertisements, a number of these markets were exposed to large numbers of targeted English advertisements. For example: Spokane, Seattle-Tacoma, and Orlando, which did not see any Spanish language ads, were exposed to over one thousand targeted English ads. In the next section, we analyze what difference Spanish and targeted political advertisements made to Latino voting.

**TABLE 6.2.** Spanish Language and Targeted English Advertisements Across Media Markets in 2000

| Market Location | Number of Spanish Language Advertisements | Number of Targeted English Advertisements |
|---|---|---|
| ATLANTA | 0 | 306 |
| CHICAGO | 56 | 691 |
| CINCINNATI | 0 | 655 |
| CLEVELAND | 0 | 1069 |
| DENVER | 69 | 10 |
| DES MOINES-AMES | 0 | 1155 |
| DETROIT | 0 | 1110 |
| FLINT-SAGINAW-BAY CITY | 0 | 1202 |
| FRESNO-VISALIA | 82 | 784 |
| KANSAS CITY | 0 | 1261 |
| LAS VEGAS | 1017 | 767 |
| LOS ANGELES | 289 | 211 |
| MIAMI-FT LAUDERDALE | 316 | 1742 |
| MILWAUKEE | 0 | 1119 |
| MINNEAPOLIS-ST PAUL | 0 | 199 |
| MOBILE-PENSACOLA | 0 | 945 |
| NASHVILLE | 0 | 810 |
| NEW ORLEANS | 0 | 618 |
| NEW YORK | 3 | 1 |
| ORLANDO-DAYTONA BEACH-MELBOURNE | 0 | 1117 |
| PHILADELPHIA | 0 | 1161 |
| SACRAMENTO-STOCKTON-MODESTO | 77 | 901 |
| SAN DIEGO | 121 | 966 |
| SAN FRANCISCO-OAKLAND-SAN JOSE | 0 | 26 |
| SEATTLE-TACOMA | 0 | 1376 |
| SPOKANE | 0 | 2169 |
| ST LOUIS | 0 | 1044 |
| SYRACUSE | 0 | 13 |
| TAMPA-ST PETERSBURG-SARASOTA | 0 | 1289 |
| WEST PALM BEACH-FT PIERCE | 0 | 1496 |

*Source:* Campaign Media Analysis Group

## THE IMPACT OF ETHNIC CAMPAIGN COMMUNICATIONS

Models of voter turnout rely on the use of indicators of socioeconomic status (SES) to explain political activity (e.g., Campbell et al. 1960; Leighley and Nagler 1992; Verba, Schlozman, and Brady 1995; Wolfinger and Rosenstone 1980). Some scholars have emphasized the importance of other factors related to participation, including social connectedness (e.g., Beck and Jennings 1982; Leighley and Vedlitz 1999; Squire, Wolfinger, and Glass 1987), psychological resources (e.g., Abramson and Aldrich 1982; Rosenstone and Hansen 1993), and group identity (e.g., de la Garza et al. 1992; Miller et al. 1981; Tate 1993). Also relevant are institutional factors (e.g., Jackman 1987; Wolfinger and Rosenstone 1980) and the political context (e.g., Aldrich 1993; Leighley and Nagler 1992). Finally, some models focus on the role elites play in mobilizing citizens to turnout (Cox and Munger 1989; Rosenstone and Hansen 1993). Studies explaining Latino turnout expanded on these traditional models to include factors specific to Latinos, such as whether individuals are born in the United States, whether individuals use Spanish or English as the language spoken at home, as well as the length of residency in the United States (Arvizu and Garcia 1996; Calvo and Rosenstone 1989; Leighley and Vedlitz 1999; Uhlaner, Cain, and Kiewiet 1989). Other studies have begun to use mobilization measures as explanatory variables in models of Latino turnout, and find that mobilization by coethnics – where the mobilizing agent is either Latino or represents a Latino organization – exerts a stronger effect on turnout than mobilization by non-Latinos (e.g., Michelson 2003; de la Garza and Abrajano this volume; Pantoja, Ramirez, and Segura 2001; Shaw et al. 2000).

Missing from the scholarship on Latino voting is an explicit recognition of the importance of mass media communications, and in particular, the significance of political advertisements on behavior. Although political commercials do not create direct opportunities for citizens to participate or reduce the costs of registering to vote, they can function as a reduction to information gathering costs by informing citizens about the political stances and capabilities of the candidates running for office. Advertisements also can increase the salience of issues and remind voters of the relevance of political participation. Moreover, it is possible that ethnic targeting in political ads can add some degree of the "personal touch" that has been found to be an important factor in the effectiveness of direct mobilization efforts.

Although few studies of the Latino electorate have looked closely at political advertisements, there is an extensive literature on the effect of political advertisements on voting behavior among the general population. Early work by Patterson and McClure (1976) focused on the effects that campaign ads had on the voting preferences of citizens. These scholars found that campaign ads did little to change the minds of voters, a finding that echoed the more general findings of minimal campaign effects in the literature (e.g., Campbell et al. 1960; Lazarsfeld, Berelson, and Gaudet 1944). However, more recent work (e.g., Shaw 1999; West 2005) has found that ads have an impact on evaluations of the candidates and vote choice. Furthermore, many studies have demonstrated that ads can have an impact on voter learning about the candidates, perceptions of candidates' chances of winning, voter turnout, and by altering the standards by which candidates are judged (e.g., Alvarez 1997; Ansolabehere and Iyengar 1995; Brians and Wattenberg 1996; Finkel and Geer 1998; Johnston et al. 1992).

With respect to our key dependent variable of turnout, the focus in the general literature has been on how the tone of the advertisement influences turnout. One school argues that negative ads demobilize the electorate by decreasing efficacy (Ansolabehere and Iyengar 1995; Ansolabehere et al. 1994). Another school claims that negative advertisements play a mobilizing role by subsidizing information (e.g., Finkel and Geer 1998; Freedman and Goldstein 1999, 2002). Because the findings with respect to tone are mixed (see Lau et al. 1999), we focus on an alternative explanation put forth by Clinton and Lapinski (2004), which they label the differential effects hypothesis.

According to this hypothesis, ads attempt to prime voters by activating the predispositions of individuals. Predispositions can be activated by catering messages to different segments of the population in the ad. For example, a campaign might air an ad about Medicaid to activate the predispositions of retired individuals, knowing that this content will not appeal to younger segments of the population. They claim that once these predispositions are activated, individuals are more likely to turn out. In this regard, advertisements targeted to Latinos should have a stronger effect on Latino turnout than general political advertisements intended for the population at large.

It is not necessarily the case that all Latinos will be more receptive to ethnically targeted advertisements. The effect of the different types of ads might depend on the process of acculturation, which can follow either an assimilationist or pluralist route. Questions of acculturation were first treated in regard to Europeans who immigrated in large numbers to the United States at the turn of the nineteenth century. According to theories of assimilation, ethnic group identity is temporary and eventually immigrants assimilate into mainstream culture. During this process, new ethnic groups begin to distance themselves from culturally distinct symbols, traditions and languages, and take on characteristics of the dominant and/or majority group (Subervi-Velez 1986; Schaefer 1979). Pluralist theories hold that ethnicity is a permanent group identity (Wolfinger 1965; Parenti 1967; Greely 1971); thus, groups continue to hold on to aspects of their culture long after their out migration.

We do not advance one theory over the other. Some Latinos may experience a more linear process of acculturation, in which assimilation into the characteristics of the dominant and/or majority group occurs. However, for other Latinos, the importance of ethnicity may not diminish. In short, we do not consider the process of acculturation for immigrants *as a whole;* instead, we allow for individual level differences in the type of acculturation, be it assimilationist or pluralist. Overall, we expect that individuals following an assimilationist route will be more receptive to general, nontargeted ads, whereas those following a pluralist route will be more receptive to targeted ads.

To test our hypothesis, we merged the aggregate-level CMAG data to individual-level data from the November 2000 Current Population Survey (CPS). The CPS is a monthly survey of households that asks a series of registration and voting turnout questions.[4] Because we focus on the impact of the ads on Latinos, respondents of Hispanic origin only are included in the study. Noncitizens were not included in the analysis because they are ineligible to vote. To determine the media market in which the respondent resides, we used data from the 2000 Census version of Tiger/line (TM) files.[5] For each respondent we have a measure of the total number, as well as the different types of ads that aired in their media market. Because the television viewing habits of individuals are not uniform, we treat the measure of advertisements aired as an indicator of maximum exposure opportunity, and like Goldstein and Freedman (2002) we consider the exposure measure, "an upper bound on the number of spots that respondents could have seen as a measure of relative exposure among respondents..." (731).[6] We also collected information on the competitiveness

---

[4] The ideal individual level survey data to use would be one that has a sizable sample of Latinos with questions measuring factors affecting turnout that have been tested in previous work on voting. Although the National Election Study contains these questions, the sample of Latinos in 2000 is of insufficient size.

[5] The CPS included forty-four out of the seventy-five media markets tracked in the CMAG data. Only those forty-four markets are included in the analysis.

[6] This is admittedly an imperfect measure, but it is a clear indicator of maximum exposure opportunity. In addition, the measure is unbiased relative to self-report measures.

of the race in the respondent's state, the closing date of registration, and states targeted for direct mobilization by the Southwest Voter Research Project.[7] The resulting dataset contains 1,061 Latino respondents.

We include a number of factors in addition to distinctive types of political campaign advertisement to explain Latino voting in the 2000 election.[8] These include controls for mobilization, age, income, education, gender, race, employment status, professional status, marital status, whether one is an employee of the government, length of residence in the community, length of time in the United States, closing date of voting registration in the state, competitiveness of the presidential election in the state, whether one speaks Spanish, whether one was born in the United States, and Latino ethnicity. Some research suggests that native-born Latinos are more likely to turn out (de la Garza and DeSipio 1992; Jackson 2002), whereas other scholarship finds the reverse (Garcia and Arce 1988; Pantoja, Ramirez, and Segura 2001). Time in the United States indicates how long the respondent has been in the United States, coded as age for U.S.-born Latinos and as years in the United States for foreign-born respondents, of which we expect longer residence should have a positive impact on turnout (Uhlaner, Cain, and Kiewiet 1989). We also separate ethnicity by grouping together Mexicans, Puerto Ricans, Central and South Americans, Cubans, and those of "other" national origins. We expect Cubans to be the most likely to vote, whereas Puerto Ricans and Mexicans will be less likely to vote in 2000 (Arvizu and Garcia 1996; Calvo and Rosenstone 1989; Jackson 2002).

The 2000 CPS did not include a question on whether an individual was asked to participate by one of the political parties or by a nonpartisan organization, so we utilize a proxy of direct mobilization with information from the Latino Vote 2000 campaign, spearheaded by the Southwest Voter Project and also composed of the Northeast Voter Registration Education Project and the United States Hispanic Leadership Institute. The measure indicates whether one of these organizations targeted a state for direct mobilization in 2000. These states included: Arizona, California, Colorado, Florida, Idaho, Nevada, New Mexico, North Carolina, Oklahoma, Oregon, Texas, Utah, and Washington. To capture the competitive context of the

---

[7] We use the average level of support for each candidate from state level tracking polls obtained from: WH 2000 General Election: State Polls. 2000. *Nationaljournal.com*. Retrieved July 9, 2001, from http://nationaljourna . . . aces/whitehouse/wh2000gen_state.htm

[8] Vote choice is not validated in the CPS surveys, and while there is likely overreporting of voting in the CPS, it is not as high as in the National Election Surveys (Leighley and Nagler 1992).

presidential campaign (Cox and Munger 1994), we created a measure of the absolute value of the difference in levels of support for Gore and Bush from state pre-election tracking polls. For institutional factors, we include the closing date of registration in the state (Wolfinger and Rosenstone 1980). A longer amount of time between the registration closing date and the election should have a negative effect on voter turnout.

In terms of the political advertisements, we measure three types of political advertising in the CMAG data. A Spanish-language advertisement is the most obvious appeal to Latinos because it sends a clear signal that the sponsor is trying to mobilize Latino citizens. Advertisements in Spanish enable the parties and/or candidates to target their message to only this segment of the electorate,[9] enabling them to focus more on the issues of importance to the Latino community. Advertisements were coded as targeted when the commercials mentioned Latinos, had a Latino narrator, or had a Latino pictured in the advertisement. All other commercials without specific Latino content and produced in English were coded as general advertisements.

To capture the moderating impact of the process of acculturation on the impact of political campaign advertisements for Latino voting, we need an indicator of an individual's process of acculturation. Although the survey did not ask detailed questions about cultural identity, we use an individual's dominant language as an indicator of which route the individual is taking. We recognize that cultural identity is a multidimensional construct; however, evidence shows that language is one of the strongest and most significant predictors of one's cultural group identity (Maria Felix-Ortiz de la Garza et al. 1995).

If an individual's dominant language is English, it is more likely that they are following an assimilationist mode of acculturation, whereas if their dominant language is Spanish, it is more likely that they are following the pluralist route to acculturation. Dominant Spanish is coded one if the respondent primarily speaks Spanish in the home, and zero otherwise. Dominant Spanish speakers make up 31.4 percent of our sample. Most scholars argue that dominant Spanish speakers should be less likely to turnout (e.g., Calvo and Rosenstone 1989; Uhlaner, Cain, and Kiewiet 1989; Johnson, Stein, and Wrinkle 2003).

In order to sort out the effects of political advertisement and acculturation among Latinos as measured by dominant language spoken, we estimated a statistical model with interaction terms of the individual's

---

[9] Non-Latinos who speak Spanish also would be exposed to the political messages.

**TABLE 6.3.** Predicting the Effect of Campaign Advertisements on Latino Voting in 2000 (probit coefficients)

| Variable | Coefficient | Standard Error |
|---|---|---|
| Mobilization | 0.1187 | 0.1493 |
| Spanish | −0.0001 | 0.0002 |
| Targeted English | −0.0002 | 0.0002 |
| General | 0.0001 | 0.0000 |
| Language* Spanish | −0.0006 | 0.0000 |
| Language* Targeted English | 0.0009+ | 0.0000 |
| Language* General | −0.0002+ | 0.0000 |
| Age | 0.0097** | 0.0042 |
| Income | 0.0298** | 0.0131 |
| Education | 0.2533** | 0.0459 |
| Gender | −0.1333+ | 0.0845 |
| Race | −0.1688 | 0.2049 |
| Employed | 0.2713** | 0.1245 |
| Professional | 0.0090 | 0.1275 |
| Married | 0.2233** | 0.0893 |
| Government Employee | 0.4517** | 0.1578 |
| Length at Address | 0.0729** | 0.0328 |
| Time in U.S. | 0.0092* | 0.0048 |
| Closing Date | −0.0421* | 0.0086 |
| Difference Gore and Bush | 0.0144** | 0.0067 |
| Language | 0.2107 | 0.1655 |
| Foreign Born | 0.0419 | 0.1342 |
| Mexican | −0.5148** | 0.2088 |
| Puerto Rican | −0.1573 | 0.2090 |
| Central American | −0.1017 | 0.2026 |
| Cuban | 0.0483 | 0.2300 |
| Constant | −0.9332* | 0.4188 |
| N | 1061 | |
| R-squared | 0.1419 | |

Significance levels: **$p \leq .05$ (two-tailed); *$p \leq .10$ (two-tailed); + $p \leq .10$ (one-tailed)

*Sources:* U.S. Census Current Population Survey 2000; Campaign Media Analysis Group

dominant language and type of advertisement, along with factors shown to influence turnout in traditional models of voting behavior. Table 6.3 presents the results of the model estimation. The main effect we are interested in is the impact of Spanish and Latino targeted advertisements for

Latinos who are primary English speakers versus those who primarily speak Spanish. We expect general advertisements in English and without specific Latino content would have a stronger impact on dominant English speakers. Alternatively, Spanish and targeted commercials would have a stronger impact on dominant Spanish speakers. The overall performance of the model is good, with 69.56 percent correctly predicted.

Many of the control variables are significant (at $p < .10$) and in the expected direction. The estimated coefficient on the measures for type of political advertisement interacted with language reflects the effect of the ads for dominant Spanish speakers, whereas the estimated coefficient on the measures for the type of political advertisement reflect the effects of the ads for dominant English-speakers. Thus, we can see that the advertisements did not have a significant effect on dominant English-speaking Latinos. However, two of the ad measures that are significant are among those whose dominant language is Spanish. More specifically, we can see that targeted ads increase the likelihood of turnout, whereas general ads decrease the likelihood of turnout.

The probit model coefficients are somewhat difficult to interpret, particularly in terms of understanding the size of the effects. Instead, to compare the substantive effect of types of political campaign commercials on the likelihood of turnout we calculate the first differences to further illuminate the findings. Furthermore, in order to determine how extensive the influence of types of campaign advertisements are on turnout among dominant Spanish speakers, we need to hold the conditioning variable of language at 1, and calculate the slope and standard error at these values (Friedrich 1982).[10] In order to test which ads are most effective, we examine the first differences for each of the measures of types of advertisements using the same scale. Table 6.4 presents the first differences of the three types of ads, moving from zero, or the minimum number of ads aired in a media market, to 1,017 ads.[11] The middle column presents the simulations with dominant English speakers as the baseline, while the last column is the simulation with dominant Spanish speakers as the baseline.

---

[10] To do this, we calculated the first differences using Clarify, developed by Tomz, Wittenberg, and King (2001). All variables were set at their mean, with the exception of the dummy variables, which were set as a married, Mexican, employed, male, born in the United States, and a nonprofessional. We calculated the first differences with dominant English speakers as the baseline by setting the language interactions and the language variable to zero. We then determined the significance and substantive effects of the ads for dominant Spanish speakers by setting language to 1 and examined the impact of moving the ads and their interaction with language (with the language component held at 1).

[11] 1,017 is the maximum of the minimum across all of the types of advertisements.

**TABLE 6.4.** First Differences of the Effect of the Different Types of Ad Variables, by the Respondent's Dominant Language

| Variables | Dominant English | Dominant Spanish |
|---|---|---|
|  | 0–1,017 ads | 0–1,017 ads |
| Spanish Ads | −0.025 | −0.172 |
| Targeted English Ads | −0.072 | 0.331* |
| General Ads | 0.017 | −0.083* |

Significance levels: *$p < .10$ (one-tailed)

Table 6.4 provides a sense of the substantive effects of the advertisements on the likelihood of voter turnout. Our discussion focuses on the targeted English and general ads among dominant Spanish speakers, because these were the only significant variables in the probit analysis. As expected, targeted English advertisements exerted the stronger effect of the two. For example, moving from zero-targeted English ads aired in a media market to 1,017 commercials increased the probability of voting by 33 percent. A very different effect is evidenced by the general ads among dominant Spanish speakers. The effect is negative and only leads to an 8 percent shift in the probability of turnout. In other words, general advertisements among dominant Spanish speakers had a demobilizing effect.

The results from our analysis provide evidence that political commercials have an impact on Latino voting turnout. But advertisements are significant to voting behavior only once we account for both the type of advertisement and the dominant language of the individual. Appeals to Latinos, either general or targeted, have no impact on voting behavior among dominant English speakers. By contrast, Latinos who are dominant Spanish speakers are influenced by the ads. However the type of effect, mobilizing versus demobilizing, varied according to the type of the ad. Targeted English language advertisements, in addition to having a mobilizing effect on turnout – encouraging voting turnout among Latinos – also exerted the strongest substantive effect.

In addition to comparing the effect of particular types of campaign advertisements on Latino voting, we examine the impact of the sheer number that were aired and how the presence of the types of commercials influenced Latino turnout in 2000. Using the results from the probit model discussed earlier, we simulated the probability of voting for dominant Spanish speakers while holding the advertisement measures at their

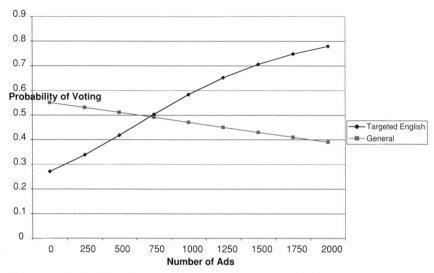

Figure 6.1. Probability of Voting by Targeted and General Ads, Dominant Spanish Speakers.

mean, and moving advertisements of interest individually.[12] Here we consider the isolated effects that both targeted English ads and general ads exerted on the likelihood of turnout.

Figure 6.1 presents the simulations with dominant Spanish speakers as the baseline. There is sharp differentiation in the direction and magnitude of the effect by ad type. Turning to the effect of targeted English ads (the blue line), when all other advertisements are held at the mean, we see the range of the probability for turning out to vote as the number of these ads increase. At zero-targeted English ads, the likelihood of voting is only 27 percent. As the number of ads increases, so does the probability of turnout. At 750 targeted English ads, the probability of voting crosses the .5 threshold. Beyond fifteen hundred, the probability of voting still increases, but starts to level off. When targeted English ads reach two thousand, the probability of turnout is now close to 80 percent. The red line in Figure 6.1 represents the probability of voting as a result of exposure to the general ads, with all other ads being held at their mean. Contrary to the effect of the targeted ads, we see a downward slope. At an exposure of zero general ads the likelihood of turnout is 55 percent, however, at two thousand ads, this probability dips down below the .5 threshold.

---

[12] We set .5 as the threshold for turnout. All other variables are set at their mean, and we use the same baselines for the dummy variables.

## MOBILIZING THE LATINO VOTE

In contrast to direct mobilization such as "get-out-the-vote" efforts, political campaign advertising has received far less attention as a tool for bringing more Latinos to the voting booth. Little is known about the range of political communications targeted to Latino voters or the efficacy of those campaign advertisements in activating voting behavior. This study has shown that campaign advertising had important effects in influencing voting behavior among Latinos in the 2000 election. Although targeted English ads increased the probability that dominant Spanish speakers would come to the polls, not all forms of advertising influenced turnout. Moreover, general ads decreased the probability of turnout among a segment of the Latino electorate.

These results have implications for future mobilization efforts. First, groups airing ads need to be mindful that the potential gains they may make in mobilization with targeted English advertisements among dominant Spanish speakers are not offset by general ads. Second, political groups need to develop more effective ways of reaching this diverse segment of the electorate. In this analysis, none of the Spanish language ads had significant effects, and only targeted ads had mobilizing effects among dominant Spanish speakers. The results from this analysis reinforce the notion that Latinos are far from a homogenous population and as a result, their receptivity to campaign media messages is similarly heterogeneous. Varying levels of acculturation, considered here through dominant language usage, indeed moderates campaign messages. In this regard, parties cannot pursue a "one size fits all" Latino ethnic strategy. Instead, effective campaign media messages will have to cater to the different degrees and intensities of Latino culture.

One interesting question raised from the results reported here is the extent to which different issue content of advertisements influences Latino voter mobilization. Distinctive content may be the underlying reason for the demobilizing influence of some of the general advertisements among dominant Spanish-language Latinos. The sample of advertisements available from the 2000 election data was of insufficient size to create a breakdown of content across the types of commercials. A second important question is the effect of partisan identification on receptivity to campaign advertisements. Although we were unable to analyze the influence of the respondent's partisanship on the mobilizing impact of various campaign advertisements, future studies should attempt to investigate the extent to which Latinos' receptivity to political communications is conditioned by their party identification. As political parties increase their targeted efforts in future elections and as surveys increase their sample size of Latinos, we might be better able to distinguish the mobilizing and demobilizing effects of different types of advertisements.

## APPENDIX

**TABLE A.** Probit on Turnout in the 2000 Election, Baseline Model

| Variable | Coefficient | Standard Error | P Value |
|---|---|---|---|
| Mobilization | .064 | .133 | .629 |
| Age | .010** | .004 | .021 |
| Income | .030** | .013 | .021 |
| Education | .251** | .047 | .000 |
| Male | −.126 | .085 | .138 |
| White | −.161 | .191 | .397 |
| Employed | .274** | .125 | .029 |
| Professional | .011 | .130 | .933 |
| Married | .219** | .089 | .014 |
| Government Employee | .443** | .152 | .004 |
| Length of Residence | .077** | .032 | .015 |
| Time in United States | .009* | .005 | .068 |
| Closing Date of Registration | −.040** | .008 | .000 |
| Difference Gore and Bush | .013** | .007 | .042 |
| Spanish Language | .147 | .121 | .223 |
| Foreign Born | .030 | .135 | .825 |
| Mexican | −.523** | .187 | .005 |
| Puerto Rican | −.168 | .195 | .389 |
| Central | −.115 | .191 | .546 |
| Cuban | .038 | .212 | .886 |
| Constant | −.941** | .391 | .016 |
| N | 1016 | | |
| Chi-Squared | 201.73 | | |
| Pseudo R-Squared | .1387 | | |
| Percent Correctly Predicted | 69.46% | | |

** Indicates significance at the .05 level and * at the .10 level.

FREDRICK C. HARRIS, BRIAN D. McKENZIE, AND
VALERIA SINCLAIR-CHAPMAN

# 7 Structuring Group Activism

## A Macro Model of Black Participation

Over forty years have passed since federal legislation began to dismantle the *de facto* racial discrimination prohibiting the participation of African Americans in the U.S. political system. The Civil Rights Act of 1964 and the Voting Rights Act of 1965 opened the door to a wealth of new opportunities for activity in mainstream forms of political participation that had long been denied to black Americans. For the first time since Reconstruction, African Americans across the nation could freely vote in elections, setting the stage for increases in black political participation. In the wake of this new political reality, blacks began to shift their energies away from protest strategies aimed at basic inclusion in the democratic process toward more conventional forms of political engagement. African Americans became active in voting in local and national elections, contacting public officials, attending political rallies and speeches, serving in local organizations and committees, and signing petitions in support or opposition to important issues that affect black communities, and a "new black politics" evolved from protest to electoral forms of political activism (Smith 1981; Rustin 1971; Preston 1987; Tate 1994).

These changes in the post–Civil Rights era raised new questions about African American political activity and generated a variety of explanations based on socioeconomic status, black political empowerment, racial group consciousness, and the importance of political context (Walton 1985; Bobo and Gilliam 1990; Tate 1991, 1994; Cohen and Dawson 1993; Dawson 1994a; Harris 1999; Shingles 1981). Although scholars emphasize the distinctive influence of each of these factors, there is unanimity in the recognition of a group imperative in African American political participation. The legacy of slavery and continuing racial discrimination provide shared historical and contemporary experiences with behavioral consequences for black Americans. Yet although the group imperative is assumed, it is neither adequately theorized nor accounted for in explanations of black political behavior. Moreover, what is missing from models of contemporary African American participation is an explicit recognition of the significance of exogenous structural forces such as social and economic distress.

The lack of attention to structural factors is rooted in the dominant strategy of inquiry driving many contemporary studies of black political behavior. Rather than examining African American activism in the aggregate, the vast share of scholarly investigation has adopted an analytical strategy with the individual as unit of analysis. This strategy has important consequences both for identifying the factors that encourage and constrain political participation among African Americans as well as for interpreting changes in black political behavior over time. In this chapter, we examine the implications of this micro strategy of inquiry, and propose instead a macro model of black political participation. We then apply the macro model to build an explanation of black political behavior and analyze how aggregate activity among African Americans has fluctuated in the post–Civil Rights era.

## BEYOND THE INDIVIDUAL LEVEL

One of the most vexing questions in the study of black political behavior addresses the fluctuations over time in levels of participation. But before assessing the reasons for change, political activity among African Americans must first be measured. Political participation is most commonly assessed by asking individuals about their involvement in politics through surveys of the African American population. Indeed, many of the most important studies of black political behavior are rooted in the venerable tradition of collecting individual-level data through survey research methods (e.g., Bobo and Gilliam 1990; Tate 1994; Dawson 1994a). For example, Dawson's 1994 study sets forth a theory of black political life in which African Americans make judgments about their political preferences based on what is best for blacks as a group. Dawson's notion of linked fate highlights the use of the "black utility heuristic" as a mechanism for processing information and assessing the benefits and costs of activity. Dawson also argues that the legacy of racial domination in the United States has shaped the "culture, norms, values, policy positions, and modes of behavior" of African Americans as a group (Dawson 1994, 13). Although the psychological, economic, and historical perspectives provide insights on African American politics, the empirical evidence nevertheless remains anchored in individual-level survey data at the expense of what Jon Elster describes as methodological collectivism. This is an approach that specifically considers "supra-individual entities" that are important explanatory forces in human behavior (Elster 1987, 6). In this regard, Dawson's approach takes an analytical leap based on individual rather than collective political behavior of blacks in reflecting the actions of blacks as a group. Micro-level evidence is used to make claims about macro-level behavior.

We argue that interpreting the reasons for political participation among African Americans and analyzing why levels of activity change over time requires a macro analytic strategy beyond the individual level. Inferences cannot rely solely on individual-level data taken in isolation from one another and other social groups. Using these data to extrapolate to the collective level without adequately considering the effects of macro-structural factors creates a set of problems in the analysis of black political participation. Hanes Walton identifies the mismatch between theory, evidence, and inference when claims about black political behavior are made with data at the individual rather than collective level (Walton 1985). The emphasis on individualism also has normative implications for how black political behavior is interpreted. As Walton observes, the "individual-centered behavioral approach in black political behavior has produced a vast literature that proposes the individual weaknesses and imperfections it uncovers are a result of Blacks' individual shortcomings and not the result of any systematic factors under which they have labored" (1985, 3). The deficiencies in black political behavior compared to that for whites is attributed to the individual shortcomings of blacks, rooted in political apathy, low educational achievement, or low levels of political efficacy.

Not only does the commitment to methodological individualism raise questions about the need to consider political context when analyzing black political behavior, but Walton's critique also highlights the need to consider macro-level factors as forces that either constrain or enhance collective political behavior. Walton notes the focus on the individual in studies of black political behavior "implies that institutional arrangements, structural devices, organizational types and legal rules do not affect political behavior as much as intrapsychic and sociopsychological forces do" (1985, 3). In this regard, by moving from the individual micro-level unit of analysis to a collective level of analysis, a macro theory of black political behavior provides a more coherent portrait of black political participation as a group phenomenon. Furthermore, it allows us to think about how macro-level political and structural forces, such as levels of black political empowerment and social and economic distress might bear on fluctuations in black political activity over time. In building a macro theory of black civic participation we move beyond methodological individualism and time-bound constraints by considering aggregate levels of black political activity as a proxy for group activism and changes in collective behavior over time.

Our macro model of black activism in the post–Civil Rights era assumes African-American participation is contingent on structural forces operating at the aggregate level of society and politics. To operationalize the model, we use the simple statistical principle of aggregation. This technique is grounded in previous scholarship on the collective dimensions of American public opinion and its response to changes in the political and economic environment (Erikson, MacKuen, and Stimson 2002; MacKuen, Erikson, and Stimson 1989; Page and Shapiro 1992). In addition, macro-level political studies have also investigated the impact of national economic conditions on aggregate voting behavior (Arcelus and Meltzer 1975; Kramer 1971, 1983; Markus 1988). These studies highlight the importance of distinguishing between individual and collective accounts of political behavior.

MacKuen, Erikson, and Stimson (1989) systematically analyze changes in aggregate partisanship and its consequences for American political behavior. In their study, macro partisanship is measured as the percentage of party identifiers who support Democrats (1128). The authors show that contrary to individual partisanship stability, aggregate levels of partisanship fluctuated from 1945 to 1987 and a one-point shift in partisanship yields a three seat gain in House elections (1129). In addition, MacKuen and colleagues demonstrate how macroeconomic and political forces affect partisan divisions in the electorate. In more recent work (Erikson, MacKuen, and Stimson 2002) the authors explain how citizens' collective responses to the economy make sense in light of their aggregate perceptions of economic events. Moreover, they contend aggregate-level partisanship responds to social and political events as the electorate views them and the collective ideological mood of the nation changes with the ebbs and flows of the political and economic environment (447).

Page and Shapiro (1992) draw attention to the disjuncture between individual and collective political attitudes. They note that unlike cross-sectional individual opinion reports, "the collective policy preferences of the American public are predominantly rational, generally stable, and form coherent and mutually consistent patterns that make sense in terms of underlying values and available information" (1992, xi). Page and Shapiro maintain that changes in the collective policy preferences of citizens respond to international events and social and economic changes reported in the media. Moreover, their study is invaluable to our understanding of macro-level behavior because it illustrates how statistical aggregation processes transform unstable individual reports of political attitudes into coherent aggregate reflections of collective opinion.[1]

These aggregation processes are important for understanding black political participation. In particular, African Americans regularly interact in various social and political settings, exchanging information about events and issues that are relevant to black communities. This interdependence often changes the quantities of political participation for blacks as a group.[2] Consequently, aggregate levels of black political activism are a function of both individual considerations and racial group concerns stimulated by interaction in black social contexts. These communal dimensions of African American political involvement have not been properly considered and operationalized in previous research efforts, and our macro-level approach to black civic participation addresses these concerns.

## SITUATING BLACK ACTIVISM

Aggregate levels of black political involvement provide a more complete depiction of black political activity as group behavior than relying on individual accounts of black participation. There are two reasons for this claim. The first emphasizes the role social interaction plays in enhancing political activism beyond the individual. The second highlights the significance of "black political entrepreneurs" in stimulating African American activism. We define black political entrepreneurs as organizations and movements that primarily seek and target blacks to support their political aims and goals. Social interaction among blacks is an important component of our civic participation model because it allows aggregate levels of black participation to exceed the sum of its individual counterparts. This interaction is sustained by indigenous organizations and institutions such as churches, civic organizations, and educational institutions, and social norms that

---

[1] Page and Shapiro justify aggregating preferences with this reply "the answer has to do with the statistical aggregation process, in which the expressed opinions of many individuals are summed or combined into a collective whole, and with social processes in which many people receive communications and think and talk with each other. These processes give collective public opinion and collective survey responses certain 'emergent' properties that are not shared by the individual opinions and responses that make them up" (14–15).

[2] Our argument is similar to Schelling (1978, 13–14), Page and Shapiro (1992, 14–15), and Erikson et al. (2002, 10–11) regarding how individual-level interactions influence aggregate political behavior and attitudes.

promote group solidarity including feelings of linked fate with other blacks, commitment to same-race relationships, or the belief in social distance from whites. We argue the existence of indigenous institutions and norms of solidarity among blacks produce higher levels of political participation for blacks as a group than would be expected if blacks were not socially interacting.

In a universe of black participation where no social interaction with other blacks occurs, there are also no institutions or organizations that are indigenous to the black population, nor are there norms of group solidarity. These are factors that enhance the political participation of blacks as a group, and in their absence African American political activity is equal to the sum of its parts. This is clearly an unrealistic portrayal of social dynamics in black communities, but analyses based on individual rather than aggregated reports of political participation are situated in this scenario precisely because they cannot account for processes enhancing the political participation of blacks as a group. Models driven by individual-level data thus ignore the group-based dynamics generated through social interactions in the black population.

In contrast, a macro model of black political participation assumes a universe where social interaction takes place between blacks. Interaction enhances the aggregate-level participation of blacks above what would be expected if there were no interaction between blacks. Consistent with Thomas Schelling's observations of contingent behavior, individuals are influenced by the actions of others in their social environment. Here, contingent behavior depends on the "system of interaction between individuals and their environment, that is between individuals and other individuals or between individuals and the collectivity" (Schelling 1978, 14). There are chains of social interaction in the universe of the black population that enhance the political participation levels in the population. In this universe there are blacks who participate in political activities without socially interacting with other blacks and there are blacks who do not participate despite their social interaction with other blacks. There are also blacks who are neither politically active nor socially connected with other blacks. However, despite different levels of social interaction within the population, the political participation of the group is greater than what would be expected if there was no interaction among blacks. Hence, when black participation is contingent on some degree of social interaction among some individual blacks but not all African Americans, the black population produces levels of participation greater than the sum of its parts.

Our macro model of black participation recognizes the dynamic nature of social interaction, and we are mindful that social interaction may expand or contract over time (Dawson 1994b). For example, during the era of legalized segregation when indigenous institutions and norms of solidarity were stronger than they are today, social interactions among blacks were vibrant, although the opportunities to participate were constrained in the context of Jim Crow. But when opportunities for black opposition to segregation expanded, those interactions facilitated black mobilization during the Civil Rights movement (McAdam 1982; Morris 1984). In the postsegregation era, when institutions and norms of solidarity are weakening, social interaction among blacks is contracting, consequently lowering the participation of blacks as a group. Despite changes in social interaction among blacks over time, we contend it still produces levels of black participation that are greater than what would occur if there were no social interaction in the black population.

The mechanism of social interaction is only part of the story of why the sum of individual black political participation is greater than its parts. We identify the importance of black political entrepreneurs as a link between social interaction and aggregation processes in black political participation. Black political entrepreneurs constitute any political group or movement from the National Association from the Advancement of Colored People (NAACP) to the Nation of Islam that is dependent on black constituencies for its viability. These entrepreneurs use resources to mobilize blacks in support of a movement or organization's goals. As strategic actors, it is more efficient for entrepreneurs to initiate political activities among blacks in a universe where blacks are socially interacting, rather than in one where there is no interaction among blacks. Thus, these entrepreneurs enhance the political participation of blacks as a group by directly and indirectly mobilizing blacks who are socially connected. For example, a group of blacks may be requested to write a letter about police brutality to their congressional representative by an NAACP official who speaks during a black church service. Or, a member of the Nation of Islam may appeal to patrons of a neighborhood barber shop to attend a rally on police brutality. Through political entrepreneurs who seek support through social interaction in the black population, the political participation of blacks as a group is enhanced beyond what we would expect in a world where blacks are not socially interacting with other African Americans.

Black political activism is thus a process of aggregation affected by macro-level economic, social, and political forces in the environment. These forces influence aggregate levels of black political participation, which are in turn influenced by social interactions supported by social solidarity norms and indigenous institutions, and mobilized by black political entrepreneurs. Social interactions and the mobilizing influences of black political entrepreneurs converge to produce levels of political participation that reflect the aggregation of political activities of blacks as a group. Our macro perspective on black political activism does not directly consider the preferences and attitudes of blacks as a determinant of black civic participation. We assume that preferences, like collective participation, vary across time, and individual blacks or segments in the black population are motivated to participate in a variety of activities linked to particular issues or ideological commitments. The ideological motivations for those activities can sway between black nationalism, feminism, class-centered ideologies, or even American patriotism, among other preferences. We make no claims of what Adolph Reed describes as a "corporate Black interest," the idea that blacks share similar group interests and that those interests influence the political participation of blacks as a group (Reed 1999). Rather, we explore how aggregate levels of black civic participation differ from their individual-level counterparts and demonstrate how macro-levels of black political involvement change over time. Next, we track our aggregate-level measures of participation over a twenty-year period from 1973 to 1994 and assess how various structural factors help to account for ebbs and flows in black political engagement.

## TRENDS IN BLACK POLITICAL PARTICIPATION

To capture macro-level trends in black political activism, we rely on simple statistical aggregation principles. Drawing on Page and Shapiro's (1992, 19–23) logic, we demonstrate how the political involvement of individual black citizens can be meaningfully amassed into a distinct social collective. The strategy considers the mobilizing capacity of black social networks and political entrepreneurs, and incorporates their overall influence on group political activism. We assume each individual has a long-term distribution of political activism that can be approximated by a normal distribution, and at various points in an individual's life, political involvement can vary from no activity to high levels of participation.[3] We aggregate the individual

---

[3] This normality assumption is used as a convenience for explanation purposes, and we are aware that the participatory behavior of some blacks cannot be characterized in a symmetric fashion, and may be better approximated by other distributions. In these cases, the alternative distributions will also have derivable central tendencies upon which the general logic of our argument will still apply. An approximately normal distribution of

participation tendencies into a macro distribution representing the average activity level of all the individual distributions. The collective central
tendency of black activism can be operationalized using a numerical average of black participatory acts or a proportional frequency in which most
individuals engaged in a particular political act (see Page and Shapiro 1992,
16–17). In terms of statistical properties, this new macro entity reflects the
micro activism tendencies of black individuals and accounts for social interaction effects among African Americans to produce a meaningful composite of group participation. This pooled quantity is an appropriate measure
of group-level activism and can be used to make inferences about collective black political involvement.

Building on our theoretical and statistical logic, we analyze nationally
representative survey data on African Americans to explore the dynamics
of black political participation. Our analyses utilize black respondents from
the Roper Social and Political Trends data set, a collection of survey questions on political participation that was asked on a quarterly basis from
1973 to 1994. We focus on civic participation beyond voting, and consider
twelve acts of political participation in our analysis. These include participation in any of the following activities in the previous twelve months: (1)
wrote to a congressman or senator, (2) attended a political rally or speech,
(3) attended a public meeting on town or school affairs, (4) held or ran for
office, (5) served on a committee for some local organization, (6) served as
an officer for an organization, (7) wrote a letter to a newspaper, (8) signed
a petition, (9) worked for a political party, (10) made a speech, (11) wrote
an article for a magazine or newspaper, and (12) joined a group interested
in better government.

We combine these activities into three indices of black political involvement, including a composite political participation index, a political work
index, and an organizational participation index. The measure of political
work is an additive index of attendance at a rally or speech, membership
in a political party, membership in a political organization such as the
NAACP, and signing a petition. The measure of organizational activity is
also an additive index including participation through service as an officer for an organization, service on a committee for a local organization,
making a speech, and attendance at a public meeting on town or school
affairs. The composite participation index includes all of the twelve civic

responses around a central tendency would occur for the collective when the responses
are aggregated (see Page and Shapiro 1992, 19–23, 28).

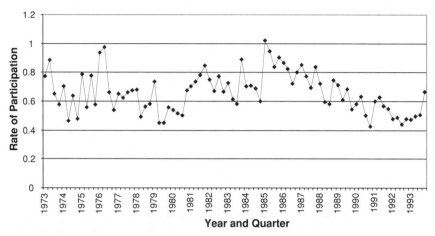

Figure 7.1. Composite Political Participation Index, 1973–1994. *Source:* Roper Social and Political Trends Data.

and political participation measured in the Roper surveys, and each of the participation measures are quarterly averages in each period between 1973 and 1994. The indices of political participation reflect the long-term tendencies of aggregate-level activism for African Americans as a group and allow us to paint a picture of how levels of black political involvement expand or contract over time.

One way to witness the dynamics of black political participation is to examine trends in aggregate-level political activism over time. Figure 7.1 displays the composite rates of participation for blacks in the twelve distinct political activities between 1973 and 1994. Perhaps the most striking finding is the low level of political activity among African Americans. At only one point over the twenty-year period does aggregate-level black activity exceed one act of political participation, and black involvement ranges between 0.4 and 1.0 political acts. In addition, the trend data show that most of the participation data points in this series were in the range of 0.4 to 0.8 acts. The composite measure of black political participation only approaches one political act in late 1976 and exceeds one act in 1985.

There is considerable volatility in rates of black participation during the post–Civil Rights era. In the early period between 1973 and 1976 black participation rates fluctuated up and down, yet show a trend of rising levels of activism. In the year following, aggregate levels of black political activism declined until 1979, the period marked by surges and declines in

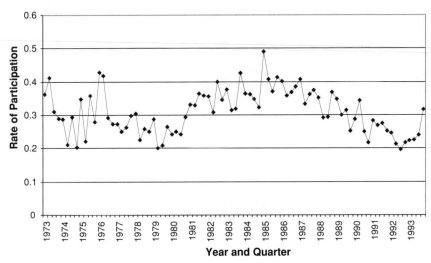

**Figure 7.2.** Political Work Participation Index, 1973–1994. *Source:* Roper Social and Political Trends Data.

black political engagement. After 1979, black participation levels drop at Reagan's first term and steadily increase between 1980 and 1982. From 1982 to 1984, black participation generally diminishes and then spikes in mid-1984. Between 1984 and 1985, black participation declines, then takes a sharp upward turn. After 1985, aggregate levels of black political involvement continue to ebb and flow, but consistently decline until 1991. By the end of 1991, black participation levels rise again and then decline throughout 1992. Finally, in 1993 black political activism levels recover and continue to rise for the rest of the period.

Now we turn our attention to examining movement trends in the black political work index, a measure including attendance at a rally or speech, membership in a political party, membership in a political organization such as the NAACP, and signing a petition. Figure 7.2 shows aggregate levels of black political work activity have fluctuated significantly since the early 1970s. In 1973, black political work levels briefly increase and then decline for the next two years. From 1975 to 1977 aggregate-level participation among blacks in political work activities decreases and increases at various points, but generally rose in this time span. Next, the trend reverses and political work activities decrease between 1977 and 1978. Volatility also characterizes aggregate black participation levels from 1978 to 1981. During this period, involvement in political work activities rises and falls in a tumultuous manner. From 1981 to 1983, we see aggregate participation levels steadily increase with the exception of a slight decrease in black activism at the end of 1982. By 1983, aggregate black political work levels begin to fluctuate again until the end of 1984; it then descends throughout most of 1985. We also see aggregate black political work levels spike during the first part of 1986 (the highest level in the series), rise and fall through 1993, but generally trend downward between 1986 and 1993. After 1993, black participation levels continue to rise in a fairly consistent pattern.

The index of organizational participation measure tells a slightly different story about black political activism. This index is a measure of organizational participation captured by service as an officer for an organization, service on a committee for a local organization, making a speech, and attendance at a public meeting on town or school affairs. Compared to the other indices, involvement in organizational modes of political activity is even more variable over time. Looking at Figure 7.3, it is clear that aggregate levels of black organizational participation ebb and flow in a more sporadic pattern than the other forms of political involvement. Specifically, black organizational participation rises at the end of 1973 and then declines until 1974. From 1974 to 1976, organizational participation rises and declines in an up-and-down pattern. By early 1977, organizational activity reaches it peak (0.46 acts) and then declines in mid 1977. Afterward, organizational participation levels increase between 1977 and 1978, falls in the end of 1978, and then rises again by early 1979. From 1979 to 1980, black participation rates steeply decline and then dramatically rise from early 1980 to 1981. The two years between 1982 and 1984 show another decline in participation, followed by two spikes in organizational involvement in early 1984 and late 1985. After 1985, there is more fluctuation in the aggregate level of organizational participation, with a familiar overall trend of declining activism after 1986.

These wildly fluctuating patterns suggest that black organizational participation is a unique form of political engagement compared to our other measures. Few African Americans engage in activism such as serving as an officer for an organization, serving on a committee, and making a speech to a group, and this accounts for the greater levels of variability observed in the black organizational participation series as compared to the index of political work.

We offer several possible explanations for these fluctuations. First, previous research demonstrates gains in black political empowerment during this time period stimulate black political participation in a variety of ways.

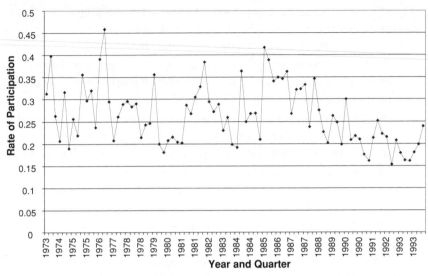

**Figure 7.3.** Organizational Work Participation Index, 1973–1994. *Source:* Roper Social and Political Trends Data.

For instance, black electoral successes brings new black voters into the electorate, nurtures feelings of political efficacy and trust in government, stimulates feelings of group consciousness, and mobilizes black constituencies (Barker and Walters 1989; Bobo and Gilliam 1990; Tate 1991; Leighley 2001). Together, these factors may account for the increases in black political activism that we observe in our data.

By contrast, at the same time black political empowerment features may encourage black political involvement, we contend that social and economic distress factors may constrain aggregate-level black political participation in the post-Civil Rights era. It is likely that macro-level structural forces such as widening economic disparities among blacks, inflation, unfavorable black employment opportunities, and the adverse economic consequences of a growing immigrant labor supply for black workers may have also decreased the level of political resources African Americans possess as a group in the years since the modern Civil Rights movement (Dawson 1994a; Cohen and Dawson 1993; Cohen 1999; Borjas 1987; Altonji and Card 1991).

Thus, the gains from black empowerment may have been simultaneously constrained by an equally powerful set of social and economic distress factors negatively impacting black communities during this period. These two sets of countervailing forces help explain why we see spikes and dips in aggregate levels of political activism at various points in our trend series. It is important to note that our claims about changes in African-American civic participation are further supported by recent research on black political behavior. Indeed, in *Countervailing Forces*, Harris, Sinclair-Chapman, and McKenzie (2006) demonstrate that trends in black political involvement in the post–Civil Rights era can be explained by a tug-of-war between the positive effects of black political power and the depressing impact of social and economic conditions in black communities. This work highlights the significance of important structural factors that bear on citizens' ability to participate in public life.

## STRUCTURING ACTIVISM

A macro model of black participation goes beyond the individual level and accounts for factors that structure activism among African Americans. We argue that the bias of methodological individualism present in many contemporary studies of black political behavior presents significant limitations in our ability to understand African American activism. We offer an alternative macro approach to theorize and model black political participation. We contend that social interaction between blacks and the behavior of black political entrepreneurs enhances the political participation of blacks as a group. This enhancement in group participation is not accounted for when only analyzing individual reports of black political involvement, but aggregating individual reports of political activities into a macro profile of black political engagement results in a more theoretically and empirically sound depiction of black activism.

The trend analysis of the Roper data on African Americans between 1973 and 1994 allows us to examine changes in black political activity over time, and represents one of the first efforts to track movement in black political involvement in the post–Civil Rights era. The limitations of previous data on black political behavior prevented scholars from understanding the dynamic properties of black participation. In contrast, we are able to show how each of our macro-level indicators of black political activism, including the composite political participation index, the political work index, and the organizational work index vary throughout the post–Civil Rights era. Black empowerment theories of political participation are rarely used in conjunction with social and economic distress arguments to analyze trends in black civic participation, but the combination of these explanations aids in understanding the dynamics of political involvement over time. By merging a countervailing forces theory of black civic participation with a distinctive analytical approach, we are able to produce a more coherent and meaningful account of black participation. Although many political behavior scholars continue to use individual-level data, our theoretical model and data analysis suggests an aggregate-level approach would be more useful for understanding why blacks as a group become involved in politics and how these levels fluctuate over time. A macro approach to black activism yields important insights about the influence of structural forces on black political involvement in America, and provides important clues to the future of African American political participation.

PAULA D. McCLAIN, VICTORIA M. DeFRANCESCO SOTO,
MONIQUE L. LYLE, NIAMBI M. CARTER, GERALD F. LACKEY,
JEFFREY D. GRYNAVISKI, KENDRA DAVENPORT COTTON,
SHAYLA C. NUNNALLY, THOMAS J. SCOTTO, AND
J. ALAN KENDRICK

# 8 Black Elites and Latino Immigrant Relations in a Southern City

## Do Black Elites and the Black Masses Agree?

The United States is becoming more racially and ethnically diverse as a function of immigration, both legal and illegal, from Asia, Mexico, and Latin America. Latinos are the fastest growing population, and in 2000, Latinos replaced African Americans as the largest minority group in the United States. Although much of the media and scholarly attention has focused on demographic changes in traditional Latino immigrant destinations such as California, New Mexico, Texas, and Arizona, the rapid growth in Latino populations is occurring across the nation. The South has undergone a particularly dramatic alteration in terms of racial composition, with six of seven states tripling the size of their Latino populations between 1990 and 2000. This settlement of Latinos in the South is no more than ten to fifteen years old, and new immigrants from Mexico and Latin America are settling in states like North Carolina, Georgia, and Tennessee (Durand, Massey, and Carvet 2000). They bring ethnic and cultural diversity to areas previously defined exclusively as black and white.

Not only have new Latino populations migrated to urban and suburban locations in the South, they also have settled in small towns and rural areas, reinforcing projections of the "Latinization" of the American South. Examples of these "New Latino Destinations" (Suro and Singer 2000) include cities such as Atlanta, Georgia; Charlotte, Greensboro-Winston

This chapter is a revision of a paper presented at the Russell Sage Foundation conference on "Immigration to the United States: New Sources and Destinations," New York, New York, February 3–4, 2005. The survey reported in this chapter was funded by a grant from The Ford Foundation (St. Benedict the Black Meets the Virgin of Guadalupe Project, Grant #1025–1445). We thank The Foundation and Dr. Melvin Oliver, former Vice President of Asset Building and Community Development, for their support of our research.

Salem, and Raleigh-Durham, North Carolina; Nashville and Memphis, Tennessee; and Greenville, South Carolina. The increases in the Latino population between 1990 and 2000 range from the 388 percent increase in the Latino population experienced in Atlanta, to growth of 809 percent in Greensboro-Winston Salem. The American South, once overwhelmingly black and white, now counts nearly 12 percent of its population as Latino.

Race has for centuries defined the legal and social history of the South, and along with it, determined the life and opportunity structures of black and white Southerners. New Latino immigrants are entering into a milieu where the black-white paradigm is the norm. What will black Southerners think about these newly arrived immigrants? Will blacks perceive Latinos as having a positive or negative effect on race relations in the South? This chapter addresses these questions on African American reactions to Latino immigrants in the Southern city of Durham, North Carolina. We address in particular black responses to the changing demography of Durham by examining attitudes of black elites toward Latino immigrants, and testing the extent to which these elite perspectives are reflected in the attitudes of the general black population. We begin with an overview of the research setting, Durham, North Carolina. We next review the literature on elite influence on public opinion and the influence of black elites on black mass public opinion, as well as scholarship on black American attitudes toward immigration in general and Latino immigration in particular. We then analyze the relationship between the attitudes of black elites and black citizens of Durham on issues related to Latino immigration.

## RACE RELATIONS IN A SOUTHERN CITY

Durham, North Carolina, was incorporated less than 150 years ago in 1869, making it a relatively new "postbellum" city in the South. As white Durham grew throughout the nineteenth and early twentieth centuries, a parallel black community, Hayti, was developing just outside of Durham proper, and the first land was sold to blacks around 1877 (Anderson 1990; Boyd 1925). Racial segregation policies were codified as early as the 1870s, suggesting Durham's racial history is similar to that of many other Southern cities. Blacks labored in Durham's mills and tobacco factories, and some members of the white business community cultivated relations with the black community. Business development within the black community also was encouraged, and in some instances, white business owners contributed money to black-owned ventures. A black entrepreneurial class in Durham grew after the founding of black-owned businesses such as North

Carolina Mutual and Provident Association, The Durham Drug Company, the Merrick-Moore-Spaulding Land Company, Lincoln Hospital, Bankers Fire Insurance Company, among others. Boyd (1925, 284) estimates the value of black property in Durham exceeded $4 million in 1923. Anderson (1990) suggests that the strong black leadership in Durham and its connections to some of the major white leaders in Durham were important for maintaining peaceful relations between blacks and whites (see also Greene 1996; Brown 1997; and Houck 1941).

At the same time, Jim Crow laws governed the public spaces and social interaction of blacks and whites in the city and on the Durham railways. Blacks in Durham protested against these segregation laws as early as 1914, and the Colored Voters League encouraged blacks to vote for quality candidates regardless of partisan affiliation in 1922. The National Negro Finance Corporation was founded two years later to assist black entrepreneurs, and in 1927, the Durham Branch of the Negro Business League actively demanded equal citizenship rights for blacks. By 1935, the Durham Committee on Negro Affairs was established to address the concerns of the black community, and throughout the Civil Rights era, it became a powerful organization exerting tremendous influence on local Durham politics.[1] As a result of the political and economic development in Durham, a strong cadre of black elites had and continues to have a great deal of political influence.

The City of Durham today is much different than it was in the early to mid-twentieth century. North Carolina has the fastest growing Latino population in the country, and whereas Charlotte has experienced the most growth, Durham's Latino population has exploded in the last ten years. Table 8.1 compares the racial composition of the City of Durham in 1990 and 2000. There were very few Latinos as recently as 1990, but by 2000, the number of Latino immigrants rose dramatically to almost nine percent (8.6 percent) of Durham's population. Where in 1990 there were just over seventeen hundred Latinos in Durham, the size of the Latino population in 2000 grew to more than sixteen thousand. Whites remain the largest racial group in Durham, comprising 46 percent of the city's population, but are no longer the majority population in the city. African Americans follow closely behind whites with 44 percent of the population in 2000.

Durham has a long-established history of biracial politics and is a city with a very prosperous upper- and upper-middle-class black community

---

[1] Now the Durham Committee on the Affairs of Black People, the organization remains a powerful force in Durham politics.

**TABLE 8.1.** Racial Composition of City of Durham, North Carolina, 1990 and 2000

|  | % in 1990 (n) | % in 2000 (n) | % change in share of population |
|---|---|---|---|
| Whites | 51.6 (70,513) | 45.5 (85,126) | −6.1 |
| Blacks | 45.7 (62,393) | 43.8 (81,937) | −1.9 |
| Latinos | 1.3 (1,713) | 8.6 (16,012) | +7.3 |
| Mexicans | 30.8 (528) | 64.2 (10,343) | |
| Puerto Ricans | 21.5 (369) | 6.7 (696) | |
| Cubans | 8.8 (150) | 14.7 (236) | |
| Other Hispanics | 38.9 (666) | 29.6 (4,737) | |
| Asian Americans | 1.9% (2,676) | 3.6% (6,815) | +1.7 |
| American Indians | 0.2 (358) | 0.3 (575) | +0.10 |
| Total Population | 136,611 | 187,035 | |

*Source:* U.S. Census

from which the black elite of Durham are drawn. Durham supports a number of black banks, libraries, hospitals, and numerous other businesses, along with North Carolina Central University, an institution with strong ties to the elite blacks in the city. Black political power in Durham is in the hands of a highly educated, and oftentimes very wealthy, black citizenry that has been very successful in achieving their objectives, primarily through political organization. Nevertheless, like other cities in the "New South," Durham has experienced a decline in industries in which blacks traditionally found work, and, as a result, a substantial proportion of the black population now works in the service industry. Many of Durham's Latino immigrants are from Mexico and other poor countries in Central America, and their reasons for immigrating to the United States are primarily economic.[2] They seek many of the same jobs and social services as blacks in Durham. As a result, Latinos and blacks in Durham often find themselves in competition with one another.

The newness and the magnitude of Latino immigration to Durham present an important set of challenges for race relations in this Southern city. Not only does the shift in the racial makeup of the population

---

[2] In a series of articles throughout 2002 chronicling the lives of area residents living in poverty, *The Herald Sun* (Durham) provided a picture of life for Latinos in Durham. Fully 26 percent of the more than sixteen thousand Latinos in Durham live below the federal poverty level, and, in order to make a good living, it is necessary for them to work more than one job (Assis and Pecquet 2002, A12).

alter the long-standing balance between blacks and whites in Durham, but the rapid influx of new workers also creates a dynamic labor market. Before analyzing the perspective of black elites in Durham toward Latino immigrants and the effects these opinions have on the attitudes of black residents of the city, we briefly review the literature addressing elite influence on public opinion.

## ELITE INFLUENCE ON BLACK ATTITUDES

American public opinion research consistently shows American citizens know little factual information about government and politics. Many scholars suggest this political ignorance does not inhibit the ability of citizens to form opinions and make political decisions. Rather, individuals rely on heuristics or cognitive shortcuts in political judgment and decision making (Popkin 1994). Taking cues from political elites is one such heuristic. Elites are more experienced and knowledgeable about political matters than ordinary citizens because they exist in positions of greater power and political influence. Despite the low levels of political knowledge in the mass public, most Americans nevertheless hold political predispositions based on individual interests, values, and ideological beliefs. This set of predispositions influence who they listen to and who they believe regarding political matters. Together with their own political awareness, these predispositions help ordinary citizens determine which political elites hold attitudes and ideas similar to their own. Once that connection is made, citizens take political cues from those elites. When divisions exist among political elites in their attitudes on a particular issue, the tendency is for individuals to adopt the position of elites they perceive to be the most consistent with their own political predispositions. When there is consensus among elites, however, "mainstream effects" occur among nonelite citizens, pushing them toward following the general elite position. In both situations, the effect will be most pronounced among those most politically aware (Zaller 1992).

Even when elites hold positions contrary to those of non-elites, their perspectives still have a great deal of influence by virtue of their privileged position in the dissemination of political information in terms of how issues are presented to the public and what images are brought to mind when issues are presented (Jacoby 2000; Kinder 2003; Popkin 1994). One particular elite frame that exerts considerable influence over mass opinion is encouraging group-centric thinking about political issues. In some instances, public opinion is guided by memberships in social groups and by reference groups they either sympathize with or resent (Nelson and Kinder 1996; Kinder 1998). If elites focus on the positive or negative moral qualifications of the intended beneficiaries, the power of group sentiment increases. If they frame issues in ways that deflect attention away from the beneficiaries, the power of group sentiment declines (Nelson and Kinder 1996, 1072). Thus, through framing, elites can effectively accentuate or attenuate the power group sentiment has in public opinion.

Although a general notion of political elites exists within the study of American politics, there is some variation regarding exactly who is included and excluded from such categorization. Some scholars opt for highly specific and constrained definitions, limiting the title of political elite to "those whose primary business is governing the nation" (Carmines and Kuklinski 1990, 266) or "individuals who work full-time within formal political channels and institutions" (Lee 2002, 9). Although the discussion about political elites often centers on elected officials, we view this as a strict designation that does not speak to the political experience of African Americans. For blacks, the opportunity to be active in mainstream political institutions is a fairly recent historical development. As a result, many of the elites in the African American community have often existed outside of formal political institutions, and come from the black community's institutions, most notably the church. For this reason, we broaden the term elite to include not only elected officials and those who work within formal, institutionalized political networks, but also those Taeku Lee (2002, 221) refers to as "counterelites," those individuals who may operate outside of conventional, institutionalized realms of politics, but who nonetheless exert political leadership and influence among ordinary citizens.

The role of black elites in the political and social life of black communities has varied. Historically, black elite efforts to highlight issues of concern to blacks in the dominant society have always been problematic, many times entangled in ideological debates among elites (Gaines 1997; Gordon 2002; Martin 1991). For many black elites the ideology of "uplift" was essential to the upward mobility of the black community. Racial uplift ideology assumed white racism would diminish as blacks became morally and materially progressive. In order for this uplift ideology to work, it became necessary to establish clear class divisions within black communities, and it was essential for black elites to distance themselves from the masses of blacks (Gaines 1997). This distancing worked to establish middle- and upper-class blacks as the morally and materially superior group. The result of this middle-class bourgeois ideology was an emphasis on class distinction, patriarchy, and pathology of the poor (Gaines 1997).

This ideology was not confined to urban centers but was also present in rural areas. The development of class distinctions was just as pronounced in the South where racial oppression and segregation established the social and political boundaries of black and white life. In an examination of black elites in rural Mississippi, Salamon found blacks in all of his rural locations were divided along class lines. "In virtually every locale a small clique of Blacks – usually the preachers, teachers, morticians, and those with light skins – managed to set themselves apart from the masses of Black sharecroppers, plantation laborers, and maids and to lay claim to a modest middle- or upper-class life-style" (Salamon 1973, 623).

Black elites have historically been successful in obtaining enhanced status for themselves and other blacks with skills and education, but were more limited in what they were able to achieve for blacks who were poor and unskilled (Gordon 2002; Stone 1986). Even so, black elites still remain an important part of the black community, especially in the political realm. One of the most important institutions historically within black communities has been the black church. It has consistently produced leaders that have come to speak for black America (Dawson 1994; Martin 1991; Reese and Brown 1995). It is the messages preached by black elites in black churches that connect religiosity with black political activity (Allen, Dawson, and Brown 1989; Brown and Wolford 1994; Hunt and Hunt 1977). Harris-Lacewell (2004) sees the role of black elites, many of whom she identifies as emerging from black churches, as multidimensional. She suggests, " . . . Black elites have the task of simultaneously speaking to, speaking for, and speaking with black masses. They are speaking to black people when they attempt to win adherents and frame the solutions to the black dilemma. They are speaking for black people when they are under the gaze of white power structures that attempt to understand and predict 'what the Negro wants' from the appeals of leaders. And they are speaking with Black people in an intricate, reciprocal cultural reproduction of ideas" (Harris-Lacewell 2004, 206).

The question of the significance of black political elites to broader black communities is one that is currently the subject of a growing body of research. Some work shows that having black representatives as descriptive representatives diminishes the substantive representation of minority interests overall (Cameron, Epstein, and Allen 1996; Lublin 1997), yet other research suggests descriptive and substantive representation can, and do, go hand-in-hand (Haynie 2001; Tate 2003). Nevertheless, there is a psychological benefit that accrues to blacks when they see black representatives in the legislature (Shingles 1981; Gay 2002). Moreover, the presence of black elites in governing institutions improves the likelihood black constituents will contact the office of a black representative, and contributes to increased levels of trust in government (Bobo and Gilliam 1990; Gay 2002; Gilliam 1996; Howell and Fagan 1988).

The research on black elites and their influence on the black mass public is considerably smaller than scholarship addressing the same questions for the general population. Nevertheless, the findings suggest the connection between black elites and black masses is somewhat tenuous. As such, black elite opinion might not be reflective of or have a significant and consistent influence on black mass opinion. Eisenger (1973) found demands for control-sharing reforms in Milwaukee, Wisconsin, emanated from black elites, although it was commonly viewed as a demand from the broader black community. The black masses in Milwaukee appeared to be indifferent to control-sharing reforms. A conclusion that can be drawn from this literature is that, unlike the broader literature on the effect of political elites on public opinion, we do not know if black elite opinion influences black mass opinion in any consistent and substantial way.

Similarly, the limited literature on attitudes of blacks toward immigration presents a mixed picture of black attitudes. Epenshade and Hempstead (1996) suggest that blacks, along with Latinos and Asian Americans, are more likely to express pro-immigration views than are non-Hispanic whites, yet these findings ran counter to earlier findings (Espenshade and Calhoun 1993). In reviewing fourteen national opinion polls concerning immigration available at the Roper Center for Public Opinion Research, Diamond (1998) found that whereas a majority of whites supported a moratorium on immigration, a majority of blacks opposed it. Conversely, a majority of blacks also favored a reduction in the level of immigration, and when the questions addressed economic costs associated with immigration, blacks were more likely to be in favor of restricting immigration than were whites.

In an analysis of 1994 Los Angeles County Social Survey data, Johnson, Farrell, and Guinn (1997) found that about one-half of non-Latino and black respondents believed they would have less or a lot less political and economic influence than they currently have if immigration continued at the present rate. Thornton and Mizuno (1999), analyzing data from the 1984 National Black Election Study, suggest blacks remain more positive toward immigrants than whites, despite perceptions of economic insecurity and feelings of economic threat. By contrast, Citrin et al. (1997) found concern about financial stress from immigration was not more significant in influencing attitudes about immigration among blacks than among whites.

The literature on black reaction to Latino immigration is even more limited. One study from Los Angeles examines the rising tensions between older, established black communities and recent immigrants, and finds black unions in Los Angeles have fiercely criticized immigration policy and the influx of Latin American immigrants into California (Miles 1994). He identifies the source of increasing tensions as competition for scarce resources in the form of jobs and social service benefits. For example, the perception and reality is black mothers are being edged out of welfare benefits by "needier" Latino mothers (Miles 1994, 118). Resentment of Latinos from job loss is not limited to those blacks in low-skilled jobs. Nonunionized Latino immigrants are replacing unionized black janitors, and black professionals, especially those who work in social services, are being displaced due to their lack of Spanish-language skills. Johnson, Farrell, and Guinn (1997) also identified a majority of black respondents who felt that more good jobs for Asian Americans and Latinos would result in fewer good jobs for blacks. In their study of black and Latino relations in Houston, Texas, Mindiola, Niemann, and Rodriguez (2002) found that as the Latino share of the population increased relations between blacks and Latinos became more contentious. Many labor-intensive industries in Houston sought out Latino immigrant workers and in the process, displaced blacks and created a sector reserved for immigrant labor. A majority of blacks believed that the overall effect of Latino immigration had a negative effect on blacks because immigrants take their jobs, depress wages, and take more from the economy than they contribute.

## DO BLACK ELITES AND THE BLACK MASSES AGREE?

The evidence on the influence of black elites on political attitudes among black Americans is not consistent, and the scholarship on black opinion on immigration and attitudes toward Latino immigrants leaves many questions unanswered. A case study of the city of Durham provides one angle into the dynamics of race relations within the context of new immigration, competition, and coalition politics. Drawing on the general literature on the influence of political elites, the more limited research on black elite influence on black opinion, and the literature on black attitudes toward immigration, we develop two hypotheses. The first posits the sector of the black community with which the elites interact will influence their view on the effects of Latino immigration. Black elites who interact with the masses will have a better understanding of the needs and concerns of the average working black person than elites who interact primarily with elites, regardless of race. The second hypothesis is concerned with whether black elite opinions on the effects of Latino immigration are similar to the opinions of blacks in general. Because black elites do not command the attention of national or even local news on a sustained basis, the only way they are able to shape public opinion is in their day-to-day interactions with people. Thus, we anticipate blacks will reflect the opinions of black elites who interact with the masses, and blacks that are part of the middle- and upper-classes will reflect the opinions of elites who interact with elites.

In order to test these hypotheses, we gathered two distinctive types of data from research subjects in Durham. In order to examine the effect of the emerging Latino population in Durham, face-to-face interviews were conducted with elites during the summers of 2002 and 2003. The pur-pose of these interviews was to determine the magnitude and domain of conflict and cooperation between blacks, Latinos, and whites in Durham by probing what issues were perceived to be of concern to the various ethnic groups, and whether perceptions of the former two issues were comparable across elites of different backgrounds. In addition the 2003 Durham Survey of Intergroup Relations (DSIR) collected data from five hundred Durham residents.[3] A randomly generated sample of phone numbers based on exchanges valid in the Durham, North Carolina, area was called, and an oversample of numbers listed in the phone directory under a Hispanic surname was called at the same time. The survey was conducted from May 4 through June 22, 2003, and interviews were con-ducted in both English and Spanish (32 percent of the interviews were con-ducted in Spanish). A race/ethnicity quota was implemented to achieve a minimum of 150 whites, 150 blacks, and 150 Latinos; the remaining fifty respondents were not under this quota restriction and represent a number of racial/ethnic backgrounds.[4] The sample of 500 consists of

---

[3] The study was conducted by the Center for Survey Research of the University of Virginia using a Computer-Aided Telephone Interviewing (CATI) system, employing random digit dialing (RDD) and dialing of directory-assisted Hispanic surname samples. We recognize the problems associated with drawing a sample from a listing of Hispanic surnames, for exam-ple, missing Hispanics with non-Hispanic last names, and those married to non-Hispanics. Given the recent nature of the Hispanic population in Durham and the high proportion of immigrants, however, we choose the sampling frame that would give us the highest probabilities of getting to a Latino respondent.

[4] A total of 4,208 phone numbers were attempted in the course of the survey and a total of 14,014 call attempts were made. The overall response rate was 21.6 percent. The American Association for Public Opinion Research (AAPOR) rate was calculated using the full call history of each number that was recorded automatically by the CATI software. The sam-ple is reasonably representative of the three racial subpopulations compared to the 2000 U.S. Census, though the distribution of respondents in the sample is slightly older, better educated, and more often female.

160 whites (32 percent), 151 blacks (30 percent), 167 Latinos (34 percent), 6 Asians (1.2 percent), and 12 who gave "Other" for their racial background (2.4 percent).[5] We analyze the black respondents to this survey in this chapter.

For the face-to-face elite interviews, we used a broad definition of elites to select individuals to participate in this study. All elite subjects were active in the Durham community as head of a community-based or political organization, an active member or leader in an organization, an elected or appointed official in Durham City, Durham County, or at the state level. Respondents were identified through news and newspaper accounts, community meetings members of the research team attended, and personal contacts through individual community activities. In some instances, snowballing techniques were used as a respondent would suggest another individual to be interviewed. A total of twenty-three interviews were conducted, and eight of the elites interviewed were black. We analyze the responses of black elites, which includes elected officials, upper-level bureaucrats, and policy specialists, as well as activists, ministers, heads of politically oriented organizations, and other "informal opinion leaders" who pay close attention to politics.

The elites who agreed to participate in the study were each asked an identical set of questions, and the survey included multiple choice and open-ended questions. The questions are grouped into five areas. First, elites were asked to provide some basic demographic information about themselves and their organization. They were also asked to briefly describe their personal experiences in Durham, their role in the organization, and the function of their organization in the community. Second, elites were asked to indicate on 5-point scales their impressions of the paired relationships among blacks, Latinos, and whites in Durham. These paired comparisons included what we refer to as undirected- and directed-form questions. The undirected-form questions ask about the relationship between group X and group Y. For each root question, the undirected-form generates three questions for the respondent to answer. For example, individuals

---

[5] Due to the use of the Hispanic surname sample and racial/ethnic quotas, sampling error is more difficult to calculate. The sample may be viewed as part of two separate populations. Within the RDD sample, the source of 276 completions, the probability of selection is known and the margin of error is ± 5.9 percent. Within the surname oversample, providing 244 completed interviews, all households listed under a resident with a Hispanic surname were attempted; however, Hispanics were included in RDD calling and non-Hispanics were included in the oversample. Non-Hispanics with Hispanic surnames had a greater change of selection than non-Hispanics in the RDD sample who do not have Hispanic surnames. If we assume this to be a more or less random occurrence, then the margin of error for each of the three racial/ethnic groups is roughly 8 percent.

were asked to characterize race relations between blacks and whites in Durham, then between Latinos and whites, and finally between blacks and Latinos. By contrast, the directed-form questions asked respondents to provide their impression of group X toward group Y. In this case, the directed-form generates six questions for each root. Respondents were asked to place the attitudes of Latinos towards blacks on a 100-point feeling thermometer; then the attitudes of blacks toward Latinos; and so forth. After each question in this portion of the survey, respondents were encouraged to further elaborate their answer. Third, the elites were asked in a series of open-ended questions about what issues they thought were of particular concern to blacks, Latinos, and whites. Respondents also were asked to discuss what issues they thought divided the various ethnic groups and about what issues they thought the groups had in common. Subsequently, elites were asked to indicate on 5-point scales their impressions about how satisfied each of the three different ethnic groups was with different aspects of life in Durham, including the performance of the schools, the police, and social service providers. Fourth, elites were asked to respond to a number of questions relating to the consequences of Latino immigration to the area and their impressions of public attitudes about this change. In general, respondents were asked to initially answer a question on a 5-point scale, and were then encouraged to further elaborate their answers. Finally, elites were asked a series of questions about Durham politics including the level of political participation of each of the different ethnic groups and the possibility of interethnic political coalitions emerging in the area. Once again, respondents were asked to initially answer a question on a 5-point scale, and were then encouraged to further elaborate their answers.

In order to see how black elites and the larger black public viewed the effects of Latino immigration, we chose similar, yet not identical, questions in each of the data sets for analysis.[6] We identified two questions from the elite surveys dealing with the perceived effects of Latino immigration. One question is, "How might you characterize race relations between Blacks and Latinos in Durham?" The responses ranged on a continuum from "poor" to "fair" to "excellent." The second question is more specific, "On a scale from one to five (where one is very negative and five is very positive), how would you characterize the effect of the growing Latino population on

---

[6] Given the nature of the two data sets and how they were collected, it is important to emphasize we cannot determine the causal order of influence between elite and mass attitudes. Rather, the data indicate the extent to which there is agreement between black mass opinion and the perspectives among black elites.

race relations in Durham?" In addition to these two questions, we used two feeling thermometer questions about Latino feelings toward blacks and black feelings toward Latinos. The thermometer was on a 100-degree scale in which 100 degrees represented a very warm or favorable feeling, 50 degrees represented no feeling at all, and 0 (zero) represented a very cold or unfavorable feeling. Given the differences in data sets, we do not posit that the elites have necessarily influenced the attitudes of those in the survey, but we are interested in seeing if there are similarities in responses from the two groups.

In order to test our first hypothesis, we divided our eight black elites into two categories, elites who interact primarily with the masses (three) and elites that interact primarily with other elites (five). Those elites who worked with community organizations were classified as interacting primarily with the masses, whereas elites who were elected officials, high-level public officials, and officials in elite private organizations we classified as elites interacting with other elites. Based on this classification, three of the black elites interacted primarily with the masses and five interacted primarily with other elites. In order to move beyond the simple marginal distributions of the small number of elite cases, we used traditional qualitative analysis techniques (see Lofland and Lofland, 1995) to systematically examine eight in-depth interviews with black elites. Appendix A provides a description of our methods for coding and analyzing the elite data.

In the DSIR data, we chose a question on how positive or negative the race relationships between blacks are in general as the dependent variable. Appendix B presents the question wording for the survey items in the DSIR. This measure parallels the question, but is not exactly the same as the question asked of the elites, and respondents in the DSIR were not asked the thermometer questions. We use five factors to explain differences in attitudes about race relationships between blacks and Latinos, including employment status, income, race relations in general in Durham, racial makeup of the respondent's residential area measured as Latinos in neighborhood, and effect of Latino immigration on black economic opportunity. We use employment status as an indicator of possible concern about economic security, and income is a measure of socioeconomic status. The presence of Latinos in their neighborhood is a measure of contact between blacks and Latinos, and the question on the effect of the Latino immigration on black economic opportunity as another measure of economic security.

In terms of perception of race relations between blacks and Latinos, 23 percent of blacks feel that they are very negative or somewhat negative,

# 158 Paula D. McClain et al.

**TABLE 8.2.** Black Elites' Perceptions of Latino Population on Race Relations in Durham

| Effect of Growing Latino Population on Race Relations | Sector of Community in which Black Elites Primarily Interact | |
| --- | --- | --- |
| | Masses | Elites |
| 1 (Very Negative) | 0 | 0 |
| 2 | 1 | 1 |
| 3 (No Impact) | 0 | 3 |
| 4 | 1 | 1 |
| 5 (Very Positive) | 1 | 0 |
| **Column Totals** | 3 | 5 |

17 percent think they are neither positive nor negative, and a healthy majority, 59 percent, feels they are somewhat positive or very positive. Blacks in Durham are distributed across the income spectrum, and 9 percent make below $15,000, whereas 9 percent make over $100,000, and 40 percent earn between $35,000 and $65,000. Seventy percent of black respondents live in neighborhoods with few or no Latinos. About half (51 percent) feel race relations in general in Durham are somewhat or very positive. Close to three-fourths (72 percent) of the black sample is working for pay,[7] and 61 percent believe blacks will have a lot less or some less economic opportunity if immigration continues at the present rate.

We test our first hypothesis that black elite opinion on the effect of Latino immigrants on black Americans will depend on the type of elite and the sector of the community with which they interact, by examining how black elites situated in distinct interaction settings feel about the effect of the Latino population on race relations. Table 8.2 shows the relationship for black elites between primary interaction location (with black masses or with other black elites) and their attitudes on the effect of Latino immigration for race relations in Durham. Because eight black elites were interviewed, the difference necessary to achieve statistical significance between social interaction settings is far greater than we could expect in these data, and the results show no statistically significant differences in the perceptions of black elites who interact primarily with the

[7] The nonworking category includes those who are unemployed, homemakers, students, and retirees.

masses and black elites that interact primarily with other elites. What does emerge, however, is that three of the five elites who interact primarily with other elites perceive no effect on race relations from Latinos, while none of the three elites that interact primarily with the black masses chose this option. Two of the three elites who interact primarily with the masses perceive Latinos as having a positive effect on race relations in Durham, whereas the other perceived the effect as negative. Thus, there appears to be no consensus among elites as to the effect of Latino immigration on race relations in general in Durham.

When asked about the feelings of blacks and Latinos toward each other, differences, although not statistically significant, do emerge. Two of the three elites who interact primarily with the black masses feel that not only do blacks have an unfavorable view of Latinos but also that Latinos have an unfavorable view of blacks. By contrast, elites who interact primarily with other elites are split on their perceptions on this question. Four of five elites feel that blacks either have no feeling at all toward Latinos, or are favorably disposed toward Latinos. Then again, three of these five elites believe that Latinos have unfavorable attitudes towards blacks, thus suggesting that they perceive blacks as more accepting of Latinos than Latinos are of blacks.

This view is clearly reflected in the responses to the open-ended questions in the interviews. Among black elites, there is an unease and concern about the growing Latino population in Durham. Many perceive an increased competition for jobs and scarce resources, and overall, black elites agree that blacks and Latinos have poor relationships in Durham. Moreover, there is no noticeable differentiation in the beliefs of black elites who interact mainly with elites and those that interact mainly with the masses. The black elites see the poor relationship as existing because of the apparent competition for resources such as jobs and social services, and both categories of elites appear equally concerned. For example, an elite that interacts primarily with other elites made the following comment on black and Latino relations:

> I mean, comments that I hear "Oh, why don't you do something about those Mexicans?" We're talking about Hispanic/Latino, but generally they describe all of them as Mexicans, which is very unfortunate because they're not all Mexicans. "Can't you pass a law to send them on back to where they came from? Most of them here are illegal. Taking our resources. Not paying for it." And these are Black folks in the . . . discussing relationships with Hispanic/Latinos. I think it's unfortunate, but that's the way it is.

Similarly, a black elite who interacts primarily with the black masses also referenced the increasing tensions between blacks and Latinos:

> Is that you know Latinos are beginning to be the minority that African-Americans used to be. Black people were feeling like you know hey they're taking our jobs, they're taking housing, they're doing this, they're doing that, Black folks don't understand because they don't understand white folks were not all speaking the same language. So I do know that with regards jobs that were entry-level positions, [unknown] labor positions, the Latinos are getting those jobs. African-Americans are not very happy about that, those that are looking for employment. I think that . . . that is posing a problem within the community as well.

What is interesting, however, is that black elites describe the relationship as improving because of what they see as a conscious attempt on their part to unify these two communities around the very issues that they previously have been divided, including public housing, jobs, and cultural diversity. Thus, the results for our first hypothesis are mixed. Elites differ on the effects of Latino immigration on race relations. A majority of elites who interact with other elites see no effect, while those who interact with the masses see an effect, but are not in agreement as to whether the effect is positive or negative. There is elite agreement on the perception of poor relations between blacks and Latinos.

We move next to analyze the data relevant to our second hypothesis that working-class blacks in Durham will reflect the opinions of elites who interact with the masses, and blacks who are part of the middle and upper classes will reflect the opinions of elites who interact with other elites. In order to test this hypothesis, we estimated a logit regression model using the data from the DSIR.[8] Table 8.3 shows the results of the ordered-logit analysis. The results show that black respondents in our survey who are not employed are more likely to feel positively about race relations between blacks and Latinos than do blacks who are employed. Substantively, nonworking blacks are about 30 percent more likely to feel race relations between blacks and Latino are positive. However, black respondents with higher incomes are slightly more likely to feel positively about race relations between blacks and Latinos. In addition, those who hold more positive feelings about race relations in Durham generally are also

---

[8] We use Clarify to compute predicted probabilities for values of the dependent variable while holding the predictor variables at their means or some other value in the ordered logit analysis (King, Tomz, and Wittenberg 2000; Tomz, Wittenberg, and King 2001, 2003).

**TABLE 8.3.** Black Respondents' Perceptions of Race Relations Between Blacks and Latinos in Durham (ordered probit estimates)

|  | Coefficient (standard error) |
|---|---|
| Employed | −.8460** (.42) |
| Income | .1911** (.0841) |
| Feelings about Durham race relations | .7793*** (.19) |
| Number of Latinos in neighborhood | .2112 (.17) |
| Perception of blacks' economic opportunities | .2749 (.18) |
| N | 125 |
| Chi-Squared | 30.09*** |
| Pseudo $R^2$ | .09 |

***$p < .01$ (two-tailed test); **$p < .05$ (two-tailed test); *$p < .10$ (two-tailed test)
*Source:* 2003 Durham Survey of Intergroup Relations

more likely to feel positively about black-Latino race relations. Substantively, blacks at the mean income level are about 7 percent more likely to feel race relations between blacks and Latinos are positive. Blacks who feel that race relations in Durham are generally positive are about 36 percent more likely to feel that relations between blacks and Latinos are positive.[9]

Our analysis also shows neighborhood contact with Latinos is not a statistically significant indicator of blacks' perceptions of race relations between blacks and Latinos in Durham. However, the estimated coefficient on this measure is positive, indicating blacks with more Latinos living in their neighborhoods tend to feel more positively about black-Latino race relations. Blacks' perceptions of the amount of economic opportunity blacks will have if immigration continues at its present rate is also not statistically significant in the model. But, like neighborhood contact, the estimated coefficient is positive, as expected, which may indicate blacks who feel continued immigration will have a positive effect on blacks' economic opportunity also feel more positively about black-Latino race relations.

What these results suggest is that although blacks who are not employed feel positively about relations between blacks and Latinos, those who are employed may be a little apprehensive about the nature of the relationship. Although the sign of the coefficient is significant for those not employed, given the distribution of the response categories, the fact

[9] The substantive effects discussed were computed using the STATA program Clarify (King, Tomz, and Wittenberg 2000; Tomz, Wittenberg, and King 2001, 2003).

that the attitudes of employed blacks are not significant gives us pause. Moreover, given the overwhelming proportion of black respondents who feel continued immigration will lead to decreased economic opportunity for blacks, it appears that at least for the moment those fears have not had an effect on their positive perceptions of black and Latino relations.

## ATTITUDES AMONG BLACK ELITES AND MASSES IN DURHAM

Our analysis of the interviews with black elites and survey data from black citizens of Durham suggest several interesting patterns of confluence between elite and mass black attitudes toward Latino immigrants. Elites who interact primarily with other elites perceive little or no effect of the new Latino immigration on race relations in Durham. It is possible that these elites have little contact with Latino immigrants or they interact with Latino elites and have a different view of the dynamics that exist between blacks and Latino immigrants in Durham. Although those who interact primarily with the masses do identify an effect, they are not in agreement as to whether the effect is positive or negative. Clearly, the masses with which each of these leaders interacts encounter a different set of dynamics between the masses of blacks and Latino immigrants, with some positive and others negative.

This finding is similar to those of Sonenshein (1993) in Los Angeles. Although black, Latino, and Asian American elites were building coalitions, the masses of these three groups were increasingly in competition for scarce resources. Yet, the black elites who interact with other elites might not be as Pollyannaish as their numeric scores indicate, for they do express some apprehension over the nature of relationships between blacks and Latino immigrants in their open-ended responses to the questions. Yet elites in general feel relations between the two groups are poor and that Latinos, by-and-large, have a negative view of blacks.

Regarding black citizens of Durham, it is clear that the public is concerned about some aspects of Latino immigration, such as diminished economic opportunity and skittish about their employment. But they are a little more positive about relations between blacks and Latinos than are the black elites. The indicators of diminished economic opportunity and employment may be gray clouds on the horizon, but they are not imminent. This suggests that, for the moment, blacks are not as negative about relations with Latinos as the elites perceive.

Yet what do these mixed results suggest about the future of black-Latino relations in our Southern location? Elites are essential to sending cues to the general populace about their attitudes toward issues and the nature of political debates. The cues that Durham black elites appear to be sending are that relations between blacks and Latino immigrants are contentious. These elite signals could result in two types of reactions. On the one hand, their anxiety could introduce more anxiety among the general black population than presently exists creating even more tensions than might already exist. On the other hand, their perceptions of contentious relations might propel them to join with white and Latino elites to intervene in and reduce these perceived tensions. If the latter reaction occurs, then it will help to mitigate whatever tensions their cues might increase, while at the same time creating venues where black, white, and Latino Durham residents can engage each other. This engagement might lead to the formation of coalitions that might be beneficial to all three groups. Therefore, the mismatch between elite and black mass attitudes might actually be a positive for black attitudes toward Latino immigration in general and black and Latino relations in particular.

The phenomenon of Latino immigration to the American South is such a recent phenomenon that it is difficult to capture not only its dynamics but also the possible effects new immigrants are having on race relations. In many ways, our study raises more questions than the data can address, and many of our answers have been far from definitive. Yet, given the recent nature of Latino immigration into the South and the absence of an established body of literature dealing with the social and political aspects of Latino immigration into this region of the country, exploratory research is a good beginning point (McClain et al. 2006). Although the data constrain us from extrapolating beyond our research setting of Durham, North Carolina, the questions explored and issues raised are critically important and require additional study in more regions of the South. Latino immigration will only increase in the coming years, and scholars of Southern politics and history need to begin to address its current and long-term effects.

## APPENDIX A: METHODS FOR CODING AND ANALYZING ELITE DATA

The first step was to develop a coding scheme for the interviews through a process of examining the data in one interview, fitting a coding scheme, and then testing the coding scheme against data in other interviews and then making the necessary revisions. The next step was to test the reliability of the interview coding by having two independent analysts recode three interviews each and compare their results with the results of the first coding. As is common in qualitative processes, particular attention was paid to comparative analysis and the development and refinement of potential hypotheses. To aid in this process, the qualitative analysis program, Atlas Ti 5.0, was used to code and analyze the data, as well as to generate network views of the various hypotheses.

When using Atlas Ti 5.0, all transcripts are loaded into the program and then coded electronically. Using Atlas offers advantages to the researcher by making the process of coding scheme development markedly easier. A single-code can be changed, merged, or deleted from all interviews by directly editing the coding list. Using traditional pen and paper methods, each interview transcript would have to be individually changed. Thus, the malleability of the program encourages a more accurate representation of the qualitative data in the coding scheme and reduces the likelihood of any coding errors because of human oversight. Perhaps the strongest advantage to using Atlas Ti 5.0 occurs after coding is complete. At this stage, Atlas has several search functions that by using the coding list, allows the researcher to search some or all of the transcripts using Boolean and semantic search strings. Moreover, these search functions allow for quantitative data to be read into the program and then linked to the transcript files. For this research, this last feature was used to filter the transcripts by demographic information contained in the quantitative data file. It also allowed us to pull out responses from elites categorized as interacting primarily with the masses and elites interacting primarily with other elites. Atlas Ti 5.0 is a systematic and efficient program for qualitative data analysis.

## APPENDIX B: QUESTION WORDING FOR 2003 DURHAM SURVEY OF INTERGROUP RELATIONS (DSIR)

Race relations between blacks and Latinos: The race relationships between blacks and Latinos in general, are they: 5 very positive; 4 somewhat positive; 3 neither positive or negative; 2 somewhat negative; 1 very negative?

Employment status: What is your employment status? Are you: (1) employed; (2) home maker; (3) unemployed; (4) student; (5) retired; (6) other (specify). Indicator was recoded to 1=employed; 0=everything else (home maker, unemployed, student, retired, and other).

Income: I am going to read you a list of income categories. Please tell me which category best describes the total income of all members of your family living in your house in 2001 before taxes. Please stop me when I get to your family's income. (1) 0–$15,000; (2) $15,001–$25,000; (3) $25,001–$35,000; (4) $35,001–$45,000; (5) $45,001–$55,000; (6) $55,001–$65,000; (7) $65,001–$75,000; (8) $75,001–$100,000; (9) $100,001 or more.

General race relations in Durham: In your opinion, racial relationships in Durham today are: (5) very positive; (4) somewhat positive; (3) neither positive nor negative; (2) somewhat negative; (1) very negative?

Residential race make-up: In your neighborhood, how many of the residents are Latino? (5) All of the residents; (4) Most of the residents; (3) Some of the residents; (2) A few of the residents; and (1) None of the residents.

Economic opportunity: What about economic opportunity? If immigration to this country continues at the present rate, do you believe black people will have more or less economic opportunity? Would you say: (5) probably would have a lot more economic opportunity than now; (4) some more opportunity than now; (3) no more or less opportunity than now; (2) some less opportunity than now; (1) a lot less opportunity than now?

# 9   Understanding the New Race Politics

## Conclusions and Challenges

With significant waves of new immigration to the United States, over-whelmingly from Asia and Latin America, the electoral significance of minority voters is becoming increasingly apparent. As the studies in this volume make clear, how increases in the racial and ethnic diversity of the voting public will influence political representation, policy outcomes, and democratic politics, more generally, remains to be seen. For example, despite the growing size of minority groups in the United States, political representation by minority officials lags far behind their numbers in the population. The 109th Congress, elected in 2004, is a specific case in point. This Congress is the most racially diverse Congress in the history of the United States. That year, voters sent a record number of minority Americans to both the United States House and Senate. The 109th House of Representatives included forty-two African Americans, twenty-four Latinos, five Asian Americans, and one American Indian, whereas the 109th Senate had one African American, two Asian Americans, and two Latinos. Nevertheless, the Senate and the House were 95 percent and 83 percent white, respectively. At the same time, nearly one-third of the U.S. population considered itself to be a race other than white. One of the most intriguing questions for the new race politics of the United States in the twenty-first century is whether those proportions will change as a function of changing patterns in minority and immigrant voting. Another interesting question is whether the growing presence of new immigrants within the population at large and among the pool of eligible voters will result in greater minority influence in state and national policymaking, regardless of whether there is greater minority representation in government. These are important and profound questions. The health of our democracy and our ability to remain a model of integration and inclusiveness for other racially and ethnically pluralistic societies may depend in part upon our political system's ability to continue to respond to and incorporate the interests and demands of an increasingly diverse citizenry. As I wrote in an earlier study,

> A continued basic level of trust in our political institutions and the continued legitimacy of our current representative system may rest in part on our ability to insure that there are significant numbers of ... minority group [representatives] in deliberative institutions who speak with distinctive ... minority voices. Moreover, once inside these institutions, we must seek to insure that these representatives are perceived and treated as equal participants, and that their ideas and views are seriously considered. This task is becoming increasingly urgent, given the rapid demographic changes that the United States is currently undergoing. (Haynie 2001: 114)

In the coming decades, our political system is likely to face another crucial test of its ability to include and incorporate nonwhite citizens. The last such challenge to our system took place over a twenty-five- to thirty-year period after the passage of the landmark 1965 Voting Rights Act. That challenge was largely a black-white affair, and was experienced first at the municipal level and gradually shifted to state legislatures in the South and Northeast, and ultimately to the U.S. House of Representatives. This next test of the system's openness will be different in three important respects. First, because of the nation's changed and changing racial and ethnic demographics, race politics in the United States can no longer be examined and fully understood by relying on black-white models exclusively. Today, the political landscape is populated with at least three racial and ethnic groups – African, Asian, and Latino Americans – who have the potential, either individually or as part of a coalition, to significantly alter politics as we currently know it. Second, it is possible that this new test of the political system will take place against the backdrop of these three groups challenging each other for political positioning and influence, while at the same time, they are challenging the system for political inclusion. Third, pressure from these groups is likely to be felt simultaneously at all levels of government. For example, their numbers in the population, their projected population growth rates, and their settlement and housing patterns, render African Americans, Asian Americans, and Latinos potential forces to be reckoned with in not only the traditional gateway urban areas, but they are also poised to become major players in statewide politics in at least seventeen states: Alabama, Arizona, California, Colorado, Florida, Georgia, Illinois, Louisiana, Maryland, Mississippi, New Jersey, New Mexico, New York, North Carolina, South Carolina, Texas, and Washington. And because these seventeen states collectively have a large number of electoral college votes and a large number of seats in the U.S. House of Representatives, these groups are positioned for potential influential roles in national politics (Jennings 1994).

The rapidly expanding presence of minority groups in the United States, and their potential for radically changing the look and substance of American politics, notwithstanding, a unifying theme of the chapters in this volume is that the future of the new American electorate is seemingly very much up for grabs. There is uniform agreement among the authors here and among scholars generally that the changing demographics and the new underlying social and structural contexts will alter, in fundamental ways, the tenor of race and ethnic politics in the United States. How exactly politics will change, and what the consequences will be for minority groups, our political institutions, and society at large, however, are yet to be determined. As Kristi Anderson argues in Chapter 2, for example, it is not all clear whether the national Democratic and Republican parties perceive themselves as having substantial enough incentives to actively seek to mobilize new Asian and Latino immigrants and integrate them into the political process.

Indeed, traditional mobilizing institutions for new immigrant populations, including political parties and labor unions, no longer exist in the same way and with the degree of strength they once did during the early twentieth century, when even larger groups of new Americans settled in the nation. This is a noteworthy development given the finding by Rodolfo O. de la Garza, Marisa Abrajano, and Jeronimo Cortina that mobilization efforts are an important predictor of turnout at both the state and national levels (Chapter 5). Specifically, they find that Latinos who are asked to are more likely to vote than those who are not asked. Janelle Wong's, Pei-te Lien's, and Margaret Conway's study of Asian American participation (Chapter 4), and Victoria DeFrancesco Soto's and Jennifer Merolla's examination of Latino voting behavior (Chapter 6) go a step further and make an additional claim. Both sets of authors argue that racially and ethnically targeted mobilization strategies are a more effective means for getting minority citizens to vote and otherwise participate in the political process than general mobilization appeals.[1] Their findings suggest that

---

[1] It is interesting that DeFrancesco-Soto's and Merolla's finding in Chapter 6 that racially and ethnically targeted mobilization strategies are a more effective means for getting minority citizens to vote, seemingly contradicts the finding by de la Graza, Abrajano, and Cortina in Chapter 6. De la Garza, Abrajano, and Cortina find that coethnic mobilization appeals do not influence turnout among Latinos. This is clearly an issue in need of additional examination and analysis.

strategies and mechanisms that are intended specifically to mobilize Asian Americans, Latinos, and African Americans such as, elite cues, coethnic mobilization drives, and large-scale non-English-language political advertising aimed directly at minority populations, may eventually render the traditional institutions irrelevant as mobilizing forces, especially if these institutions fail to adapt to what appears to be new electoral realities.

Another set of reasons why it is difficult to predict the future path or place of this new more racially and ethnically diverse American electorate involves factors internal to each of the minority groups, especially Asians and Latinos. It is not at all clear whether Asians and/or Latinos will become identifiable and politically relevant voting blocs similar to what we have seen with African Americans. And if such electoral blocs were to materialize, it isn't clear with which party, if either, the blocs would be aligned.

One of the factors complicating the strategies to mobilize Americans grouped by race and ethnicity is the tenuousness and contextual specificity of racial group identity among Asian and Latino Americans. Unlike the case with African Americans, these groups of Americans are apparently less likely to be unified in terms of political outlook and party and candidate preference. Dennis Chong and Dukhong Kim (Chapter 3) find, for instance, that whereas African Americans' views on questions of race and representation are strongly influenced by their assessment of the economic standing of minority groups and by perceptions of the amount of discrimination these *groups* experience, Latino and Asian Americans' views are more likely to be influenced by *personal* experiences with discrimination.

The internal diversity of these larger racial categories in terms of ethnic background, national origin, language, religion, and economic circumstances, creates additional hurdles for pan-ethnic group consciousness and political cohesion. Both Asian Americans and Latino Americans are good examples of how internal group diversity matters. One of the most interesting findings of the Wong, Lien, and Conway study of Asian Americans is that, unlike the case with native-born Asians, being born and educated outside of the United States is negatively associated with some types of political participation. Similarly, DeFrancesco Soto and Merolla find that Latinos' receptivity to political advertisements varies by their level of acculturation. Specifically, they find that general (i.e., non-group-targeted) advertisements play a more significant role in mobilizing dominant English-speaking Latino Americans than they do in mobilizing Latino Americans who speak Spanish most of the time.

Another pertinent question about the future of racial and ethnic politics in the United States is whether the relationship among minority groups will be characterized more by cooperation or by conflict. It has long been the conventional wisdom among political scientists that shared minority group status would be the nucleus around which African, Asian, and Latino Americans would form powerful and influential political coalitions. Scholars have assumed that common political interests, similar ideological worldviews, and mutual respect would be the ties that would bind these groups together (Henry 1994; McClain and Stewart 2006; Sonnenshein 1994). And it has widely been expected that politics and public policy would be transformed by the presence and active engagement of these coalitions in the political process. For example, in an earlier study, James Jennings suggested that the emergence of coalitions among communities of color could be the basis for conceptualizing and enacting different policy paradigms. As he put it, "political cooperation among blacks, Latinos, and Asians can help in the development of progressive social agendas that benefit all groups, including working class whites" (Jennings 1994, 5). There are well-known instances of such coalitions forming in a few large metropolitan areas. It is clear that these coalitions have met with some success in electing minority candidates and incorporating racial and ethnic minorities and their interests into the political system. Chicago, Los Angeles, San Francisco, and Washington, DC, are a few of the cities in which biracial or multiracial coalitions have been successful (Browning, Marshall, and Tabb 1984; McClain and Stewart 2006). One of the most recent visible examples of multiracial coalition political success is the 2005 mayoral race in Los Angeles, in which Antonio Villaraigosa was elected the city's first mayor of Latino descent. In that election, a large percentage of African and Asian American voters, 48 and 44 percent, respectively, joined with 84 percent of Latino voters to give Villaraigosa a dramatic victory over incumbent mayor James Hahn.

What is the future of multiracial coalitions? Successes like the one in Los Angeles notwithstanding, there is ample evidence to suggest that future relations among racial and ethnic minority groups could be more conflictual than cooperative. For instance, in Chapter 8 of this volume, Paula McClain and her colleagues uncover a potential source of tension between African Americans and Latinos. It is well established in the literature that elite attitudes and behaviors are important determinants of successful multiracial coalitions. In their study of Durham, North Carolina, McClain et al. find that black elites sometimes send cues to the black masses that suggest that relations between the two groups are more contentious than the masses might themselves perceive or experience them to be based on their day-to-day interactions. They argue that the concern exhibited by black leaders could contribute to blacks having negative attitudes and opinions about Latinos and result in more anxiety within the black community, which in turn might reduce the likelihood of positive interactions between the two groups.

Using data and case studies from six cities, Compton, the District of Columbia, Houston, Los Angeles, Miami, and New York City, Nicolas Vaca, in a 2004 study, identified several additional factors that might threaten the formation of effective multiracial political coalitions. Among the factors that he identifies are language barriers, perceived and real competition for certain types of jobs, and differing attitudes about affirmative action (Vaca 2004). To these potential sources of intergroup conflict, Gary Segura and Helena Alves Rodrigues add "affective indifference" or a "general lack of affinity" that the groups have for each other as another threat to multiracial coalitions (Segura and Rodrigues 2006, 389). Segura and Rodrigues call attention to the fact that successful coalitions "must operate at the mass level . . . in order to influence electoral and policy outcomes" (Segura and Rodrigues 2006, 389). Ill feelings or hostility among the masses can undermine any objective underlying incentives or motivations that might ordinarily result in cooperation.

## CHALLENGES FOR POLITICAL SCIENCE

The uncertainties that exist about the future path of the new race politics raise interesting questions and challenges for political science and the other social sciences. In a recent review essay on the state of the scholarship on racial minority group politics, Gary M. Segura and Helena Alves Rodrigues observed that for most of the extant race and ethnic politics research, the African American experience is the default analytical framework for investigating the political experience of all racial and ethnic minorities in the United States. They write:

> As a consequence of both the historical demography of the United States and the relative paucity of research on other racial groups, scholarly understandings of race and its consequences for American politics have been achieved largely through the analytical lens of a black-white dynamic. . . . When discussions move beyond these groups, political scientist often mistakenly presume that arguments and findings with respect to African-Americans extend to other racial and ethnic groups. Moreover, racial and ethnic interactions between Anglos and other minority groups are assumed to mimic – to some degree – the black-white experience. (Segura and Rodrigues 2006: 376)

Broadening the study of racial and ethnic politics to account for the nation's changed political landscape is one of the crucial challenges political science must engage. The authors in this volume have taken some initial steps toward meeting this challenge. They have suggested and argued that in order to understand the dynamics of this new race politics, analysts need to go beyond traditional models of political behavior that were developed primarily to explain the political attitudes, public opinion, and the voting patterns of the white majority. For example, it is clear from these studies that we must break out of our overreliance on theories and frameworks that tend to overemphasize the importance of individual-level social and economic resources that are correlated with political participation. Elucidating the importance of political context, broadly conceived, must inform inferences about voting behavior among racial and ethnic minorities. Specifically, it is vital that analysts account for factors such as differences in state-level electoral structures, the presence of mobilizing agents, and the competitiveness of elections.

It is also clear that political scientists need to direct new attention to the significance of institutions. We need to develop parsimonious theories and robust analytical models that will help us understand how the racial and ethnic classifications that have been a feature of American society from the very beginning of the republic have provided political actors and ordinary citizens with incentives to make racially based choices in designing all sorts of institutions, and how early institutions set into motion patterns of procedure, expectations, and behaviors that can have important consequences for the structure of subsequent institutions and the decisions, policies, and changes they produce (Lieberman 1995; Katznelson 2005; Quadagno 1994; Skocpol 1995).

At the same time that we are pursuing broad, general theories, scholars of race and ethnic politics must be vigilant about insuring the distinctiveness of the various race and ethnic politics subfields. That is, while there are many similarities among racial and ethnic minorities, and although there are many theories and models that explain phenomena across multiple groups, African American, Asian, black, and Latino politics are separate entities with distinct theoretical foundations and frameworks (McClain and Garcia 1993). For example, ethnic identification, language, and a variety of citizenship status related issues are integral to the study of Asian, black, and Latino voting and political participation, but not necessarily to examinations of African American political behavior. It is important that distinctions such as these be accounted for when it is relevant to do so, and that scholars avoid the temptation to assume group similarities or differences.

Finally, if we are to make sense of the dynamics and consequences of this new race politics, we should take care to situate the study of race and ethnic politics within, and connect it to, the study of American politics more broadly conceived. At its core, American politics is largely the politics of race and ethnicity. Understanding race and ethnic politics is a prerequisite for fully understanding American politics.

# References

Abramson, Paul R., and John H. Aldrich. 1982. "The Decline of Electoral Participation in America." *American Political Science Review* 76: 502–21.

Aiken, Leona S., and Stephen G. West. 1991. *Multiple Regression: Testing and Interpreting Interactions*. Newbury Park, CA: Sage.

Alba, Richard. 1992. *Ethnic Identity: The Transformation of White America*. New Haven, CT: Yale University Press.

Alba, Richard, and Victor Nee. 1997. "Rethinking Assimilation Theory for a New Era of Immigration." *International Migration Review* 31 (Winter): 826–74.

Alba, Richard, and Victor Nee. 2003. *Remaking the American Mainstream: Assimilation and Contemporary Immigration*. Cambridge, MA: Harvard University Press.

Aldrich, John H. 1993. "Rational Choice and Turnout." *American Journal of Political Science* 37: 246–78.

Aleinikoff, T. Alexander. 2001. "Policing Boundaries: Migration, Citizenship, and the State," in Gary Gerstle and John Mollenkopf, editors, *E Pluribus Unum? Contemporary and Historical Perspectives on Immigrant Political Incorporation*. New York: Russell Sage Foundation.

Alex-Assensoh, Yvette, and A. B. Assensoh. 2001. "Inner-City Contexts, Church Attendance, and African-American Political Participation." *Journal of Politics* 63: 886–901.

Allen, Richard L., Michael Dawson, and Ronald E. Brown. 1989. "A Schema-Based Approach to Modeling an African-American Racial Belief System." *The American Political Science Review* 83: 421–41.

Allswang, John M. 1977. *Bosses, Machines, and Urban Voters*. Baltimore, MD: Johns Hopkins University Press.

Altonji, J., and Card, D. 1991. "The Effects of Immigration on the Labour Market Outcomes of Natives," in John M. Abowd and Richard B. Freeman, editors, *Immigration, Trade, and The Labour Market*. Chicago: University of Chicago Press.

Alvarez, R. Michael, and Jonathan Nagler. 1999. "Is the Sleeping Giant Awakening? Latinos and California Politics in the 1990's." Presented at the Annual Meeting of the Midwest Political Science Association.

Alvarez, R. Michael and Lisa Garcia Bedolla. 2003. "The Foundations of Latino Voter Partisanship: Evidence from the 2000 Election." *The Journal of Politics* 65: 31–49.

Alvarez, R. Michael. 1997. *Information and Elections*. Ann Arbor: University of Michigan Press.

Ancheta, Angelo N. 1998. *Race, Rights, and the Asian American Experience*. New Brunswick, NJ: Rutgers University Press.

Andersen, Kristi. 1979. *The Creation of a Democratic Majority 1928–1936*. Chicago: University of Chicago Press.

Andersen, Kristi. 1994. "Women and the Vote in the 1920s: What Happened in Oregon." *Women and Politics* 14: 43–56.

Andersen, Kristi, and Jessica Wintringham. 2003. "Political Parties, NGOs, and Immigrant Incorporation: A Case Study." Presented at the Midwest Political Science Association meetings.

Anderson, Jean Bradley. 1990. *Durham County*. Durham, NC: Duke University Press.

Ansolabehere, Stephen, Shanto Iyengar, Adam Simon, and Nicholas Valentino. 1994. "Does Attack Advertising Demobolize the Electorate?" *American Political Science Review* 88: 829–38.

Ansolabehere, Stephen, and Shanto Iyengar. 1995. *Going Negative: How Political Advertisements Shrink and Polarize the Electorate*. New York: The Free Press.

Arcelus, Francisco, and Allan H. Meltzer. 1975. "The Effect of Aggregate Economic Variables on Congressional Elections." *American Political Science Review* 69: 1232–39.

Arvizu, John R., and F. Chris Garcia. 1996. "Latino Voting Participation: Explaining and Differentiating Latino Voting Turnout." *Hispanic Journal of Behavioral Sciences* 18:104–28.

Assis, Claudia, and Julian Pecquet. 2002. "Hispanics' Search for a Better Life Pushes Durham into Poverty." *The Herald Sun*, September 25, A12.

Baretto, Matt, Rodolfo O. de la Garza, Jongho Lee, Jaesung Ryu, and Harry P. Pachon. 2002. "A Glimpse Into Latino Policy and Voting Preferences." Policy Brief, The Tomas Rivera Policy Institute.

Barker, Lucius, and Ron Walters, eds. 1989. *Jesse Jackson's 1984 Presidential Campaign*. Urbana: University of Illinois Press.

Barnes, Jessica S., and Claudette Bennett. 2002. *The Asian Population: 2000*. Census 2000 Brief (C2KBR/01–16). Washington, DC: U.S. Department of Commerce, Bureau of the Census.

Barreto, Matt A., Gary M. Segura, and Nathan D. Woods. 2004. "The Mobilizing Effect of Majority-Minority Districts on Latino Turnout." *American Political Science Review* 98: 65–75.

Barreto, Matt, Nathan D. Woods, and Gary M. Segura. 2002. "Rest Assured? Estimating the Potential Mobilizing or Demobilizing Effects of Overlapping Majority-Minority Districts." Presented at the Annual Meeting of the Midwest Political Science Association, Chicago, IL.

Basch, Linda, Nina Glick Schiller, and Christina Szanton Blanc. 1994. *Nations Unbound*. Langhorne, PA: Gordon and Breach.

Bass, Loretta E., and Lynne M. Kasper. 2001. "Impacting the Political Landscape: Who Registers and Votes among Naturalized Citizens?" *Political Behavior* 23:1 (June): 101–30.

Beck, Paul A., and M. Kent Jennings. 1982. "Pathways to Participation." *American Political Science Review* 76: 94–108.

Benhabib, Seyla. 2002. *The Claims of Culture: Equality and Diversity in the Global Era.* Princeton, NJ: Princeton University Press.

Bibby, John F. 1996. *Politics, Parties, and Elections in America, 3rd ed.* Chicago: Nelson-Hall Publishers.

Bloemraad, Irene. 2006. "Citizenship Lessons from the Past: The Contours of Immigrant Naturalization in the Early Twentieth Century." *Social Science Quarterly,* 87(5): 927–53.

Bobo, Lawrence, and Franklin D. Jr. Gilliam. 1990. "Race, Sociopolitical Participation, and Black Empowerment." *American Political Science Review* 84: 377–93.

Borjas, George J. 1987. "Immigrants, Minorities, and Labor Market Competition." *Industrial and Labor Relations Review* 40: 382–92.

Boyd, William Kenneth. 1925. *The Story of Durham, City of the New South.* Durham, NC: Duke University Press.

Brians, Craig Leonard, and Martin P. Wattenberg. 1996. "Campaign Issue Knowledge and Salience: Comparing Reception from TV Commercials, TV News and Newspapers." *American Journal of Political Science* 40: 172–93.

Brischetto, Robert, and Rodolfo O. de la Garza. 1983. *The Mexican American Electorate: Political Participation and Ideology.* Austin, TX: Center for Mexican American Studies and Southwest Voter Research and Education Project.

Brown, Leslie. 1997. *Common Spaces, Separate Lives: Gender and Racial Conflict in the Capital of the Black Middle Class.* Ph.D. Durham, NC: Duke University. Archives Ph.D. B878C.

Brown, Ronald, and Monica Wolford. 1994. "Religious Resources and African American Political Action." *National Political Science Review* 4: 30–48.

Browning, Rufus, Dale Rogers Marshall, and David H. Tabb. 1984. *Protest is Not Enough: The Struggle of Blacks and Hispanics for Equality in Urban Politics.* Berkeley: University of California Press.

Buehler, Marilyn H. 1977. "Voter Turnout and Political Efficacy among Mexican-Americans in Michigan." *Sociological Quarterly* 18: 504–17.

Burnham, Walter Dean. 1970. *Critical Elections and the Mainsprings of American Democracy.* New York: Norton.

Burns, Nancy, Kay Lehman Schlozman, and Sidney Verba. 2001. *The Private Roots of Public Action: Gender, Equality, and Political Participation.* Cambridge, MA: Harvard University Press.

Cain, Bruce E., D. Roderick Kiewiet, and Carole J. Uhlaner. 1991. "The Acquisition of Partisanship by Latinos and Asian Americans." *American Journal of Political Science* 35: 390–422.

Cain, Bruce, Jack Citrin, and Cara Wong. 2000. *Ethnic Context, Race Relations, and California Politics.* San Francisco: Public Policy Institute of California Monograph.

Calvo, Maria Antonia, and Steven Rosenstone. 1989. "Hispanic Political Participation." (Latino Electorate Series). San Antonio: Southwest Voter Research Institute.

Cameron, Charles, David Epstein, and Sharyn O'Halloran. 1996. "Do Majority-Minority Districts Maximize Substantive Black Representation in Congress?" *The American Political Science Review* 90: 794–812.

Campbell, Angus, Philip Converse, Warren Miller, and Donald Stokes. 1960. *The American Voter.* New York: Wiley.

Cassel, Carol A. 2002. "Hispanic Turnout: Estimates from Validated Voting Data." *Political Research Quarterly* 55: 391–408.

Chan, Sucheng. 1991. *Asian Americans: An Interpretive History*. Boston: Twayne.

Chang, Gordon H. 2001. "Asian Americans and Politics: Some Perspectives from History," in Gordon H. Chang, editor, *Asian Americans and Politics: Perspectives, Experiences, Prospects*. Stanford, CA: Stanford University Press.

Cheng, Lucie, and Philip Yang. 1996. "The 'Model Minority' Deconstructed." In Roger Waldinger and Mehdi Bozorgmmehr, eds., *Ethnic Los Angeles*. New York: Russell Sage Foundation.

Cho, Wendy K. Tam. 1999. "Naturalization, Socialization, Participation: Immigrants and (Non-) Voting." *Journal of Politics* 61: 1140–55.

Chong, Dennis. 1991. *Collective Action and the Civil Rights Movement*. Chicago: University of Chicago Press.

Chong, Dennis. 2000. *Rational Lives: Norms and Values in Politics and Society*. Chicago: University of Chicago Press.

Chong, Dennis, and Dukhong Kim. 2006. The Experiences and Effects of Economic Status Among Racial and Ethnic Minorities." *American Political Science Review* 100 (August): 335–51.

Chong, Dennis, and Reuel Rogers. 2005. "Racial Solidarity and Political Participation." *Political Behavior* 27 (December): 347–74.

Citrin, Jack, Donald P. Green, Christopher Muste, and Cara Wong. 1997. "Public Opinion Toward Immigration Reform: The Role of Economic Motivations." *The Journal of Politics* 59: 858–81.

Clinton, Joshua D., and John Lapinski. 2004. "'Targeted' Advertising and Voter Turnout: An Experimental Study of the 2000 Presidential Election." *Journal of Politics* 66: 69–97.

Cohen, Cathy J. 1999. *The Boundaries of Blackness: AIDS and the Breakdown of Black Politics*. Chicago: University of Chicago Press.

Cohen, Cathy J., and Michael C. Dawson. 1993. "Neighborhood Poverty and African-American Politics." *American Political Science Review* 87: 286–302.

Conway, M. Margaret. 2000. *Political Participation in the United States*. Third Edition. Washington, DC: Congressional Quarterly Press.

Cose, Ellis. 1995. *The Rage of a Privileged Class*. New York: Harper-Perennial.

Cox, Gary W., and Michael C. Munger. 1989. "Closeness, Expenditures, and Turnout in the 1982 U.S. House Elections." *America Political Science Review* 83: 217–31.

Dahl, Robert. 1961. *Who Governs: Democracy and Power in an American City*. New Haven, CT: Yale University Press.

Davidson, Russell, and James G. MacKinnon. 1993. *Estimation and Inference in Econometrics*. New York: Oxford University Press.

Dawson, Michael, Ronald Brown, and Richard Allen. 1990. "Racial Belief Systems, Religious Guidance, and African American Political Participation." *National Political Science Review* 2: 22–44.

Dawson, Michael. 1994. *Behind the Mule*. Princeton, NJ: Princeton University Press.

Dawson, Michael. 1994b. "A Black Counterpublic? Economic Earthquakes, Racial Agenda(s), and Black Politics." *Public Culture* 7: 195–223.

de la Garza, Rodolfo O. 2004. "Latino Politics." *Annual Review of Political Science* 7: 91–123.

de la Garza, Rodolfo O., and Louis DeSipio. 1992. *From Rhetoric to Reality: Latino Politics in the 1990 Elections.* Boulder, CO: Westview.

de la Garza, Rodolfo O., and Marissa A. Abrajano. 2002. "Get Me to the Polls on Time: Latino Mobilization and Turnout in the 2000 Election." Paper presented at the Annual Meeting of the American Political Science Association, Boston, MA.

de la Garza, Rodolfo O., and Robert R. Brischetto, with Andrew Hernandez and David Vaughan. 1985. *The Mexican American Electorate: A Demographic Profile.* Austin, TX: University of Austin Press.

de la Garza, Rodolfo O., and Fujia Lu. 1999. "Explorations into Latino Voluntarism," in Diana Campoamor, William A. Diaz, and Henry A. J. Ramos, editors, *Nuevos Senderos: Reflections on Hispanics and Philanthropy.* Houston: Arte Publico Press.

de la Garza, Rodolfo O., and Louis DeSipio. 1993. "Save the Baby, Change the Bathwater, and Scrub the Tub: Latino Electoral Participation after Twenty Years of Voting Rights Act Coverage," in F. Chris Gareia, editor, *Pursuing Power: Latinos and the Political System.* Notre Dame, IN: University of Notre Dame Press.

de la Garza, Rodolfo O., and Louis DeSipio. 1997. "The Best of Times, the Worst of Times: Latinos and the 1996 Elections." *Harvard Journal of Hispanic Policy* 10: 3–26.

de la Garza, Rodolfo O., and Louis DeSipio. 2004. *Muted Voices: Latinos and the 2000 Election.* Lanham, MD: Rowman and Littlefield.

de la Garza, Rodolfo O., C. Dunlap, J. Lee, and J. Ryu. 2002. *Latino Voter Mobilization in 2000: Campaign Characteristics and Effectiveness.* Claremont, CA: Tomas Rivera Policy Institute.

de la Garza, Rodolfo O., Charles W. Haynes, and Jaesung Ryu. 2002. "An Analysis of Latino Turnout Patterns in the 1992–1998 General Elections in Harris County, Texas." *Harvard Journal of Hispanic Policy* 14: 77–95.

de la Garza, Rodolfo O., Louis DeSipio, F. Chris Garcia, John A. Garcia, and Angelo Falcon. 1992. *Latino Voices: Mexican, Puerto Rican, and Cuban Perspectives on American Politics.* Boulder, CO: Westview.

de la Garza, Rodolfo, Martha Menchaca, and Louis DeSipio. 1994. *Barrio Ballots: Latino Politics in the 1990 Elections.* Boulder, CO: Westview.

de Tocqueville, Alexis. 1969. *Democracy in America.* J. P. Mayer (Ed.), George Lawrence (Tran.). New York: Doubleday.

DeFrancesco, Victoria M. 2004. "Identity Fluidity in the Voting Booth: Social Group Identification and Latino Vote Choice." Presented at the Annual Meeting of the American Political Science Association, Chicago, IL.

Demo, David H., and Michael Hughes. 1990. "Socialization and Racial Identity among Black Americans." *Social Psychology Quarterly* 53 (December): 364–74.

DeSipio, Louis. 1996. *Counting on the Latino Vote: Latinos as a New Electorate.* Charlottesville: University of Virginia Press.

DeSipio, Louis, and Jennifer Jerit. 1998. "Voluntary Citizens and Democratic Participation: Political Behaviors among Naturalized U.S. Citizens." Paper Presented at the Annual Meeting of the Midwest Political Science Association, Chicago, IL.

DeSipio, Louis. 2001. "Building America, One Person at a Time: Naturalization and Political Behavior of the Naturalized in Contemporary American Politics," in Gary Gerstle and John Mollenkopf, editors, *E Pluribus Unum? Contemporary and Historical Perspectives on Immigrant Political Incorporation*. New York: Russell Sage Foundation.

DeSipio, Louis. 2001. "Do Angry Naturalized Citizens Make Better Citizens? Context of Naturalization and Participation in Latino Communities." Presented at 2001 American Political Science Association Meeting.

DeSipio, Louis. 2002. "Are Naturalized Citizens Leading Latinos to Electoral Empowerment? Voting Among Naturalized Latinos Registered to Vote in the 2000 Election." Presented at 2002 American Political Science Association Meeting.

Diamond, Jeff. 1998. "African-American Attitudes Towards United States Immigration Policy." *International Migration Review* 32: 451–70.

Diaz, William A. 1996. "Latino Participation in America: Associational and Political Roles." *Hispanic Journal of Behavioral Sciences* 18: 154–74.

Doherty, Brendan J., and Melissa Cully Anderson. 2003. "Presidential Message Tailoring: Courting Latino Voters in the 2000 Presidential Advertising Campaign." Presented at the Annual Meeting of the American Political Science Association, Philadelphia, PA.

Durand, Jorge, Douglas S. Massey, and Fernando Charvet. 2000. "The Changing Geography of Mexican Immigration to the United States: 1910–1996." *Social Science Quarterly* 81: 1–16.

Easton, David. 1953. *The Political System: An Inquiry into the State of Political Science.* New York: Alfred A. Knopf.

Eisenger, Peter K. 1973. "Support for Urban-Control Sharing at the Mass Level." *American Journal of Political Science* 17: 669–94.

Elster, Jon. 1987. *Making Sense of Marx.* New York: Cambridge University Press.

Erie, Steven P. 1990. *Rainbow's End: Irish-Americans and the Dilemmas of Urban Machine Politics, 1840–1985.* Berkeley: University of California Press.

Erikson, Robert S., Michael B. MacKuen, and James A. Stimson. 2002. *The Macro Polity.* New York: Cambridge University Press.

Espenshade, Thomas J. and Charles A. Calhoun. 1993. "An Analysis of Public Opinion toward Undocumented Immigration." *Population Research and Policy Review* 12: 189–224.

Espenshade, Thomas J., and Katherine Hempstead. 1996. "Contemporary American Attitudes Toward U.S. Immigration." *International Migration Review* 30: 535–70.

Espiritu, Yen Le. 1992. *Asian American Panethnicity.* Philadelphia: Temple University Press.

Finkel, Steven E. and John G. Geer. 1998. "A Spot Check: Casting Doubt on the Demobilizing Effect of Attack Advertising." *American Journal of Political Science* 42: 573–95.

Fix, Michael, and Jeffrey S. Passel. 2003a. "A New Citizenship Day." Washington, DC: Urban Institute, http://www.urban.org/url.cfm?ID=900671.

Fix, Michael, Jeffrey S. Passel, and Kenneth Sucher. 2003b. "Trends in Naturalization." Washington, DC: Urban Institute, http://www.urban.org.

Foley, Michael W., and Dean R. Hoge. 2003. "Do Churches Promote Civic Participation? New Evidence on the Role of Local Worship Communities in the Civic Incorporation of Immigrants." Paper presented at American Political Science Association Meeting.

Foner, Nancy. 2001. *Islands in the City: West Indian Migration to New York*. Berkeley: University of California Press.

Fong, Timothy. 1998. *The Contemporary Asian American Experience*. Upper Saddle River, NJ: Prentice Hall.

Freedman, Dan, and Sasha Johnson. 2002. "New Voters: Shadow Falls Between Registration and Voting," *National Voter*, September/October 2002.

Freedman, Paul, and Ken Goldstein. 1999. "Measuring Media Exposure and the Effects of Negative Campaign Ads." *American Journal of Political Science 43*: 1189–1208.

Friedrich, Robert J. 1982. "In Defense of Multiplicative Terms in Multiple Regression Equations." *American Journal of Political Science* 26: 797–833.

Frymer, Paul. 1999. *Uneasy Alliances: Race and Party Competition in America*. Princeton, NJ: Princeton University Press.

Gaines, Kevin. 1997. *Uplifting the Race: Black Leadership, Politics, and Culture in the Twentieth Century*. Chapel Hill: University of North Carolina Press.

Gamm, Gerald H. 1990. *The Making of the New Deal Democrats: Voting Behavior and Realignment in Boston, 1920–1940*. Chicago: University of Chicago Press.

Garcia, John A. 2003. *Latino Politics in America: Community, Culture, & Interests*. Lanham, MD: Rowman and Littlefield.

Garcia, John A., and Carlos H. Arce. 1988. "Political Orientations and Behaviors of Chicanos: Trying to Make Sense Out of Attitudes and Participation," in F. Chris Garcia, editors, *Latinos and the Political System*. Notre Dame, IN: University of Notre Dame Press.

Gay, Claudine. 2002. "Spirals of Trust? The Effect of Descriptive Representation on the Relationship between Citizens and their Government." *American Journal of Political Science* 46: 717–32.

Gay, Claudine. 2004. "Putting Race in Context: Identifying the Environmental Determinants of Black Racial Attitudes." *American Political Science Review* 98 (November): 547–62.

Gerstle, Gary, and John Mollenkopf, eds. 2001. *E Pluribus Unum? Contemporary and Historical Perspectives on Immigrant Political Incorporation*. New York: Russell Sage Foundation.

Gilliam, Frank. 1996. "Exploring Minority Empowerment: Symbolic Politics, Governing Coalitions, and Traces of Political Style in Los Angeles." *American Journal of Political Science* 40: 56–81.

Goldstein, Ken, and Paul Freedman. 2002. "Campaign Advertising and Voter Turnout: New Evidence for a Stimulation Effect." *The Journal of Politics* 64: 721–40.

Gordon, Karen Ferguson. 2002. *Black Politics in New Deal Atlanta*. Chapel Hill: University of North Carolina Press.

Gordon, Milton M. 1964. *Assimilation in American Life*. New York: Oxford University Press.

Graves, Scott, and Jongho Lee. 2000. "Ethnic Underpinnings of Voting Preference: Latinos and the 1996 U.S. Senate Election in Texas." *Social Science Quarterly* 81: 226–36.

Gray, Virginia, Russell Hanson, and Herbert Jacob. 1999. *Politics in the American States: A Comparative Analysis*, 7th ed. Washington, DC: CQ Press.

Greene, Christina. 1996. *Our Separate Ways: Women and the Black Freedom Movement in Durham, NC 1940s–1970s*, Ph.D. in History. Durham, NC: Duke University. 39 Archives G7990.

Guerra, Fernando, and Luis Ricardo Fraga. 1996. "Theory, Reality, and Perpetual Potential: Latinos in the 1992 California Elections," in Rodolfo O. de la Garza and Louis DeSipio, editors, *Ethnic Ironies: Latino Politics in the 1992 Elections* (pp. 131–45). Boulder, CO: Westview.

Gujarati, Damodar N. 1995. *Basic Econometrics*. 3rd edition. New York: McGraw-Hill.

Gurin, Patricia, Shirley Hatchett, and James S. Jackson. 1989. *Hope and Independence: Blacks' Response to Electoral and Party Politics*. New York: Russell Sage Foundation.

Gutmann, Amy. 2003. *Identity in Democracy*. Princeton, NJ: Princeton University Press.

Hajnal, Zoltan, and Mark Baldassare. 2001. "Finding Common Ground: Racial and Ethnic Attitudes in California." Report. Public Policy Institute of California, San Francisco, CA.

Hardy-Fanta, Carol. 1993. *Latina Politics, Latino Politics: Gender, Culture, and Political Participation in Boston*. Philadelphia, PA: Temple University Press.

Harles, John C. 1993. *Politics in the Lifeboat: Immigrants and the American Democratic Order*. Boulder, CO: Westview Press.

Harris, Fredrick C. 1999. *Something Within: Religion in African-American Political Activism*. New York: Oxford University Press.

Harris, Fredrick C., Valeria Sinclair-Chapman, and Brian D. McKenzie. 2006. *Countervailing Forces in African-American Civic Activism, 1973–1994*. New York: Cambridge University Press.

Harris-Lacewell, Melissa. 2004. *Barbershops, Bibles, and BET: Everyday Talk and Black Political Thought*. Princeton, NJ: Princeton University Press.

Haynie, Kerry L. 2001. *African American Legislators in American States*. New York: Columbia University Press.

Henig, Jeffrey, and Dennis E. Gale. 1987. "The Political Incorporation of Newcomers to Racially Changing Neighborhoods." *Urban Affairs Quarterly* 22: 399–419.

Henry, Charles P. 1994. "Urban Politics and Incorporation: The Case of Blacks, Latinos, and Asians in Three Cities," pp. 17–28 in James Jennings, editor, *Blacks Latinos, and Asians in Urban America: Status and Prospects for Politics and Activism*. Westport, CT: Praeger.

Hero, Rodney E. 1986. "Explaining Citizen-Initiated Contacting of Government Officials: Socioeconomic Status, Perceived Need, or Something Else?" *Social Science Quarterly* 67: 626–35.

Hero, Rodney E. 1992. *Latinos and the U.S. Political System: Two-Tiered Pluralism*. Philadelphia: Temple University Press.

Higham, John. 1992. *Strangers in the Land: Patterns of American Nativism, 1860–1925*. New Brunswick, NJ: Rutgers University Press.

Hill, Kevin A., and Dario Moreno. Forthcoming. "Battleground Florida," in Rodolfo O. de la Garza and Louis DeSipio, editors, *Muted Voices*. Lanham, MD: Rowman and Littlefield.

Hochschild, Jennifer L. 1993. "Middle Class Blacks and the Ambiguities of Success." In Paul M. Sniderman, Philip E. Tetlock, and Edward G. Carmines, editors, *Prejudice, Politics, and the American Dilemma.* Stanford: Stanford University Press.

Hochschild, Jennifer L. 1995. *Facing Up to the American Dream: Race, Class, and the Soul of the Nation.* Princeton, NJ: Princeton University Press.

Hogg, Michael A., and Dominic Abrams. 1988. *Social Identifications.* London: Routledge.

Houck, Thomas H. 1941. "A Newspaper History of Race Relations in Durham, North Carolina, 1910–1940. A.M. Thesis, Durham, NC: Duke University. H835.

Houghland, James, and James Christenson. 1983. "Religion and Politics: The Relationship of Religious Participation to Political Efficacy and Involvement." *Sociology and Social Research* 67: 406–20.

Howell, Susan, and Deborah Feagan. 1988. "Race and Trust in Government." *Public Opinion Quarterly* 52: 343–50.

Hritzuk, Natasha, and David K. Park. 2000. "The Question of Latino Participation: From an SES to a Social Structural Explanation." *Quarterly* 81: 151–66.

Huckfeldt, Robert, and John Sprague. 1992. "Political Parties and Electoral Mobilization: Political Structure, Social Structure, and the Party Canvass." *American Political Science Review* 86: 70–86.

Hum, Tarry, and Michaela Zonta. 2000. "Residential Patterns of Asian Pacific Americans." In Paul M. Ong, editor, *The State of Asian Pacific America: Transforming Race Relations.* LEAP Asian Pacific American Policy Institute and UCLA Asian American Studies Center.

Hung, Chi-kan Richard. 2002. "Asian American Participation in Civil Society in U.S. Metropolitan Areas." Paper presented at the Meeting of the American Political Science Association, Boston, MA.

Hunt, Larry L., and Janet G. Hunt. 1977. "Black Religion as Both Opiate and Inspiration of Civil Rights Militance: Putting Marx's Data to the Test." *Social Forces* 56: 1–14.

Huntington, Samuel P. 2004. *Who Are We? The Challenges to America's National Identity.* New York: Simon and Schuster.

Ignatiev, Noel. 1987. *How the Irish Became White.* New York: Routledge.

Jackman, Robert W. 1987. "Political Institutions and Voter Turnout in the Industrialized Democracies." *American Political Science Review* 81: 405–24.

Jackson, Byran O. 1987. "The Effects of Racial Group Consciousness on Political Mobilization in American Cities," *Western Political Quarterly* 40: 631–46.

Jackson, Robert A. 2002. "Latino Electoral Participation." Florida State University Working Paper.

Jacobson, Matthew Frye. 1998. *Whiteness of a Different Color: European Immigrants and the Alchemy of Race.* New Haven, CT: Yale University Press.

Jacoby, William G. 2000. "Issue Framing and Public Opinion on Government Spending." *American Journal of Political Science* 44: 750–67.

Jamieson, Amie, Hyon B. Shin, and Jennifer Day. 2002. *Voting and Registration in the Election of November 2000.* Current Population Reports (P20–542). Washington, DC: U.S. Department of Commerce, Bureau of the Census.

Jennings, James. 1994. *Blacks, Latinos, and Asians in Urban America.* Westport, CT: Praeger.

Johnson, James H., Walter C. Farrell, Jr., and Chandra Guinn. 1997. "Immigration Reform and the Browning of America: Tensions, Conflict, and Community

Instability," in Charles Hirschman, Philip Kasinitz, and Josh DeWind, editors, *The Handbook of International Migration*. New York: Russell Sage Foundation Publications.

Johnson, Martin, Robert M. Stein, and Robert Wrinkle. 2003. "Language Choice, Residential Stability, and Voting among Latino Americans." *Social Science Quarterly* 84: 412–24.

Johnston, R. J., A. Blais, H. E. Brady, and J. Cret. 1992. *Letting the People Decide: Dynamics of a Canadian Election*. Stanford, CA: Stanford University Press.

Jones-Correa, Michael, and David L. Leal. 1996. "Becoming 'Hispanic': Secondary Panethnic Identification among Latin American-Origin Populations in the United States." *Hispanic Journal of Behavioral Sciences* 18: 214–54.

Jones-Correa, Michael, and David Leal. 2001. "Political Participation: Does Religion Matter?" *Political Research Quarterly* 54: 751–70.

Jones-Correa, Michael. 1998. *Between Two Nations: the Political Predicament of Latinos in New York City*. Ithaca, NY: Cornell University Press.

Jones-Correa, Michael. 2005. "Bringing Outsiders In: Questions of Immigrant Incorporation." In Christina Wolbrecht and Rodney E. Hero, editors, *The Politics of Democratic Inclusion*. Philadelphia: Temple University Press.

Junn, Jane. 1999. "Participation in Liberal Democracy: The Political Assimilation of Immigrants and Ethnic Minorities in the United States." *American Behavioral Scientist* 42(9): 1417–38.

Junn, Jane. 2003. "Mobilizing Group Consciousness: Some Consequences Under Which Ethnicity Has Political Consequences." Paper presented at the Nation of Immigrants Conference, University of California, Berkeley.

Kaiser Family Foundation. 1995. *The Four Americas: Government and Social Policy Through the Eyes of America's Multi-Racial and Multi-Ethnic Society*. Washington, DC.

Kaiser Family Foundation. 1999. *National Survey on Latinos in America*. Washington, DC: Author.

Karpathakis, Anna. 1999. "Home Society Politics and Immigrant Political Incorporation: The Case of Greek Immigrants in New York City." *International Migration Review* 33: 55–79.

Kasinitz, Philip. 1992. *Caribbeans in New York: Black Immigrants and the Politics of Race*. Ithaca, NY: Cornell University Press.

Katznelson, Ira. 2005. *When Affirmative Action Was White: An Untold History of Racial Equality in Twentieth Century America*. New York: W.W. Norton & Company.

Key, V. O. 1949. *Southern Politics in State and Nation*. New York: Knopf.

Kim, Claire. 2000. *Bitter Fruit: The Politics of Black-Korean Conflict in New York City*. New Haven, CT: Yale University Press.

Kinder, Donald R. 1998. "Opinion and Action in the Realm of Politics," in D. T. Gilbert, S. T. Fisk, and G. Lindzey, editors, *The Handbook of Social Psychology, 4th edition*. Oxford: Oxford University Press.

Kinder, Donald R. 2003. "Communication and Politics in the Age of Information," in David O. Sears, Leonie Huddy, and Robert Jervis, editors, *Oxford Handbook of Political Psychology*. Oxford: Oxford University Press.

King, Desmond. 2000. *Making Americans: Immigration, Race, and the Origins of the Diverse Democracy*. Cambridge, MA: Harvard University Press.

King, Gary, Michael Tomz, and Jason Wittenberg. 2000. "Making the Most of Statistical Analyses: Improving Interpretation and Presentation." *American Journal of Political Science* 44: 347–61.

Kramer, Gerald H. 1971. "Short-Term Fluctuations in U.S. Voting Behavior, 1896–1964." *American Political Science Review* 65: 131–43.

Kramer, Gerald H. 1983. "The Ecological Fallacy Revisited: Aggregate versus Individual Level Findings on Economics and Elections, and Sociotropic Voting." *American Political Science Review* 77: 92–111.

Kwoh, Stewart, and Mindy Hui. 1993. "Empowering Our Communities: Political Policy." In Paul M. Ong, editor, *The State of Asian Pacific America: Transforming Race Relations*. LEAP Asian Pacific American Policy Institute and UCLA Asian American.

Lau, Richard R., Lee Sigelman, Caroline Heldman, and Paul Babbitt. 1999. "The Effects of Negative Political Advertisements: A Meta-Analytic Assessment." *American Political Science Review* 93: 851–76.

Lazarsfeld, Paul, Bernard Berelson, and Helen Gaudet. 1944. *The People's Choice*. New York: Duell, Sloane, and Pearce.

Leal, David. L., Matt A. Barreto, Jongho Lee, and Rodolfo O. de la Garza. 2005. "The Latino Vote in the 2004 Election." *PS: Political Science and Politics* 38(1): 41–50.

Lee, Taeku. 2000. "Racial Attitudes and the Color Line(s) at the Close of the Twentieth Century." In Paul M. Ong, editor, *The State of Asian Pacific America: Transforming Race Relations*. Los Angeles, CA: LEAP Asian Pacific American Policy Institute and UCLA Asian American Studies Center.

Lee, Taeku. 2002. *Mobilizing Public Opinion: Black Insurgency and Racial Attitudes in the Civil Rights Era*. Chicago: University of Chicago Press.

Lieberman, Robert. 1995. "Race and the Organization of Welfare Policy," in Paul E. Peterson, editor, *Classifying by Race*. Princeton, NJ: Princeton University Press.

Leighley, Jan E., 2001. *Strength in Numbers? The Political Mobilization of Racial and Ethnic Minorities*. Princeton, NJ: Princeton University Press.

Leighley, Jan E., and Arnold Vedlitz. 1999. "Race, Ethnicity and Political Participation: Competing Models and Contrasting Explanations." *The Journal of Politics* 61: 1092–1114.

Leighley, Jan E., and Jonathan Nagler. 1992. "Individual and Systematic Influences on Turnout: Who Votes? 1984" *Journal of Politics* 54: 718–38.

Lien, Pei-te, Christian Collet, Janelle Wong, and Karthick Ramakrishnan. 2001. "Asian Pacific American Politics Symposium: Public Opinion and Political Participation." *PS: Political Science and Politics* 34: 625–30.

Lien, Pei-te, M. Margaret Conway, Taeku Lee, and Janelle Wong. 2001b. "The Pilot Asian American Political Survey: Summary Report." In James Lai and Don Nakanishi, editors, *The National Asian Pacific American Political Almanac, 2001–02*. Los Angeles: UCLA Asian American Studies Center.

Lien, Pei-te, M. Margaret Conway, and Janelle Wong. 2004. *The Politics of Asian Americans*. New York: Routledge.

Lien, Pei-te. 2001a. "Race, Gender, and the Comparative Status of Asian American Women in Voting Participation." In Gordon Chang, editor, *Asian Americans and Politics: Perspectives, Experiences, and Prospects*. Stanford, CA: Stanford University Press.

Lien, Pei-te. 1994. "Ethnicity and Political Participation: A Comparison between Asian and Mexican Americans." *Political Behavior* 16: 237–64.

Lien, Pei-te. 1997. *The Political Participation of Asian Americans: Voting Behavior in Southern California*. New York: Garland Publishing.

Lien, Pei-te. 1998. "Does the Gender Gap in Political Attitudes and Behavior Vary Across Racial Groups?" *Political Research Quarterly* 51: 869–94.

Lien, Pei-te. 2000. "Who Votes in Multiracial America? An Analysis of Voting and Registration by Race and Ethnicity, 1990–96," in Yvette Alex-Assensoh and Lawrence Hanks, editors, *Black and Multiracial Politics in America*. New York: New York University Press.

Lien, Pei-te. 2001b. *The Making of Asian America through Political Participation*. Philadelphia: Temple University Press.

Lien, Pei-te. 2003. "Religion and Political Adaptation Among Asian Americans: An Empirical Assessment From the Multi-Site Asian American Political Survey," in Tony Carnes and Fenggang Yang, editors, *Asian American Religions: Borders and Boundaries*. New York: New York University Press.

Lien, Pei-te. 2004. Asian Americans and Voting Participation: Comparing Racial and Ethnic Differences in Recent U.S. Elections. *International Migration Review* 38: 493–517.

Liff, Bob. 2000. "Local Contests Are Overshadowing Big Race." *New York Daily News*, November 5.

Lin, Jan. 1998. *Reconstructing Chinatown: Ethnic Enclaves and Global Change*. Minnesota: University of Minnesota Press.

Lofland, John, and Lyn H. Lofland. 1995. *Analyzing Social Settings: A Guide to Qualitative Observation and Analysis, 3rd edition*. Belmont, CA: Wadsworth Publishing Company.

Lublin, David. 1999. *The Paradox of Representation: Racial Gerrymandering and Minority Interests in Congress*. Princeton, NJ: Princeton University Press.

MacKuen, Michael, Robert S. Erikson, and James A. Stimson. 1989. "Macropartisanship." *American Political Science Review*, 83: 1125–42.

Marinucci, Carla. 2000. "Republicans Go All-out to Sway the Latino Votes / GOP, Bush Planning Separate Advertising Campaigns." *San Francisco Chronicle*, January 14.

Markus, Gregory B. 1988. "The Impact of Personal and National Economic Conditions On the Presidential Vote: A Pooled Cross-Sectional Analysis." *American Journal of Political Science* 32: 137–54.

Martin, Ben L. 1991. "From Negro to Black to African-American: The Power of Names and Naming." *Political Science Quarterly* 106: 83–107.

Massey, Douglas S., and Nancy A. Denton. 1993. *American Apartheid: Segregation and the Making of the Underclass*. Cambridge, MA: Harvard University Press.

Massey, Douglas S., and Nancy A. Denton. 1988. "Suburbanization and Segregation in U.S. Metropolitan Areas." *American Journal of Sociology* 94: 592–626.

Matthews, Donald R., and James W. Prothro.1966. *Negroes and the New Southern Politics*. New York: Harcourt, Brace, and World, Inc.

McAdam, Doug. 1982. *Political Process and the Development of Black Insurgency, 1930–1970*. Chicago: University of Chicago Press.

McClain, Paula D., and John A. Garcia. 1993. "Expanding Disciplinary Boundaries: Black, Latino and Racial Minority Group Politics in Political Science," in Ada W.

Finifter, editor, *Political Science: The State of The Discipline II*. Washington, DC: American Political Science Association.

McClain, Paula D., and Joseph Stewart Jr. 2006. *Can We All Get Along? Racial and Ethnic Minorities in American Politics*, fourth edition. Boulder, CO: Westview Press.

McClain, Paula D., Niambi M. Carter, Victoria M. DeFrancesco Soto, Monique L. Lyle, Jeffrey D. Grynaviski, Shayla D. Nunnally, Thomas J. Scotto, J. Alan Kendrick, Gerald F. Lackey, and Kendra Davenport Cotton. 2006. "Racial Distancing in a Southern City: Latino Immigrants' Views of Black Americans." *Journal of Politics* 68, 3 (August): 571–84.

McCubbins, Matthew, and Thomas Schwartz. 1984. "Congressional Oversight Overlooked: Police Patrols Versus Fire Alarms." *American Journal of Political Science* 2: 165–79.

Michelson, Melissa R. 2002. "Turning Out Latino Voters." Presented at the Annual Meeting of the American Political Science Association, Boston, MA.

Michelson, Melissa. 2003. "Getting Out the Latino Vote: How Door-to-Door Canvassing Influences Voter Turnout in Rural Central California." *Political Behavior*. 25: 247–63.

Miles, Jack. 1994. "Blacks vs. Browns." In *Arguing Immigration: Are New Immigrants a Wealth of Diversity . . . or a Crushing Burden?*, ed. Nicolaus Mills. New York: Simon & Shuster.

Miller, Arthur H., Patricia Gurin, Gerald Gurin, and Oksana Malanchuk. 1981. "Group Consciousness and Political Participation." *American Journal of Political Science* 25: 494–511.

Min, Pyong Gap, and Jung H. Kim (Eds). 2002. *Religions in Asian America*. Walnut Creek, CA: AltaMira Press.

Mindiola, Jr., Tatcho, Yolanda Flores Niemann, and Nestor Rodriguez. 2003. *Black-Brown Relations and Stereotypes*. Austin: University of Texas Press.

Minnite, Lorraine C., and John H. Mollenkopf. 2001. "Between White and Black: Asian and Latino Political Participation in the 2000 Presidential Election in New York City." Presented at 2001 Meeting of the American Political Science Association.

Money, Jeannette. 1999. *Fences and Neighbors: The Political Geography of Immigration Control*. Ithaca, NY: Cornell University Press.

Morris, Aldon D. 1984. *The Origins of the Civil Rights Movement: Black Communities Organizing for Change*. New York: Free Press; London: Collier Macmillan.

Morris, Aldon D., Shirley J. Hatchett, and Ronald E. Brown. 1989. "The Civil Rights Movement and Black Political Socialization," in, Roberta S. Sigel, editor, *Political Learning in Adulthood: A Sourcebook of Theory and Research*. Chicago: University of Chicago Press.

Nakanishi, Don T. 1991. "The Next Swing Vote? Asian Pacific Americans and California Politics," in Byran O. Jackson and Michael B. Preston, editors, *Racial and Ethnic Politics in California*. Berkeley, CA: IGS Press.

Nakanishi, Don T. 1998. "When the Numbers Do Not Add Up: Asian Pacific Americans and California Politics," in Michael Preston, Bruce E. Cain, and Sandra Bass, editors, *Racial and Ethnic Politics in California* (Volume 2). Berkeley, CA: University of California Institute of Government Studies.

Nakanishi, Don T. 2001. "Beyond Electoral Politics: Renewing a Search for a Paradigm of Asian Pacific American Politics," in Gordon Chang, editor, *Asian*

*Americans and Politics: Perspectives, Experiences, and Prospects*. Stanford, CA: Stanford University Press.

Nelson, Thomas E., and Donald R. Kinder. 1996. "Issue Frames and Group-Centrism in American Public Opinion." *The Journal of Politics* 58: 1055–78.

Ngai, Mae M. 2004. *Impossible Subjects: Illegal Aliens and the Making of Modern America, 1924–1965*. Princeton, NJ: Princeton University Press.

Nie, Norman H., Jane Junn, and Kenneth Stehlik-Barry. 1996. *Education and Democratic Citizenship in America*. Chicago: University of Chicago Press.

Novak, Robert. 2000. "Golden State Attracts Green." *Chicago Sun Times*, October 22.

Omi, Michael, and Howard Winant. 1994. *Racial Formation in the United States: from the 1960s to the 1990s*, second edition. New York: Routledge.

Ong, Paul. ed. 2000. *Transforming Race Relations*. Los Angeles: LEAP Asian Pacific American Public Policy Institute.

Ong, Paul, Don T. Nakanishi. 1996. "Becoming Citizens, Becoming Voters: The Naturalization and Political Participation of Asian Pacific Immigrants," in Bill Ong Hing and Ronald Lee, editors, *Reframing the Immigration Debate*. Los Angeles, CA: LEAP Asian Pacific American Public Policy Institute and UCLA Asian American Studies Center.

Page, Benjamin I., and Robert Y. Shapiro. 1992. *The Rational Public: Fifty Years of Trends in Americans' Policy Preferences*. Chicago: University of Chicago Press.

Pantoja, Adrian D., Ricardo Ramirez and Gary M. Segura. 2001. "Citizens by Choice, Voters by Necessity: Patterns in Political Mobilization by Naturalized Latinos." *Political Research Quarterly* 54: 729–50.

Park, David K., and Carlos Vargas Ramos. 2002. "Paradigms of Minority Political Participation in the United States Research in Micropolitics." *Decision-Making Deliberation and Participation* 6: 253–93.

Patterson, Thomas E., and Robert McClure. 1976. *The Unseeing Eye: The Myth of Television Power in National Elections*. New York: Paragon Books.

Peel, Roy V. 1935. *The Political Clubs of New York City*. New York: G.P. Putnam Sons.

Petty, R. E., and J. T. Cacioppo. 1986. *Communication and Persuasion: Central and Peripheral Routes to Attitude Change*. New York: Springer-Verlag New York, Inc.

Popkin, Samuel L. 1994. *The Reasoning Voter: Communication and Persuasion in Presidential Campaigns*. Chicago: University of Chicago Press.

Portes, Alejandro, and Min Zhou. 1993. "The New Second Generation: Segmented Assimilation and Its Variants." *Annals of the American Academy of Political and Social Science* 530 (November): 74–96.

Portes, Alejandro, and Rubén G. Rumbaut. 1996. *Immigrant America: A Portrait*, 2nd ed. Berkeley: University of California Press.

Preston, Michael B. 1987. "Introduction," in Michael B. Preston, Lenneal J. Henderson, Jr., and Paul L. Puryear, editors, *The New Black Politics: the Search for Political Power, second edition*. White Plains, NY: Longman.

Putnam, Robert. 2000. *Bowling Alone*. New York: Touchstone (Simon and Schuster).

Quadagno, Jill. 1994. *The Color of Welfare: How Racism Undermined the War on Poverty*. New York: Oxford University Press.

Ramakrishnan, S. Karthick. 2005. *Democracy in Immigrant America: Changing Demographics and Political Participation*. Stanford, CA: Stanford University Press.

Ramirez, Ricardo. 2002. "Getting Out the Vote: The Impact of Non-Partisan Voter Mobilization Efforts in Low Turnout Latino Precincts." Unpublished Manuscript, Public Policy Institute of California.

Reed, Adolph, Jr. 1999. *Stirrings in the Jug: Black Politics in the Post Segregation Era.* Minneapolis: University of Minnesota Press.

Reese, Laura, and Ronald E. Brown. 1995. "The Effects of Religious Messages on Racial Identity and System Blame among African-Americans." *The Journal of Politics* 57: 24–43.

Rogers, Reuel. 2000. "Afro-Caribbean Immigrants, African Americans, and the Politics of Group Identity," in Yvette M. Alex-Assensoh and Lawrence J. Hanks, editors, *Black and Multiracial Politics in America.* New York: New York University Press.

Rogers, Reuel. 2006. *Afro-Caribbean Immigrants and the Politics of Incorporation: Ethnicity, Exception, or Exit.* New York: Cambridge University Press.

Rogers, Reuel, and Dennis Chong. 2004. "We Are They: Immigration, Identity, and Assimilation in the United States." Unpublished manuscript. Northwestern University.

Rosenstone, Steven J. 1982. "Economic Adversity and Voter Turnout." *American Journal of Political Science* 26: 25–46.

Rosenstone, Steven J., and John Mark Hansen. 1993. *Mobilization, Participation, and Democracy in America.* New York: Macmillan.

Rumbaut, Ruben G. 1997. "Assimilation and Its Discontents: Between Rhetoric and Reality." *International Migration Review* 31 (Winter): 923–60.

Rustin, Bayard. 1971. "From Protest to Politics: The Future of the Civil Rights Movement." In *Down the Line: The Collected Writings of Bayard Rustin.* Chicago: Quadrangle Books.

Salamon Lester M., and Stephen Van Evera. 1973. "Fear, Apathy, and Discrimination: A Test of Three Explanations of Political Participation." *The American Political Science Review* 67: 1288–1306.

Salamon, Lester M. 1973. "Leadership and Modernization: The Emerging Black Political Elite in the American South." *Journal of Politics* 35: 615–46.

Sanjek, Roger. 1998. *The Future of Us All: Race and Neighborhood Politics in New York City.* Ithaca, NY: Cornell University Press.

Schaefer, R. T. 1979. *Racial and Ethnic Groups.* Boston: Little, Brown.

Schelling, Thomas C. 1978. *Micromotives and Macrobehavior.* New York: W.W. Norton and Company.

Schlozman, Kay Lehman, Sidney Verba, and Henry Brady. 1999. "Civic Participation and the Equality Problem," in Theda Skocpol and Morris P. Fiorina, editors, *Civic Engagement in American Democracy.* Washington, DC: Brookings Institution Press; New York: Russell Sage Foundation.

See, Letha A. (Lee). 1986–87. "International Migration and Refugee Problems: Conflict between Black Americans and Southeast Asian Refugees." *The Journal of Intergroup Relations* 14: 38–50.

Seelye, Katharine. 2001. "Poverty Rates Fell in 2000, But Income Was Stagnant." *The New York Times.* September 26, A12.

Segura, Gary M., and Helena Alves Rodrigues. 2006. "Comparative Ethnic Politics in the United States: Beyond Black and White," in Nelson W. Polsby, editor, *Annual Review of Political Science, Vol. 9.* Palo Alto, CA: Annual Reviews.

Shaw, Daron R. 1999. "A Study of Presidential Campaign Event Effects from 1952 to 1992." *Journal of Politics* 61: 387–422.

Shaw, Darren, Rodolfo O. de la Garza, and Jongho Lee. 2000. "Examining Latino Turnout in 1996: A Three-State, Validated Survey Approach." *American Journal of Political Science* 44: 338–46.

Shingles, Richard D. 1981. "Black Consciousness and Political Participation: The Missing Link." *The American Political Science Review* 75: 76–91.

Singer, Audrey. 2004. "The Rise of New Immigrant Gateways." Washington, DC: Brookings Institution, http://brookings.edu.

Skocpol, Theda. 1995. "African Americans in U.S. Social Policy," in Paul E. Peterson, ed., *Classifying by Race*. Princeton, NJ: Princeton University Press.

Skocpol, Theda. 2003. *Diminished Democracy From Membership to Management in American Civic Life*. Norman: University of Oklahoma Press.

Smith, Robert C. 1981. "Black Power and the Transformation from Protest to Politics." *Political Science Quarterly* 96: 431–43.

Smith, Tony. 2000. *Foreign Attachments: The Power of Ethnic Groups in the Making of American Foreign Policy*. Cambridge, MA: Harvard University Press.

Sommers, Laurie Kay. 1991. "Inventing Latinismo: The Creation of "Hispanic" Panethnicity in the United States." *The Journal of American Folklore* 104: 32–53.

Sonenshein, Raphael. 1994. *Politics in Black and White: Race and Power in Los Angeles*. Princeton, NJ: Princeton University Press.

Spencer, David E., and Kenneth N. Berk. 1981. "A Limited Information Specification Test." *Econometrica* 49 (July): 1079–85.

Spencer, Thomas T. 1976. *Democratic Auxiliary and Non-Party Groups in the Election of 1936*. Ph.D. Thesis, University of Notre Dame.

Squire, Peverill, Raymond E. Wolfinger, and David P. Glass. 1998. "Residential Mobility and Voter Turnout." *American Political Science Review* 81: 45–66.

Sterne, Evelyn Savidge. 2001. "Beyond the Boss: Immigration and American Political Culture from 1880 to 1940," in Gary Gerstle and John Mollenkopf, editors, *E Pluribus Unum? Contemporary and Historical Perspectives on Immigrant Political Incorporation*. New York: Russell Sage Foundation.

Stone, Clarence N. 1986. "Atlanta: Protest and Elections are Not Enough." *PS: Political Science and Politics* 19: 618–25.

Subervi-Velez, Federico A. 1986. "The Mass Media and Ethnic Assimilation and Pluralism: A Review and Research Proposal with Special Focus on Hispanics." *Communication Research* 13: 71–96.

Subervi-Velez, Federico A., and Stacey Connaughton. 1999. "Targeting the Latino Vote: The Democratic Party's 1996 Mass-Communication Strategy," in Rodolfo O. de la Garza and Louis DeSipio, editors, *Awash in the Mainstream: Latino Politics in the 1996 Elections* (pp. 47–71). Boulder, CO: Westview Press.

Suro, Roberto, and Audrey Singer. 2002. "Latino Growth in Metropolitan America: Changing Patterns, New Locations." *Brookings Institution Center on Urban and Metropolitan Policy and The Pew Hispanic Center* (July): 1–18.

Suro, Roberto. 1998. *Strangers Among Us: How Latino Immigration is Transforming America*. New York: Alfred A. Knopf.

Tajfel, Henri. 1981. *Human Groups and Social Categories*. Cambridge: Cambridge University Press.

Tajfel, Henri, and John C. Turner. 1979. "The Social Identity Theory of Intergroup Behaviour," in W. G. Austin and S. Worchel, editors, *Psychology of Intergroup Relations*. Chicago: Nelson-Hall.

Takaki, Ronald. 1989. *Strangers from a Different Shore: A History of Asian Americans*. New York: Little, Brown.

Tate, Katherine. 1991. "Black Political Participation in the 1984 and 1988 Presidential Elections." *American Political Science Review* 85: 1159–76.

Tate, Katherine. 1993. *From Protest to Politics: The New Black Voters in American Elections*. New York: Russell Sage Foundation.

Tate, Katherine. 2003. *Black Faces in the Mirror: African Americans and their Representatives in the U.S. Congress*. Princeton, NJ: Princeton University Press.

Thornton, Michael C., and Yuko Mizuno. 1999. "Economic Well-Being and Black Adult Feelings toward Immigrants and Whites, 1984." *Journal of Black Studies* 30(1): 15–44.

Tichenor, Daniel J. 2002. *Dividing Lines: The Politics of Immigration Control in America*. Princeton, NJ: Princeton University Press.

Tomz, Michael, Jason Wittenberg, and Gary King. 2001. CLARIFY: Software for Interpreting and Presenting Statistical Results, version 2. Cambridge, MA: Harvard University Press.

U.S. Bureau of the Census. *1990 Census of Population*. Washington, DC: Author.

U.S. Bureau of the Census. *2000 Redistricting File*. Washington, DC: Author.

U.S. Census Bureau. 2004. "U.S. Interim Projections by Age, Sex, Race, and Hispanic Origin," http://www.census.gov/ipc/www/usinterimproj/Internet Release Date: March 18, 2004.

Uhlaher, Carole J., Bruce E. Cain, and D. Roderick Kiewiet. 1989. "Political Participation of Ethnic Minorities in the 1980s." *Political Behavior* 11: 195–231.

Uhlaner, Carole J. 1996. "Latinos and Ethnic Politics in California: Participation and Preference." In Anibal Yanez-Chavez, editor, *Latino Politics in California*. San Diego, CA: Center for U.S.-Mexican Studies.

Uhlaner, Carole Jean. 1989. "'Relational Goods' and Participation: Incorporating Sociability into a Theory of Rational Action." *Public Choice* 62: 253–85.

Vaca, Nicolas C. 2004. *The Presumed Alliance: The Unspoken Conflict Between Latinos and Blacks and What It Means for America*. New York: Harper Collins.

Vallely, Richard M. 2005. "Why Then But Not Now? Immigrant Incorporation in Historical Perspective." Paper presented to CSDP Workshop, Princeton, NJ.

Verba, Sidney, and Norman H. Nie. 1972. *Participation in America: Political Democracy and Social Equality*. New York: Harper Row.

Verba, Sidney, Kay Lehman Schlozman, and Henry Brady. 1995. *Voice and Equality: Civic Voluntarism in American Politics*. Cambridge, MA: Harvard University Press.

Waldinger, Roger. 1996. "From LAX to Ellis Island: Immigrant Prospects in the American City." *International Migration Review* 30:4, 1078–87.

Walton, Hanes, Jr. 1985. *Invisible Politics: Black Political Behavior*. Albany: State University of New York Press.

Waters, Mary. 1990. *Ethnic Options: Choosing Identities in America*. Berkeley: University of California Press.

Waters, Mary. 1999. *Black Identities: West Indian Immigrant Dreams and American Realities*. Cambridge, MA: Harvard University Press.

Weinstein, Jeremy M. 1999. "Abandoning the Polity: Political Parties and Social Capital in American Politics." Presented at APSA Meeting, 1999.

Welch, Susan, Lee Sigelman, Timothy Bledsoe, and Michael Combs. 2001. *Race and Place*. Cambridge: Cambridge University Press.

Wilson, William J. 1980. *The Declining Significance of Race, second edition*. Chicago: University of Chicago Press.

West, Darrell M. 2005. *Air Wars: Television Advertising in Election Campaigns, 1952–2004*. Washington, DC: CQ Press.

Wilcox, Clyde. 1990. "Religious Sources of Politicization among Blacks in Washington, D.C." *Journal for the Scientific Study of Religion* 29: 387–94.

Wolfinger, Raymond, and Steven J. Rosenstone. 1980. *Who Votes?* New Haven, CT: Yale University Press.

Wong, Janelle. 2006. *Democracy's Promise: Immigrants and American Civic Institutions*. Ann Arbor: University of Michigan Press.

Wong, Janelle S. 2000. "The Effects of Age and Political Exposure on the Development of Party Identification Among Asian American and Latino Immigrants in the United States." *Political Behavior* 22: 341–71.

Wong, Janelle S. 2002. "The Role of Community Organizations in the Political Incorporation of Asian American and Latino Immigrants." Paper presented at the Conference on Race and Civil Society, Racine, WI.

Wong, Janelle. 2005. "Mobilizing Asian Americans: A Field Experiment." *Annals of the American Academy of Political and Social Sciences* 601(September): 102–14.

Yans-McClaughlin, Virginia. 1977. *Family and Community: Italian Immigrants in Buffalo 1880–1930*. Ithaca, NY: Cornell University Press.

Yoo, David K. (Ed). 1999. *New Spiritual Homes: Religion and Asian Americans*. Honolulu: University of Hawai'i Press, in association with UCLA Asian American Studies Center, Los Angeles.

Young, Iris Marion. 2002. *Inclusion and Democracy*. New York: Oxford University Press.

Zaller, John R. 1992. *The Nature and Origins of Mass Opinion*. Cambridge: Cambridge University Press.

# Index